WINNING

WINNING

The Guide to a Life of
Peace and Purpose

Travis Moody

WINNING
THE GUIDE TO A LIFE OF PEACE AND PURPOSE

iUniverse books may be ordered through booksellers or by contacting:

iUniverse
1663 Liberty Drive
Bloomington, IN 47403
www.iuniverse.com
1-800-Authors (1-800-288-4677)

ISBN: 978-1-4917-8598-0 (sc)
ISBN: 978-1-4917-8597-3 (e)

Library of Congress Control Number: 2015921207

Print information available on the last page.

iUniverse rev. date: 05/12/2016

This book is dedicated to all the men who have provided coaching and mentoring to me and to all the men who I have had the privilege of coaching as well.

CONTENTS

Part 3: Peace in Health

Part 4: Peace in Finances

Part 5: Peace in Purpose

PREFACE

I had always dreamed of living a successful life. I had completed my MBA at one of the top business schools in the United States and had a good career with a Fortune 500 company in Seattle. I had spent a couple of years researching and planning for an opportunity to buy a company. I found a small company in Atlanta that met the criteria, and I went after it. I quit my job in Seattle and moved to Georgia to pursue my dream. The company turned out to be difficult to buy, and the deal fell through. I spent all our savings and the equity in our home. I used credit cards to charge living and business expenses during my four months in Atlanta and incurred legal and consulting expenses associated with buying the business. I was so presumptuous about how this deal would make me rich that, in the middle of all of this, I took out a 100 percent mortgage for a 4,800-square-foot dream home in Atlanta.

Now, there was nothing wrong with my desire to own a business or with leaving my job to pursue this dream. However, along the way, I ignored God's warnings that I was stepping out of His will. He gave me unease about using credit cards, but I ignored it. He provided obstacles in getting the mortgage, but I manipulated the system and even provided false information to get the loan. If I had been honest, the loan would have been denied, and I would have saved myself much heartache.

After four months of hard work, I finally came to my senses and realized that this business deal would not happen. We were left with no money, no income, and more than $100,000 in debt. The home that was supposed to be our dream home became a nightmare. We had a huge mortgage on a home that we could not afford to live in, maintain, or even sell.

Carol and I had been married almost ten years at the time, but this was the first time I had seen her cry because of something I had done. I remember her saying, "Travis, people look at where we live and think that we have it made, but I cannot even afford to go to Walmart to get basic needs for our family. We are living a lie." She never placed blame, but nonetheless, this hurt me. I felt like I had failed my wife, and I felt that my God had failed me. I was mad at God. I could not understand why He'd allowed this to happen.

Do not get me wrong. I was not in denial. I knew it was my fault, but God had always protected me from my own foolishness. I could not understand why He did not stop me or, better yet, why He didn't make it work out in my favor. Isn't that what the Bible says? I had always paid my tithes. I had tried to live right. It seemed like the wicked people were always winning. Why couldn't I win? If God was in control, why did I have to lose? Some of you might be going through some difficult times, and maybe you are asking God the same questions right now. I struggled with these feelings and wrestled with God over them for about a year. I felt like a failure and that I had wasted wealth that I could never get back.

After a year of struggling with this, Carol finally suggested we go to this financial class to learn what God says about money. I thought, *Why should I go to this class?* Arrogantly, I thought, *I have a Duke MBA and manage millions of dollars, and I'm the head of the financial team at church. All they are going to tell me is that I need to tithe and things will work out.* I didn't need to hear that, because I was already tithing, and things weren't working out. Reluctantly, I went to this class, and what I learned about money shocked me.

I had been in church my whole life, and all I had ever heard was that I was supposed to give 10 percent to the church. But no one had ever told me how to handle the other 90 percent, and that's what got us in trouble. We discovered God had a lot to say about the subject. What I learned during that period positioned us to get out of what seemed like an unwinnable battle with debt. Over the next three years, we were able to pay off more than $100,000 in debt. Our experience with getting out of debt was just a start to us learning the keys to winning in life.

ACKNOWLEDGMENTS

There is no winning in life without a loving Savior, Christ Jesus, and great family, friends, and mentors. For your unconditional love and support as we live this adventure, I would like to thank my wife, Carol, and our kids, Erica, Travis Jr., Donovan, and Gilana. I appreciate my parents, Essie Moody and the late Herbert Moody, for being a source of wisdom and guidance.

A special thank-you goes to my senior pastors, John and Leslie Siebeling, for providing a church environment that allows me to grow spiritually, impact lives, and live out the dream God gave to me. And also to Pastor Mundo Meneses and The Life Church family for all you do to support me personally and allow me to weave stewardship and generosity ministry into a growing local church.

God has blessed me with so many amazing mentors, uncles, friends, ministry partners, and coaches who have helped me along my life's journey. You have given me the encouragement, motivation, and training necessary to win in life and coach others as well. The entire list is too extensive to write, but it includes Roosevelt Hancock, Keith Holmes, Bill Curry, Roy "Soup" Campbell, Jeff Woodard, Rob Clement, Andrew Young, Howard Dayton, Frank Smith, David Lenoir, Dan Henley, and Curtis Garrison.

To all the men I have been privileged to serve as a mentor and coach, I want you to know that I take this responsibility very seriously and I am honored you have given me the opportunity to speak into your lives. William Turner, Joe Bryant, Malvin

Jones, Khary Goodwin, Frank Monahan, Dathan Thomas, James Kanadet, David Stratton, Jonathan Hampton, Dwayne Bufford, Kelly Henderson, Jason Pettis, and others, thank you for trusting me as your life coach.

INTRODUCTION

One day, I was spending my usual prayer time with God, and I was pleasantly surprised by the message I sensed that God was communicating to me. I wasn't surprised by the fact that God was speaking to me, as I had often felt God speaking to me before. He had often encouraged me when I needed to be more thankful or be more patient. He had often warned me to be strong or to have more faith. But what I sensed He was saying to me this day was something new. It was only four words, but it stopped me in my tracks. I sensed God was saying to me, "Let's have some fun."

I wasn't sure what this meant, but it put a smile on my face. I'm not sure what surprised me more—the fact that God cared about me having fun or the fact that He wanted to have fun with me. Either way, I couldn't help smiling.

I thought about what really made life fun for me. My thoughts went to times when I was just hanging out with my family. Whether we were playing card games around the house or going on vacation, those times with my loved ones made life fun. I also realized life is more fun when I'm healthy spiritually, relationally, physically, emotionally, and financially. The game of life is a lot like sports. It's a lot more fun when you are winning.

We all want to win in life. Some people make it sound so simple and easy. "Just give your life to God, and you will be happy." That sounds good, but it's only the beginning to winning in life. Having a relationship with Christ guarantees our success in eternity, but what about winning in *this* life?

Winning in this life and winning in eternity are two different things. You can win in this life but lose in eternity, and you can win in eternity (go to heaven) but lose in this life. It does not have to be a choice of one or the other. In fact, God's desire is that we have both. God doesn't want us to just survive this life so that we can enjoy eternity. He also wants for us the same thing that we all want for ourselves: to win in this life (Mark 10:29–30).

I spent most of my early years playing sports, including playing football on a Division I team. Whether it was football, basketball, or my favorite card games, my objective was to win. Winning made sports more fun. Who doesn't like winning? For me, there was no sense in playing any sport unless I was aiming to win, and more times than not, I won.

Although my official playing days ended in the eighties when I played my last college football game, I found that the same rules that apply to sports apply to life. Life is more fun when you win. But unlike with sports, many people don't know how to win when it comes to life. There is no huge scoreboard letting you know where you stand. There is no coach patrolling the sideline and calling the plays. Many of us are just going through life being defeated. Often times we do not even realize that we are in competition.

In recent years, several high-profile National Football League players have had legal troubles with domestic violence. These great athletes who manage to perform with a high level of discipline on the field have not translated that same discipline off the field. Perhaps it is because on the field, they understand the rules of the game, keep score, and have the benefit of good coaches, while off the field, they are left with navigating through life on their own.

I have learned that life is a competition and requires all the same components involved in winning any good sporting event. It's not just talent that determines who wins. It also requires a good game plan, a strong desire to win, good coaches, and a commitment to execution.

These things have helped me to win in life. By winning in life, I mean winning in my spiritual life, in relationships, in my health, and in my financial life. I learned that ultimately winning in life also includes living a life of significance with a purpose that is much bigger than me.

I decided to write this book in order to help coach readers through a winning life and to provide a tool for those who want to coach others. It is written as my personal letter to you, the reader. In this book, I discuss the keys that will help you move from just surviving life to living a life of success and, even better, a life of significance.

The book starts with a self-assessment so that you can determine where you currently are on your journey to winning in five key areas of life. The rest of the book is dedicated to explaining in more detail what it means to win in each of these five areas.

This book can be used by individuals or by small groups. At the end of each section, there is a list of questions to help guide discussions.

Whether you are reading it as an individual or as part of a group, my hope is that this book will help guide you to a life of joy, peace, and significance and help you to guide others there as well.

CHAPTER 1

THE PEACE FOUNTAIN

One of the most peaceful sounds water flowing through a fountain. We have all marveled at the beauty of water fountains. We put them in our offices, our homes, and our gardens. I love watching the multilevel water fountains. It is so peaceful and calming. It is also a good picture of the winning life God wants for us.

"The LORD gives strength to his people; the LORD blesses his people with peace" (Psalm 29:11).

Just like the multilevel water fountain, there are multiple areas in our lives in which God wants us to experience peace. As we experience this peace, we win in this area of our life. I call these the *five tiers of peace*:

1. Peace with God
2. Peace in relationships
3. Peace in health
4. Peace in finances
5. Peace in purpose

These five tiers are in order of priority. Think of the five tiers as a multilevel water fountain, like the one illustrated here.

THE PEACE FOUNTAIN

LEVEL 1 - SURVIVAL { PEACE WITH GOD

PEACE IN RELATIONSHIPS

PEACE IN HEALTH

LEVEL 2 - SUCCESS {

PEACE IN FINANCES

LEVEL 3 - SIGNIFICANCE { PEACE IN PURPOSE

If there is no water flowing in the top tier, then obviously the bottom tiers will eventually dry up. Water flows in one direction. The higher tier has to fill completely in order to have water flow into the lower tiers.

As stewardship pastor at my church, one of my responsibilities is to provide money coaching to those needing help with their personal finances. A couple came to me for money coaching because they were experiencing chaos in their finances. They were in debt and struggling to pay their bills each month. Both the husband and wife were frustrated and wanted our help getting peace in their finances. What I found was that they didn't have a money problem at all. They had a relationship problem. They had separate bank accounts and handled money separately. There was no common vision for handling money. The issue in their relationship resulted in chaos in their finances. They had to address their marriage issues in order to have peace in their finances. Water has to flow freely in the higher tiers in order to have water flowing in the lower tiers. They only felt it in their financial tier because it dried up first. We also must have water flowing in each of those tiers in order to experience all God has for us.

2

Peace and Prosperity

Something that I have been intrigued about is prosperity teaching. I often hear ministers say God wants me to prosper, but it always seems to end with me giving more money to their ministry. I would hear prosperity equated to a big house, luxury cars, vacation homes, diamond rings, expensive clothes, and eating out at fine restaurants. This didn't feel right to me, and I asked God, "Is this really what You mean for us?"

To get answers, I did a word search to study what God meant by this term *prosperity*. I studied every scripture I could find on the subject. I found the word used over sixty times in the Bible. I was surprised to find out that prosperity has little to do with material possessions. In many cases, the word *prosperity* was interchangeable with the word *peace*. A Hebrew word used for prosperity was *Shalom*, meaning "peace." *Shalom* means the absence of chaos, being complete, and lacking for nothing. It means to have peace on all sides, including financial peace. I was convinced through scripture that God wants us to have peace. It included financial peace, but it was so much bigger than that. God wants us to have peace and prosperity in every area of our life.

I asked myself, "Can the world give us peace?"

Jesus tells us, "Peace I leave with you; my peace I give to you—not as the world gives, do I give to you" (John 14:27).

The world tells you to go out and get the big house and big car and then you will have peace, but any peace you get out of these things is temporary at best. When we get those things through the use of debt, our peace is very short-lived. To those around us, we look like we really have it going on, but in reality, we are in financial chaos. Although we have all the luxuries of life, we struggle to pay our bills, have no investments, and have no peace in our finances. In contrast, God offers us true peace.

"The peace of God, which surpasses all comprehension, will guard your hearts and your minds in Christ Jesus" (Philippians 4:7).

God promises peace *in* the storm, not the absence of storms. Jesus tells us, "These things I have spoken to you, so that in me you may have peace. In the world you have tribulation, but take courage; I have overcome the world" (John 16:33).

Our situations in life will not always be positive. The Bible tells us that bad things happen to both the righteous and the unrighteous. In spite of that, it's clear that God's will for you is peace. Proverbs 10:22 says, "It is the blessing of the LORD that makes rich, and He adds no sorrow to it."

God does not bless you with a house and then bring sorrow when it's time to pay the mortgage. If we're not experiencing peace in our day-to-day lives, then it's quite possible that we have not allowed God to control a particular area of our lives.

Each of us has to determine where we are today in each of these five peace tiers and then whether we are willing to trust God to provide us peace.

Peace Self-Assessment

Use the following self-assessment to evaluate areas of your life where you are consistently doing the behaviors that will bring you freedom, peace, and strength. Ask yourself, "Am I ... consistently?" or "Do I ... consistently?" Answer either "yes" or "no." Be honest.

Peace with God	Yes	No
1. Accept Jesus as payment for my sins and know for certain that if I died today I would go to heaven		
2. Confident in who I am in Christ		
3. Spend time with God daily		
4. Planted (attending and serving) in a healthy local church		
5. Consistently give at least 10 percent of my gross income to God through my local church		

6. Master sin in my life

7. Submit to every change God wants to make in my life and humbly ask Him to remove my character defects

8. Have at least one wise, spiritually mature person with whom I regularly and openly share details of my life for the purpose of guidance and accountability

9. Have a positive attitude

Loving Relationships

1. Maintain sex in the context of marriage between husband and wife (Note: if you are single and are not having sex, then answer "yes")

2. Provide regular affirmation for loved ones ("I love you," "I'm proud of you," "You are good at ..." etc.)

3. Pray for each loved one daily

4. If married, committed to marriage and loving my spouse

□ Have regular intimacy with my spouse

□ Avoid emotional relationships with anyone other than my spouse

□ Know and regularly meet my spouse's needs

□ Have a weekly date with my spouse

□ Tell my spouse, "I love you," daily

5. If a parent, committed to loving and caring for children

□ Provide regular and appropriate touch to them daily

□ Regularly speak words of love and encouragement to them

☐ Spend individual time weekly with each child

☐ Provide financially for their care

☐ Regularly teach life skills to kids

6. Spend time with at least one close lifelong friend

Good Health (Physical, Mental, and Emotional)

1. Have regular doctor checkups and follow doctor's recommendations

2. Avoid abuse of drugs and alcohol

3. Take one day a week off as the Sabbath Day unto the Lord (day of rest)

4. Exercise regularly (e.g., getting the heart rate up to 124–144 b.p.m. for at least twenty minutes at least three times a week and do strength building at least two times a week)

5. Consistently eat healthy, not overeating and minimizing unhealthy foods

6. Have no unaddressed heart (emotional) wounds, offering forgiveness to those who have hurt me

Financial Peace

1. Use a written balanced budget and consistently spend less than I earn

2. Know how much is earned, where my money is spent, my credit rating, and my financial net worth

3. Maintain three to six months of expenses in emergency savings

4. Have a plan and aggressively work toward being or remaining debt-free

5. Earn and handle money with honesty and integrity

6. Earn income doing what God gifted me to do and what I am passionate about

7. Have adequate insurance and an estate plan in order

8. Invest 10 to 15 percent of my income for the future

9. Live with a margin

Living on Purpose

1. Have and pursue my big God-given dream

2. Actively and intentionally mentor/disciple others

3. Do something meaningful to express love to someone other than myself and my family

4. Live a godly/blessed/prosperous life others desire

5. Give above the tithe toward building God's kingdom and continuously grow in generosity

6. Have and execute a written vision, plan, and goals

Applying the Assessment

It's important to note that it is when we display the behaviors discussed in the assessment that we receive peace. However, this is not intended to be a plan for how to please God. When we accept Jesus, God is already pleased with us. There is nothing we can do to make Him love us less or more. We couldn't please God through our works even if we tried. No matter how hard we try to be good, we cannot succeed at it. Thank goodness we don't have to. Jesus did it for us so we can stop trying. This is more about how we let the Spirit of God impact our lives.

Romans 8:5 says, "Those who live according to the flesh have their minds set on what the flesh desires; but those who live in accordance with the Spirit have their minds set on what the Spirit desires."

Having our minds set means we have to start with a choice. We have to make our minds up that we desire what God wants for us and are open to Him changing our hearts.

Focusing on saying no to our sinful nature doesn't work. We continuously fail at it. It's not productive, and it wears us out.

The apostle Paul, who was one of the most significant men of God and who wrote most of the New Testament, struggled in the same way that many of us do. In Romans 7:18–19, he reveals how he was baffled by his own inability to do what was right. He said, "The good I want to do I don't find myself doing, but the evil I do not want to do is the very thing I find myself doing … what a wretched man I am." If Paul couldn't will himself to do good, then what chance do we have?

Well, there is hope for us. In a matter of a few sentences, it seems like Paul did a 180-degree turn. Instead of "what a wretched man I am," Paul goes on a rant about how strong he is in Christ. He finishes off with Romans 8:37–39, saying,

> "No, in all these things we are more than conquerors through him who loved us. For I am convinced that neither death nor life, neither angels nor demons, neither the present nor the future, nor any powers, neither height nor depth, nor anything else in all creation, will be able to separate us from the love of God that is in Christ Jesus our Lord."

Wow! A huge change. What was it that made such a big difference between Paul in Romans 7 and Paul in Romans 8? The same thing that changed Paul from a "wretched man" to one among those who are "more than conquerors" is the same thing that changes us.

The difference in Romans 7 and Romans 8 is the Holy Spirit. The Holy Spirit is only mentioned once in Romans 7 but seventeen times in Romans 8. It's God's Spirit who changes us and gives us life and peace.

Instead of relying on your ability to say no to your sinful nature, I am encouraging you to say yes to your spiritual nature.

The nine things listed in this first section are things that feed your spiritual nature. When we feed our spiritual nature, it allows God's Spirit to change us.

In 2 Corinthians 3:17, it says, "… where the Spirit of God is there is freedom [peace]."

In each of the peace tiers are behaviors that allow God's Spirit to change that area of our lives. The peace or freedom is in the behavior not the results. It's not when we are debt free that we experience peace in our finances, but when we spend less than we earn and wisely manage the difference. Our peace starts with a change in our mind and behaviors. When we set our minds on what the Spirit desires, the peace of God will flow in every area of our lives.

We will come back to your assessment results later, but for now, I will spend the next parts of the book on further explanation of each question of this assessment.

PART 1

PEACE WITH GOD

11

CHAPTER 2

PEACE WITH GOD

The first peace tier is peace with God. In any water fountain, there has to be a water source. If there is no source, water in the tiers will eventually dry up.

The Bible often uses flowing water to represent the Spirit of God (Isaiah 44:3). Jesus spoke to a Samaritan woman at a well and asked her for a drink of water. She wondered why Jesus, a Jew, would ask her for a drink of water. In those days, Jews did not associate with Samaritans.

Jesus responded, "If you knew the gift of God and who it is that asks you for a drink, you would have asked him and he would have given you living water" (John 4:10).

Jesus wants to provide us this same living water. Whether we realize it or not, we thirst for this water. We try to fill that thirst with the enemy's many counterfeits, but nothing but God's living water can truly satisfy us.

It's impossible to have peace without a relationship with God. If it were possible, rich and famous people would never be miserable.

It all starts here. Jesus is the Source. The only way for us to have peace with God is through Christ.

It's when we allow God's Spirit to flow through us like living water that we can experience the peace God intends for us. We allow His Spirit to work in us by taking these steps.

Accept Jesus as Payment for Your Sins

The first step to gain peace with God is to begin a relationship with Him. We do this when we accept Jesus as payment for our sins. Jesus said, "I am the way and the truth and the life. No one comes to the Father except through me" (John 14:6). Jesus is called the Prince of Peace. His very name is peace, and He is the source of peace.

When my son was small, I remember having a conversation with him about heaven. I asked, "Do you think Daddy deserves to go to heaven?"

He said, "You do a lot of good things and go to church and treat people good. Yes, you deserve to go to heaven."

I told him that I appreciate him saying those nice things about me, but none of those things give me the right to go to heaven.

God tells us that the only way to go to heaven is to be free of sin. That's the deal. If you are free from sin, you get to go to heaven. I asked him, "Do you think I have ever sinned in life?"

He said, "Yes, everyone sins."

"That's right," I said.

Scripture tells us that all have sinned and fall short of God's expectation (Romans 3:23). God gives us the choice to sin or not. But He is clear that if you sin even just once, you lose your right to live in heaven. But because God loves us so much and didn't want us separated from Him for eternity, He provided a way.

Jesus came in the form of a man, lived a perfect life without sin, went to the cross, died, and was buried. His death was payment for our sins. Three days later, He was resurrected from the grave. This is called the gospel or the story of Jesus's death, burial, and resurrection. Jesus saves us from an eternity separated from God.

So many of us are trying to obtain righteousness by our own strength. We think if we can avoid drinking, cussing, and treating people badly, then we can work ourselves into righteousness. The problem with this is we will inevitably fail. This futile exercise wears us out.

Hebrews 4:10 tells us, "… for anyone who enters God's rest also rests from his own work." We can stop trying to make ourselves good. Jesus has already done this for us. We can't change ourselves. It's God's Spirit that changes us. All we have to do is let Him. When we apply the spiritual disciplines discussed in this book (reading scriptures, being around other believers, praying, getting planted in church, and so on), we are allowing God's spirit to change us.

I love the way my pastor, John Siebeling, explains it in his book, *Fresh Start with God*:

> God loved you and me so much that He gave His only Son, Jesus Christ. The Bible says that Jesus came in the form of a man and walked this earth, the same earth we're walking today. He was tempted in every way so He could fully relate to us, but He never gave in to the temptation and therefore lived a sinless life. He became the sacrifice for our sins by dying on the cross. All of the things we have ever done wrong, all of our mistakes, all of our sin—past, present, future—was placed on Jesus. Then He took our place on the cross and was crucified. He was laid in a tomb and three days later, by the power of the Holy Spirit He rose from the dead. He overcame our sin.
>
> The Bible teaches that through the cross we receive forgiveness from our sin and through the resurrection we have new life and a new beginning—a fresh start.

"If you confess with your mouth, 'Jesus is Lord,' and believe in your heart that God raised him from the dead, you will be saved. For it is with your heart that you believe and are justified, and it is with your mouth that you confess your faith and are saved" (Romans 10:9–10).

These verses give us the practical steps to a fresh start with God. It starts with believing. In our heart, we believe the story I just described. We believe God loves us and sent Jesus. We believe Jesus gave His life on the cross and rose from the dead. We may not fully understand it all, but something inside our hearts says, "This is true." When we believe in our heart, then we can "confess" or pray with our mouth. We pray and declare our love for God and invite His presence into our life. From that moment, our lives are changed! The Bible says we are "saved," meaning we're united with God through Jesus Christ.

I encourage you, if you are reading this right now and you are insecure or unsure of where you stand in your relationship with God, take a minute and pray this prayer:

God, thank you for the amazing plan you have for my life. I come today to ask you to fill me with your presence. Thanks for sending your Son, Jesus, to die on a cross for me so I could receive forgiveness from my sin. Thank you for raising Jesus from the dead so I could have new life. I ask you to forgive me of my sin, cleanse me, and make me new. Come live inside of me and give me the strength to live for you. In Jesus' name, amen.

There you go! You just made a fresh start with God.

When we pray and accept Jesus, asking Him to forgive us, we are accepted by God and we become His children.

Be Confident in Who You Are in Christ

Traditional religion gives us a list of things we have to do so God will like us. But Jesus says, "I have already done everything so we can get to know each other." You don't have to do, do, do. You just have to accept what is already done.

Really there are two paths you can choose in your relationship with God. The first is to spend the rest of your life trying to earn God's approval by your own efforts, doing or not doing certain things. This is a very hard path because we can never be perfect and will end up falling short, feeling condemned and far from God. The second is to enjoy God's approval by accepting what Jesus Christ has already done. You can't earn God's love, acceptance, or approval. You already have it.

Our confidence needs to be in God, not in ourselves. Be confident of who you are in Christ. Having spiritual confidence means knowing and believing what the Bible says about you.

Jesus was confronted by opposition, trying to trap Him with the question, "What is the greatest commandment?" His answer really broke our faith down into one simple sentence: love God and love others as yourself.

"Jesus replied: 'Love the Lord your God with all your heart and with all your soul and with all your mind.' This is the first and greatest commandment. And the second is like it: 'Love your neighbor as yourself'" (Matthew 22:37–39).

It was the perfect answer and gives us a road map to follow in order to live a significant life. But His answer implies something huge that we cannot overlook.

It implies we love ourselves. People who do not love themselves cannot effectively love others. You have to have a healthy self-image in order to focus on others.

I counseled a husband who was struggling in his marriage. He wanted to work on the marriage and build a better relationship with his wife, but the root of his problem was that he had a problem loving himself. Until he learned how to love himself, he couldn't effectively love his wife. In order to have peace, I have to see myself as God does and not how others see me.

When Satan tempted Christ, he started by trying to cast doubt on Jesus's identity. He said, "If you are the Son of God ..." Jesus didn't need man's approval (John 2:24–25). He was self-confident. His value was not in how others viewed Him. Jesus knew exactly who He was and was able to resist Satan's foolishness. Satan tries the same trick with us. He wants to cast doubt on who we are in Christ. He knows if we doubt who we are, we will be less effective in accomplishing the things of God.

Jesus combated this attempt to cause doubt by quoting what the Bible says. We have to do the same. It doesn't matter who the world says I am, only who God says I am. We have to know what God says about us and put it in our hearts.

Listen to what God says about you:

- John 1:12: You are God's child.
- John 1:16: God calls you blameless.
- John 15:15: You are Christ's friend.
- John 15:16: You have been chosen and appointed to bear fruit.
- Romans 8:28: You are assured that all things work together for good.
- Timothy 1:7: You have not been given a spirit of fear but of power, love, and a sound mind.
- Philippians 4:13: You can do all things through Christ, who strengthens you.
- Romans 8:37: You are a champion.
- Romans 8:38–39: You cannot be separated from the love of God.

When Satan tries to tap me on my shoulder and say, "You don't deserve God's love," I reply, "I know. You are right."

He pushes, "How can God love you with what you did last night?"

I say, "That's what's so crazy."

There is nothing I can do to make God love me more or less. I am the apple of God's eye. When He tweets, it's about me. I am all over His Instagram. My face is on God's refrigerator. How can I say I have no value when God loved me so much that He gave up His only Son for me?

Scripture tells us that when we are saved, nothing can separate us from the love of God—not death or Satan, not our past sins or future sins. There is nothing in all of creation that can separate you from God's love (Romans 8:38–39).

Take some time to look up each of these verses and pray these thoughts over your life. Be confident in how God made you. Find self-worth in what God says and not what others say. Remember, we have to love ourselves before we can effectively love others. Incorporate confessing and memorizing these scriptures into your weekly goals, which we will discuss later.

CHAPTER 3

SPEND TIME WITH GOD DAILY

Since Jesus commanded us to 'Love the Lord your God with all your heart and with all your soul and with all your mind,' then we should do this. But what does it mean to love God? The Bible speaks of several specific ways to spend time with God to express love to Him. Here are a few.

Search scripture

> "Now the Berean Jews were of more noble character than those in Thessalonica, for they received the message with great eagerness and examined the Scriptures every day to see if what Paul said was true" (Acts 17:11).

We shouldn't just take others' words for who God is and what He says. God loves it when we search scripture for ourselves. It shows Him we want to know more about Him.

Learn God's Word

> "Moses summoned all Israel and said: 'Hear, Israel, the decrees and laws I declare in your hearing today. Learn them and be sure to follow them'" (Deuteronomy 5:1).

Nothing has benefited me more than learning the Bible. It's God's Word. How can we know what to do if we don't know His Word?

It encourages us, gives us direction, and teaches us His way. It's the Word of God that saves us.

Worship God

> "Yet a time is coming and has now come when the true worshipers will worship the Father in the Spirit and in truth, for they are the kind of worshipers the Father seeks. God is spirit, and his worshipers must worship in the Spirit and in truth" (John 4:23–24).

Give God praise. Celebrating who He is and what He has done for us. If you don't like worshipping, then you will not like heaven because all we will do there is worship God.

Pray

> "Do not be anxious about anything, but in every situation, by prayer and petition, with thanksgiving, present your requests to God. And the peace of God, which transcends all understanding, will guard your hearts and your minds in Christ Jesus" (Philippians 4:6–7).

When we pray, we are just talking with God. Tell Him what's on your mind and what you are in need of.

I heard someone say, "The way we spell love is T-I-M-E." We love our spouse when we spend time with them. It is the same with our Kids and our friends. Loving God is no different. God wants to spend time with us in relationship. When we spend time with God in relationship, it lets Him know that we love Him.

I encourage every man I mentor to have daily alone time with God. I encourage them all to give God the best time of their day. Whenever you are the freshest is when you should spend time with God. For me, this is the morning time. At the end of the day, I can barely think. I don't want to give God that time when I'm at my worst.

Scripture tells us that this daily time with God is a key to having success in life.

"Keep this Book of the Law always on your lips; meditate on it day and night, so that you may be careful to do everything written in it. Then you will be prosperous and successful" (Joshua 1:8).

This is my time to journal my thoughts from the previous day, read my Bible and journal notes, pray for things that concern me, and pray for those around me. I love this time with God. It gives me energy, hope, encouragement, and direction. It prepares me to take on my day with confidence.

Jesus did the same thing. He would often take time away from everyone to spend it with God.

"Very early in the morning, while it was still dark, Jesus got up, left the house and went off to a solitary place, where he prayed" (Mark 1:35).

Jesus needed this time with God, and so do we. Spend time each day reading God's Word, for it is the pathway to God's will and direction, taking us from a place of uncertainty to a place of peace.

Tips for Spending Time with God

1. Choose a Bible with a translation that works for you.
2. Have a designated place and time. Don't give God the leftover time.
3. Pick a reading plan.
4. Be consistent. It takes only twenty-one days to make a habit.
5. Use extra materials to help your understanding (e.g., a Bible dictionary, commentaries, web searches, and so on).
6. Start with thanksgiving and praise (three minutes).
7. Read the scriptures for who, what, when, where, how, and why (five minutes).

8. Ask the following (two minutes):
   a. What is God saying to the people at that time?
   b. What timeless principle is addressed?
   c. How can I apply this principle to my life?
9. Journal what you are reading and what God is saying to you (ten minutes).
10. Pray for the following (ten minutes):
    a. Your vision/needs (spiritual, relational, health, financial, and purpose)
    b. Your family and friends
    c. Your church
    d. God's kingdom

CHAPTER 4

GET PLANTED IN A HEALTHY LOCAL CHURCH

One of the most important things to do to grow in your relationship with God is to find a healthy, life-giving church and get connected through attending and serving each week. It's not enough just to go to church. Being planted means that you become a contributor at church and not just a consumer. You become the church and take on responsibility for carrying out the vision of the church. It is no longer *that* church or *their* church; it becomes *your* church.

At our church, we call this getting planted in God's house. Psalm 92:12-14 paints a great picture of what happens when we are planted in the house of God. "The righteous will flourish like a palm tree, they will grow like a cedar of Lebanon; planted in the house of the LORD, they will flourish in the courts of our God. They will still bear fruit in old age, they will stay fresh and green"

This scripture tells us when we are planted in God's house, our lives will flourish. We grow in our relationship with God and get a vision for our lives.

Pastor John Siebeling explains it like this. "We are like a seed and the environment of the local church is like the soil. Without good soil, the seed doesn't fulfil its purpose. But when we are planted in a healthy church environment, we grow and produce" (Siebeling, Fresh Start with God, 51). Every Christian needs a local church family. In fact, a Christian without a church is a contradiction.

There are at least five benefits from being planted in God's house:

- **You can build relationships.**

Church is a place to build positive relationships. Who we spend time with is the best indicator of where our lives are headed. At church, you can find people you can do life with who are going in the same direction as you. We can't do life by ourselves. We need others, and they need us.

- **You will have opportunities to make a difference.**

When we are a part of a church, we are able to partner with God and others to make an impact in our communities and our world. At our church, we have adopted several schools and have decided to help provide food to almost three thousand elementary-age children. This is a big effort, but it is shared throughout our church. Some people work with planning and gathering the food. Others separate and prepare the food to distribute, while others do maintenance on the food trucks or deliver food to the schools. Everyone has a part. This task would be daunting if any one of us decided to do it by him or herself. Our time, talents, and financial resources go further when we are connected with others with a goal of impacting people's lives. The church gives us a chance to make a huge difference in the lives of others.

- **You receive support and encouragement.**

Being connected with a church family strengthens us. We have people who can support us and encourage us when we need it. It's tough doing life by ourselves. As grown as we all like to think we are, we still need others to encourage us from time to time. Your church family is there for that reason. It's not just the pastor's responsibility to support and encourage church members when needed. It's the role of the entire church. That's why it's so important not to just attend church but to become a part of the church by serving and connecting with others in the church.

There was a family in our church who lost a loved one and was upset that the church didn't provide more support. The problem was this family was not planted in the church. They did not serve on any teams or join any of our connect groups. They usually got to church late and were the first ones out the door when church ended. No one knew them, and they didn't know anyone. When they got to a point where they needed encouragement and support from their church family, they did not get what they were hoping for and needed.

I remember when I first joined my church but was not connected. I thought to myself, *I don't have anyone from church in my cell phone, and no one from church has me in theirs.* I had not been to anyone's home, and no one had been to mine. I made a decision that this needed to change. I made a commitment to be intentional about building relationships at my church. This is a key part of being planted in church. Because of our commitment to get planted, we receive support and encouragement from our church family that keeps our lives flourishing.

- **You get a vision for your life.**

Church is where we hear God's Word spoken to us and over us. It's a place where the vision God has for you can be revealed, nurtured, and encouraged. In many cases, God will use those in spiritual authority over us to speak vision over our lives. When we are not planted in a church, our vision gets lost in all the surrounding noise. When you are planted in a healthy church, you are encouraged by others to pursue your dreams. You have a chance to practice and hone your God-given spiritual gifts. A vision for your life is formed and nurtured. I'm convinced if we had not been planted in church, I would have never written my first book or taught my first financial seminar. I remember talking to a pastor at my church about my story, and he suggested I publish my first book. Another pastor asked me to teach a financial small group. The vision that I have for my life would never have happened if I had not been planted in a church where these men could speak into my life. If you are in a place where you don't have a vision for your life, start by getting planted in a healthy local church.

- **You will grow in your relationship with God.**

Being planted in a healthy local church is important in your spiritual growth. Psalm 92:12–14 says, "The righteous will flourish like a palm tree, they will grow like a cedar of Lebanon; planted in the house of the LORD, they will flourish in the courts of our God. They will still bear fruit in old age, they will stay fresh and green …"

We know whatever is being fed will grow and what is not being fed will die. The local church is a place we can be fed and grow. It is like a seed being planted in good soil where a farmer can nurture, water, and prune for growth. When we are planted in a healthy local church, we will grow strong, flourish in life, and continue to be productive even as we grow older.

We had a great couple in our church who transferred because of a job relocation out of state. They continued to give financially to our church six months after the move. I called them to see how things were going. They confirmed that they hadn't found a church yet. I encouraged them to get planted in a local church soon and when they did to begin giving their weekly offering to that church immediately instead of to us. I told them we appreciate their generosity toward our church, but it's more important for them to get planted in a local church and begin giving there. God expects us to financially support the church where we are getting spiritually fed and encouraged. This couple agreed and seemed to appreciate that we cared more about their spiritual growth than we did about receiving their money.

Here are a few things to consider when looking for a healthy local church.

- Word—God's Word is believed to be the standard and is preached in a way that you understand it and can apply it to your daily life.

- Worship — God's presence is tangible, and there is a freedom to connect with Him. The worship style shouldn't be your primary consideration; worship is an attitude and heart issue.
- Vision — The church is going somewhere. You can see where it's going and desire to be involved. It values reaching out to and serving its community.
- Leadership — The leaders of the church are strong, committed, humble people with good character.
- Atmosphere — The environment is life-giving, encouraging, fun, friendly, and Spirit-filled.

Being planted in God's house puts us in position to be blessed by Him and to receive His peace. If you have not done so already, I encourage you to get planted in a thriving, life-giving local church.

CHAPTER 5

HONOR GOD WITH YOUR FINANCES

There is no such thing as being right with God and wrong with money. This sounds like a harsh statement, but these following scriptures seem to support it.

- "The seed falling among the thorns refers to someone who hears the word, but the worries of this life and the deceitfulness of wealth choke the word, making it unfruitful" (Matthew 13:22).
- "For where your treasure is, there your heart will be also" (Matthew 6:21).
- "No one can serve two masters. Either you will hate the one and love the other, or you will be devoted to the one and despise the other. You cannot serve both God and money" (Matthew 6:24)
- "For the love of money is a root of all kinds of evil. Some people, eager for money, have wandered from the faith and pierced themselves with many griefs" (1 Timothy 6:10).

We honor God with our finances when we commit to giving Him the first part of our income.

Proverbs 3:9 says, "Honor the Lord by giving him the first part of all your income."

Most Christians are familiar with the term *tithe* but may not understand what it really means. The term *tithe* literally means "a tenth part," just like the word *half* means 50 percent or a *quarter* means 25 percent. The most often used definition of tithing is bringing the first 10 percent of my gross income to God through my local church. Tithing gives us a vision for giving systematically. It provides a clear benchmark for action. The truth is everything we have belongs to God, not just 10 percent but 100 percent. Tithing is a tangible way we show God that we honor, love, and trust Him.

Giving Willingly and Cheerfully

At my local church, we have an expectation of members to give, but we do not put pressure on people to give. We do this for two reasons. First, we don't believe it would be effective. Eventually, members would begin to distrust us and hold back from being generous, knowing the pressure will soon come. Secondly, we don't put pressure on people to give because it's unbiblical. In 2 Corinthians 9:7, it says, "Each one should give what he has decided in his heart to give, not reluctantly or under pressure for God loves a cheerful giver!"

God doesn't want people giving out of obligation any more than He would want us to pray or go to church out of obligation. He cares more about our heart. This scripture says He loves a cheerful giver.

I believe it is also true that a cheerful giver loves God. Giving is a true test of the heart. If we are struggling in giving financially, maybe the truth is we just *like* God. When we aren't giving cheerfully, we are expressing to God, "You are all right. You do a lot of good things, and I want to go to heaven and all. I really like You but not as much as I love money." We love money and the things it allows us to buy so much that we hate to part with it—even for Jesus.

One of the saddest stories in the Bible is the story of the rich young ruler who came to Jesus and asked how he could get into heaven. Jesus responded that he must follow the commandments given by Moses.

The ruler replied, "I have done all these since birth."

When Jesus heard this, He said to him, "You still lack one thing. Sell everything you have and give to the poor, and you will have treasure in heaven. Then come, follow me." (Luke 18:18–23)

Jesus knew this man's true heart. The rich young ruler loved money more than he loved God. Scripture says, "When he heard this, he became very sad, because he was very wealthy."

This is a strange saying, "He became very sad, because he was very wealthy." Most of us would think the opposite, that being very wealthy would make us happy. How can being wealthy make us sad? Money makes us sad when it serves as our god.

When given the choice between God and wealth, he chose wealth. Money was his god.

Every time I read this, I find myself hoping for another ending. I'm pulling for the ruler to make the right decision. I want to scream out, "You are standing in front of the King of Kings. Choose Him. Choose life." But every time I read it, I'm disappointed again. He chose to let money serve as his god. He chose sadness instead of peace and death instead of life.

Jesus said, "No one can serve two masters; for either he will hate the one and love the other, or he will be devoted to one and despise the other. You cannot serve God and Money" (Luke 16:13).

Jesus spent so much time and energy talking about money because He knew it would be our toughest battle. When we consistently put God first in our finances, we win the battle against money and show God He is first in our lives.

Tithing Is for Babies

I love the way Jesus talked about tithing in Matthew 23:23. He said, "Of course you should tithe, but also take care of the more important things." Jesus' response shows us that tithing is just a baby step for Christians. Even to us, in any other area of life, we consider 10 percent to be insignificant. We don't get excited when there is a 10 percent off sale at our favorite store. We don't complain with 10 percent sales tax. We don't even complain about a 15 percent tip to a server at a restaurant. The only time 10 percent becomes a big deal is when we are giving it to the church. Tithing is not the goal. It's just the beginning.

Tithing Builds Our Faith

"Trust in the Lord with all your heart and lean not on your own understanding" (Proverbs 3:5).

Putting God first in our finances gives God a chance to prove He exists and wants to bless us.

Our Lord wants us to trust and test Him. Giving never makes financial sense. I always get questions like, "Should I tithe even though I'm in debt?" My response is, "It depends on whom you trust. Do you trust that you can do more with 100 percent than God can do with 90 percent? If you do, then don't tithe." But I always follow up with the question, "How is that working for you?" because I know it doesn't work.

A few years ago, Carol and I went through our own personal financial struggle. We had over $100,000 in personal debt. It was a rocky start, but after the first two years, we felt pretty good about our progress. We had paid down a lot of the debt and could see the light at the end of the tunnel.

I had been meditating on Proverbs 3:5 and had an internal sense that something big was about to happen. I received a call from my boss that he was coming to town for a visit and thought to myself, *This is it. I'm about to be promoted.*

When we met, he said the words, "Travis, we are going to have to let you go."

I was shocked. I really thought I was going to be promoted, but I was fired.

Carol was a stay-at-home mom with our four children so I was the breadwinner in our family. During this time, our only income was my $275.00 per week unemployment check. We decided that we would continue to trust God. We honored God with our $27.50 per week tithe and committed to not using credit cards or taking loans. We had learned our lesson and decided we would not try to *help God out*.

We realized that at some point we had to decide we would obey God even if it meant we would lose everything else we loved. We agreed if we lost the house, so be it. Our faith was in God, and if He didn't show up, we were guaranteed to fail. We would obey Him anyway.

He never failed us. Every time the house payment was due, we made a payment. Once, I thought we were at the end of our resources and we received a large tax refund.

I wasn't too concerned about finding a job, because I had a good résumé and I interview well. In fact, I had never interviewed for a job without coming away with a job offer. So I started my job search. I went on my first interview but came away with no job. The second and third interviews resulted in no job offers as well. This went on for six months, but Carol and I never panicked. As much as this goes against my personality, we both felt this sense of peace.

At the end of the six months, I received a job offer making more money than I had before. By the end of the year, we were able to pay off the remaining debt. Remember, this was a year that I didn't work for six months. What this taught me is that God is a God who can be counted on. He built my faith. You don't have to tell me that I can trust Him, because now I know it for myself. If I had tried to help God by not tithing and using credit cards or getting loans, I would have never learned this lesson. God proved to us that He exists and that He wants to bless us, and He wants to bless you too.

Is God Really Number One?

It's easy to say God is first, but does our spending reflect it? Show me your checkbook and I will show you your priorities. If you are serious about living for God, you've got to make Him the number-one priority in every area of your life. When you write your check, you say to God, "Regardless of what else I've said or done this week, this is how I really feel about You."

We can't take care of our wants and needs and give God the leftovers. After spending what we want and paying our bills, we scrape together what's left and offer it to God and then have the audacity to ask Him to meet all of our needs. We can't put God at the end or our priority list and expect Him to bless us. We can't violate His principles and expect His promises. When He is truly first in our lives, it is reflected in our finances.

Don't Fool Yourself

I'm amazed at the number of people who say they tithe compared to those who do actually tithe. I'm not talking about those who don't believe in tithing. I'm talking about those who say they understand that a tithe is 10 percent of their gross income and say they are committed to it.

I was a consultant at a church that conducted a survey of members and asked questions like, "How many times a week do you attend church?" and "How often do you serve in a ministry?" One of the questions was, "Do you tithe 10 percent of your gross income to your local church?" The results baffled me. It seemed on most questions, people responded with total accuracy, but when it came to the tithing question, the results were astonishing. Seventy percent of the members said that they were tithers, yet only 10 percent of the members gave at least $800 per year. This was shocking to me since the average annual income in this church was around $42,000. It was an anonymous survey, so there was no benefit to lying. Why would people be untruthful about this question and not the other questions?

I have even had people I am counseling tell me that they tithe when I'm looking right at their paychecks and giving statements. It baffles me. I really don't think they are just blatantly being untruthful. An article in the *New York Times* explains how if you tell yourself something long enough, your mind begins to believe it as truth.

(Dupree, "Can You Become a Creature of Habit?"). This could explain why people respond the way they do when asked about their giving. It seems that most people have manipulated their minds to convince themselves that they are tithers even when they are not.

So, to help you make a simple and clear determination of your giving, I have added a giving percent calculation tool below. I know this sounds elementary, but indulge me by taking the time to actually complete this exercise.

Giving Percent Calculation

- What was your last year's income based on line 22 of last year's tax 1040? Put that number below on line 1.
- What did you give to your local church based on last year's contribution statement? Put that number below on line 2.

Actual	Example
Line 1 —_____	$65,000
Line 2 —_____	$4,000

Then divide line 2 by line 1 and place that number on line 3.

Line 3 — My Giving Percent _____

This is your actual giving percent. If this amount is less than 10 percent, then you did not tithe. If the government does not think you are a tither, then certainly God does not. The important thing is to stop fooling ourselves into believing God is our top priority when it's clear He is not.

I don't want you to feel condemnation because of your giving. Just start where you are and commit to grow from there.

How to Start?

Now you have to make a decision. Will you trust God with your finances? If you have not done so, I encourage you to begin today. Don't overthink it. Just trust God and see if He is trustworthy.

To help encourage people to trust God with their finances at my church, we do a ninety-day tithing challenge. Here is how it works.

- You make a commitment to trust God with your whole tithe for the next ninety days.
- You agree to meet with a money coach and/or attend our financial small groups.
- If you don't feel God has kept up His end of the deal at the end of the ninety days, we will give you back every penny of the tithes you gave during those ninety days, no questions asked.

You have nothing to lose but a whole lot to gain. Even if your church doesn't have a money-back guarantee, I encourage you to test God at His word for the next ninety days. It shows God that He is your top priority and that you love Him and trust Him.

Now this doesn't mean you can handle the other 90 percent any kind of way and God will still bless you financially. You must manage the other 90 percent responsibly as well. If personal finances are a struggle for you, you should join a financial small group study to get things in order. I will discuss more about how to manage the 90 percent in a later chapter.

But for now, commit to tithing consistently by giving at least 10 percent of your gross income to God through your local church.

Small Group Discussion Questions

1. What did you read in chapters 1 through 5 that interests you most?

2. What surprised you most as you took the self-assessment?

3. Would you say you have peace with God? Why or why not?

4. Do you feel you are planted in a healthy local church? If not, what can you do to be more planted in a healthy local church? (Attending, serving, giving, etc.)

5. On a scale of 1–10 with 10 being the highest, how would you rate the consistency and effectiveness of your daily time with God?

    • How can you improve your daily time with God?

6. What scripture concerning who God says you are stands out to you the most? Why?

7. Did you complete the giving calculation on page 37? If no, why not? If yes, did your giving percent surprise you?

8. How has putting God first or not putting God first in your finances impacted your life?

CHAPTER 6

MASTERING SIN IN MY LIFE

I received an e-mail from a man at my church who, no matter how hard he tried, kept falling into a sinful behavior. He felt horrible every time he did. He tried hard to be a good guy. When he was doing well, he felt God was there with him. When he did bad, he felt God was distant from him. He was tormented by this up-and-down struggle with sin and wanted to get off the seesaw of condemnation with God.

Even though he felt he was on a seesaw with God, God was not on the other side. God was actually there watching over him during the ups and downs.

Scripture tells us that we all sin and fall short of His glory. When I accept Him as my savior, my sin is forgotten at that moment and forever. God will not love me more or less based on whether I sin or not. He took away my sin when He died on the cross once and for all.

So, if my sins are forgiven, why fight temptation? The truth is my sin doesn't limit me from experiencing life with God in heaven, but my sin will limit me from experiencing life with God on earth. God wants us to master sin in our lives.

"[Sin] is crouching at your door, it desires to have you, but you must master it" (Genesis 4:7).

Mastering sin is not for Him; it's for you. The enemy dresses sin up and tries to make the choice to sin seem reasonable and appealing. But in the end, all sin leads to death and God's way leads to life.

God wants you to master sin because He knows that His way is best for you. God wants you to master sin so that you can live the abundant life of peace He intended for you to have. You must defeat sin, or it will be defeat you.

We tend to minimize our sins. If someone asked us whether we are being mastered by something, we would be quick to answer, "No, I have it all under control." Here is a quiz to determine whether something is mastering you.

1. Do your family and friends say you have a problem?
2. Is it hard for you to go a week without being involved in this situation?
3. Do you rearrange your schedule for it?
4. Does it isolate you from others?
5. Do you continue even though you are hurting yourself or others?
6. Do you hide it?

If you answer yes to three or more, then there may be something in your life that's mastering you that God wants to free you from.

Mastering sin would be a lot easier if it wasn't for one small thing—Satan.

Satan's biggest deception is that he does not really exist or that he can be recognized by a red suit and pitchfork. Satan is real, and he is God's enemy. By studying Genesis 3, we can see how Satan works. Satan has six goals as it relates to you.

Satan's Six Goals:

1. To deceive (Genesis 3:1)—He is the father of lies. He distorts the truth to make sin appear reasonable and appealing. He tries to trick us into meeting a legitimate need in an illegitimate way or to do the right thing at the wrong time. He tries to convince us that there is a better way than God's way. He tricks us into to taking what appears to be shortcuts, making a small compromise for a big return. But even small compromises can get us way off track.

2. To discredit (Genesis 3:5) — Satan tries to discredit God and the followers of God. He tells us, "God doesn't have your best interests at heart." Here are three truths about God:

   a. Only God wants what's best for us.
   b. Only God knows what's best for us.
   c. Only God gives what's best for us.

3. To distract (Genesis 3:6) — He distracts us with things. It could be good things. He just wants to keep us distracted from God's best. It could have us focused on a pretty girl, a new promotion, a bigger lifestyle, and so on. He will even provide us with some of the things. The more he can distract us with stuff, the less we are focused on achieving what God has for us. Just like he did with Eve, the liar makes the forbidden apple look good and blinds us to all the good fruit God makes available to us.

4. To divide (Genesis 3:8, 12) — Satan wants to divide us from God and each other. This is why he attacks marriages and families. He knows if we are unified with God and each other, then there is nothing we can't accomplish. His strategy is to divide and conquer. The minute Adam and Eve ate from the forbidden fruit, they were separated from God spiritually. They immediately went and hid from their creator. This is what sin does in our lives. When God confronted Adam, he immediately threw Eve under the bus. He said, "That woman you gave me." Adam blamed everyone but himself. Eve did it, God did it, and Satan did it. He blamed everyone he could in the garden. There was no more unity. It was now every man for himself. Satan was successful in dividing them.

5. To discourage (Genesis 3:10) — After they ate from the tree, Adam and Eve hid from God when they heard Him coming. "I heard you coming, and I hid because I was afraid because I was naked." They had always been naked, but once they had sinned, they felt shame and guilt. They were discouraged. This is what sin does to us; it makes us feel inadequate. Satan believes if he discourages you, then you will leave God. It worked for a while with Adam and Eve because they hid from God.

6. To destroy (Genesis 3:21–22) — Satan's ultimate goal is to kill and destroy us. He knew that the punishment for eating from the tree was death. Adam and Eve immediately died spiritually. They no longer had the connection with God that they had enjoyed. Scripture tells us in 1 Peter 5:8 that the devil prowls around like a roaring lion looking for someone to devour. Satan knows if he can keep us separated from God, then he will accomplish his intent to destroy us.

I'm not telling you this so that you feel defeated. I'm telling you this to help you understand the key to winning in this area of your life.

How do you fight the temptation of the liar? How do you master sin? We have to recognize the pattern of sin and cut it off.

GEICO, the insurance company, ran a series of commercials called "Happier Than." They highlighted several humorous characters who were happy for various reasons. One of the most popular ads had the line, "Happier than a camel on Wednesday." It featured a camel traveling through an office, asking people if they knew what day it was and shouting, "Hump Day!" I love these commercials. One of my favorites was one stating, "Happier than an antelope with night-vision goggles." It had a lion trying to sneak up and attack a couple of antelopes. The antelopes were not worried because they could see the lion with their night-vision goggles. They teased the lion, saying, "This is embarrassing. We can see you, Carl." By using night-vision goggles, they were able to take away all the great lion's power to sneak up on them.

This is how God wants us to approach Satan. He wants us to put on our night-vision goggles so we can clearly see the enemy coming. When we can clearly see the enemy, it takes away his power. We take away his power when we recognize that sin always follows the same pattern.

Sin Pattern: See → Desire → Take → Hide

Here are three examples of this pattern.

1. Adam and Eve (Genesis 3:6, 8)

"When the woman *saw* that the fruit of the tree was good for food and pleasing to the eye, and also *desirable* for gaining wisdom, she *took* some and ate it. She also gave some to her husband, who was with her, and he ate it.

Then the man and his wife heard the sound of the LORD God as he was walking in the garden in the cool of the day, and they *hid* from the LORD God among the trees of the garden." (emphasis added)

Adam and Eve saw the fruit, desired to eat, took it, and then hid when God came looking for them.

2. Achan's Story (Joshua 7:20–21)

"When I *saw* in the plunder a beautiful robe from Babylonia, two hundred shekels of silver and a bar of gold weighing fifty shekels, I *coveted* them and *took* them. They are *hidden* in the ground inside my tent, with the silver underneath." (emphasis added)

Achan saw the plunder, coveted or desired it, took it, and then hid it in his tent.

3. David (2 Samuel 11:2–8)

"King David *saw* Bathsheba, he *desired* her even though she was another man's wife, he *took* her and had sex with her, then he had her husband killed to *hide* what he had done." (emphasis added)

Satan is the father of lies. The liar makes the apple look good and blinds you to the fruit in the basket. He distorts the truth to make sin appear reasonable and appealing.

It starts with having us *see* the wrong thing.

Then we *desire* the wrong thing.

Then we *take* the wrong action.

And finally we *hide* it.

When we follow this pattern, the results are predictable. We are no match for temptation. We become easy prey for the enemy to knock us off. Just as the sin pattern is predictable, so is the pattern God gives us for mastering sin. God told Cain, "If you follow the right pattern, you will master sin."

God's Pattern for success: Vision → Hope → Action → Accountability

Vision — See What God Sees

"Where there is no revelation, the people cast off all restraint" (Proverbs 29:18).

How do we form or maintain God's vision? It starts with what we see. Eve saw the fruit, Achan saw the plunder, and David saw Bathsheba. We have to be careful what we see or watch. We have to guard what we allow into our minds. It starts with what we see, and then it gets into our mind and eventually into our heart. Scripture tells us we must guard our heart because out of it springs life. Whatever is in our heart eventually controls our behavior.

We have to ask ourselves, "How does this line up with the vision God has for my life?" When Satan approached Eve, he questioned Eve with God's words. He asked, "Did God really say you couldn't eat from the tree?" Eve responded, "God said not to eat or touch the tree." I think at this point Satan knew he had her because she had misquoted God. God never said not to touch the fruit from the tree. Eve added words to God's words, showing that she didn't know exactly what God had said. It provided room for Satan to create a new vision for her. I'm sure at this moment, he was salivating. Satan probably thought to himself, "I got her now because she doesn't know the word of God."

In order to resist temptation, we have to know the Word of God. In Psalm 119:11, David says, "I have hidden your word in my heart."

What does God say about your life? God will never lead us in a way that contradicts His word. We have to know the Word of God in order to understand the vision He has for us.

Hope—Desire What God Desires

To master sin, the second thing we have to do is put our hope in God. Hope gives us a reason to believe our vision will come to pass. Without hope, we fail. We have a choice as to whom or what to put our hope in. We could put our hope in our youth, our own abilities, other people, our wealth, and so on. But it's only when we put our hope in God that will we have peace.

Isaiah 40:30–31 says, "Even youths grow tired and weary, and young men stumble and fall; but those who hope in the LORD will renew their strength. They will soar on wings like eagles; they will run and not grow weary, they will walk and not be faint."

When we were struggling financially, Carol and I took the Crown Financial Bible study. Looking at our debt, we almost lost hope. When our finances looked impossible, we had to decide who we would put our hope in. In the class, we read and memorized scriptures concerning finances.

We took this small box and on the outside placed scriptures that spoke to God's promises concerning our finances, such as Philippians 4:19, which says, "And my God will meet all your needs according to the riches of his glory in Christ Jesus."

These words gave us hope. Even though we had all kinds of doubts that God would change our situation, we held on to His promises. It was all we had to put our hope in.

On the inside of the box, we placed nineteen strips of paper, each with one of our prayer requests written on it.

Some of our prayers were things like

- pay off $100,000 of debt,
- repair the roof on the porch,
- get a new car,
- give $4,000 above my tithe to my church's annual campaign,
- save $5,000 in my children's college fund,
- save $10,000 in the emergency fund,
- pay off our home, and
- Travis working in full-time ministry.

We made a decision to put our hope in God. We didn't have a backup plan. If God didn't show up, we were guaranteed to fail.

Once a year, we look in this box to review our prayers. We highlight in yellow the prayers that God has answered. At this point, fourteen of the nineteen prayers are highlighted in yellow.

If I knew then what I know now, there are three things I would have done.

1. Stop worrying

I spent a lot of time and energy worrying, when God had everything under control. My worrying did nothing to help my situation.

2. Continue to do my part and trust God to do His part

My part was to manage responsibly what God had given me. I couldn't dwell on past mistakes. I just had to be faithful going forward.

3. Dream bigger dreams

I realize now that my prayers weren't big enough. God has answered our prayers. But as I think back on it, I can't help but wonder, "Why didn't I ask for more?" Why in the world would I just ask for $5,000 in my kids' college fund? Why didn't I ask for $100,000? I couldn't see far past my situation. My vision was not nearly big enough. At that time, $10,000 in my emergency fund seemed like a million dollars. Giving $4,000 to my church seemed like a pipe dream.

What I know now is that God certainly answers prayers. He loves to bless us when our hearts are centered on Him. God is a big God, and He wants to bless us in big ways. He is not limited to our situations and what we see. We can't lower God to our vision. He wants to lift us to His vision.

In John 15:7, Jesus says, "If you remain in me and my words remain in you, ask whatever you wish, and it will be done for you."

God wants us to depend on Him to provide our heart's desires. He loves to answer our prayers. He is the only one who can provide it. He is on our side and wants what's best for us. It's up to us to stop worrying about things we can't change, continue to do what we know to do, and start asking and trusting Him to answer big prayers.

Choose to be like David, who decided to put his hope in God's word. David said in Psalm 119:114, "You are my refuge and my shield; I have put my hope in your word."

Take a minute to answer these two questions:

1. What am I hoping for? (List your requests.)
2. Whom or what do I put my hope in? (List scriptures that give you confidence that what you are hoping for will happen.)

Take Action

The third step in mastering sin is to take action toward what you are hoping for. This step requires both faith and patience.

"We do not want you to become lazy, but to imitate those who through faith and patience inherit what has been promised" (Hebrews 6:12).

Faith is confidence that God can move in our lives today (Hebrews 11:1). Faith always requires patience. Faith is day after day of believing and doing. *Doing* is the key word. Too many times we believe we are having faith for something, but we are not putting our faith to work. Faith is our hope in action. The action we take by faith gives our hope something to work with.

James 2:26 says, "As the body without the spirit is dead, so faith without deeds is dead."

If I have faith for better health, then I have to do my part by eating better, exercising, and so on. If I have faith to get out of debt, then I have to live on a budget. We have to do our part while trusting God will do His part.

It's our hope in God's Word that gives us the patience to act in faith. "… remembering without ceasing your work of faith, labor of love, and patience of hope in our Lord Jesus Christ in the sight of our God and Father" (1 Thessalonians 1:3).

Maybe you are like me and are praying and hoping for some big things in your life. I'm not talking about the little things that I have control over. I have some things I'm praying for that the only way for them to happen is if God shows up and does something I can't do.

In 2 Kings 4, a widow was so far in debt that her creditors were about to take her sons and force them into slavery. She needed a miracle, so she cried out to the man of God, Elisha, for help.

It was Elisha's response to her request that taught me a key lesson in receiving a miracle blessing from God. He responded with two questions, "How can I help you?" and "What do you have in your house?"

See, Elisha knew that in order for God to perform a miracle in our lives, he had to deal with two parts. So in essence, he was asking, "What's in your control that you can use to show God you are serious about Him showing up in your life?" God has a part, but we also have a part. It's when we do our part by faith that we unleash God to do His part.

Like many of us, the widow initially thought, *I don't have anything; that's why I'm coming to you.* Then she remembered, "I only have a little oil." Elisha realized that God could use her little oil to perform something great. He told her, "Now go and get all the jars you can get, start filling them with oil." She did just what she was told, and God performed a miracle. She filled so many jars she was able to pay off all her debts and have enough for her family to live on.

This miracle inspires me because I have some big things I'm believing God for in my life. I have one big thing that I'm believing God for in particular. It means so much to me that I decided I would pray and fast one day a week for God to answer my prayer. I did this to show God I'm serious about Him moving in my life. It's been over two years since I started this. The more I do my part, the more confidence I have in God doing His part. About six months after I started my fast commitment, I decided to take it to another level. I decided that I would commit to fast and pray one day a week even after God answered my prayer to thank Him for answering my prayer. So regardless of when He answers my prayer, I'm committed to fasting and praying one day a week for the rest of my life. This may sound like a big commitment, but if you only knew what I'm asking God to do in my life, you would understand how small a commitment this really is. Doing my part lets God know that not only am I serious but I trust Him and I'm thankful for Him.

I'm sure you have some big things you are hoping for as well. My challenge to you is to think not only about God's part but also about your part.

There is an exercise that I started that really keeps me focused throughout the year, and I want to encourage you to try it as well. Take an index card and list the things you are hoping for God to do in your life. Write at the top "God's Part." On the back, write "My Part" and list the things you could do to show God you are serious about Him working in your life.

For example, if you are praying for God to touch the heart of a loved one. That's out of your control. Only God can do that. But what if you commit to praying and fasting for this person one day a week? It shows God you are serious.

Many of us are like the widow and downplay what we can do to move us closer to our miracle. We want to put it all on God. But we have to do our part. Remember, faith is day after day of believing and doing.

So what are you willing to *do* by faith? If you have faith for a better marriage, commit to taking your wife out once a week or saying "I love you" daily. If you have faith for a lower cholesterol level, commit to walking thirty minutes three times a week. If you have faith for a promotion at work, commit to showing up fifteen minutes early each day.

No matter how little the amount of oil you have, if you commit it to God, I'm convinced He will do the same as He did for the widow. He will take your small part and perform big miracles in your life.

Accountability — Seek Godly Wisdom

The final step in the sin pattern is to hide it. Adam and Eve hid behind fig leaves. Achan hid the treasures he had taken, and David hid the fact that he had slept with Bathsheba.

I tell my kids when they do something and don't want us to know, then there is a good chance they are in sin. Sin has to be in the dark. With sin comes shame. We have to hide it. We don't want others to know.

"God is light; in him there is no darkness at all" (1 John 1:5).

God's final step to master temptation to sin is to have spiritual accountability. Having spiritual accountability is the opposite of hiding. It's shining light in a place of darkness.

I counseled a young married man who was upset that his wife would look through his phone. I told him he needed that. He thought she should just trust him. I told him I've been married over twenty years and have never so much as looked at another naked person, but I don't trust myself. I know that I need accountability. My wife can look through my phone, computer, and calendar anytime she wants.

We all need accountability. Without it we become easy prey for the enemy. Remember the scripture "… the devil prowls around like a roaring lion looking for someone to devour" (1 Peter 5:8).

How does a lion prowl around? He sneaks around waiting for the one who is separated from the others. He waits until it is all alone and in no position to get away, and then he preys on it. When we are by ourselves and have no accountability or covering, then we become easy prey for the enemy. We need spiritually mature men and women with which to share our struggles.

Satan wants you to keep it in the dark. He knows as soon as it comes to the light he has lost power. The liar wants us weighed down in the dark, keeping secrets like I'm having an affair, I watch porn, I had an abortion, I have an addiction, I sell drugs, I like men, I like women, I steal money, I don't like my spouse, I'm addicted to food, I'm abusive, I've been abused, I hate myself, I'm considering suicide, I hate my spouse, I'm deep in debt, and so on. The weight of it alone is killing us. We are not intended to carry such a burden. We can't continue to hold up the facade.

The minute we share our struggles with someone who provides spiritual accountability, it's like a weight being lifted off our shoulders. I'm not talking about secretly sharing it with others who are just our partners in crime and will conceal our secrets. All of us have this one friend we know we can tell our dirt to because he or she has dirt as well. We just become keepers of each other's dirt. This person is not going to give godly advice and hold you accountable.

On the other end of the spectrum, you can't just share your stuff with anybody. Find some spiritually mature person you can trust who will not be judgmental but will provide godly advice and will lovingly hold you accountable for God's vision for your life.

Mastering sin doesn't mean that you never sin in life. It starts with you knowing what your temptations are. Then you have to know how God wants you to live and want the same thing for yourself. Finally, you take actions toward the vision God has given you and ask some mature, godly person to hold you accountable for moving toward that vision.

You Can't Play Around with Temptation

I was in a meeting when I saw what looked like a cookie on the snack tray. I had been committed to limiting my sweets to once a week in order to improve my health and fitness. I saw some of the people in the meeting eating them and thought, *That looks like a really good cookie.* By the second break, I went over to investigate more. Indeed, it looked like a really good cookie. There was some fresh fruit there as well, but it didn't look as good as the cookie. By the end of the meeting, I saw the cookies were still there so I went over and said, "I will just try a bite to see how good it is." I took one and bit it. It was okay, but it didn't actually taste as good as I had imagined. I thought about throwing the rest away, but I continued to eat the whole cookie. Here is what I learned.

You can't play around with temptation. You have to respect temptation without surrendering to it. I know I'm tempted by sweets. Instead of continuing to look at them and think about them, I should have stayed away. It wasn't the first look that got me in trouble but the second and third looks. I'm a former football player so let me use a football analogy. I know I must play good defense as well as good offense to win a football game. The same is true for mastering sin.

Playing Good Defense

Playing defense is setting appropriate boundaries. One of the things I hate in football is this thing called *prevent defense.* It's when the defense decides to protect the end zone by putting all the players back near the end zone. I hate this play because it allows the offense to get as many yards as they can prior to getting in the end zone. The problem with this defense is that it weakens the defense and allows the offense to get right near the end zone, and more times than not, they eventually score. That's how many of us play defense against temptation to sin. We say, "I'm not going to have sex, but I will do everything up to the point of sex." Just like the prevent defense, this fails almost every time. It's never effective to set boundaries right at the end zone.

This is especially true for men; our bodies are naturally built to complete the action. We can't set it in motion and plan to stop before the end zone. When we do, we have already lost the game. Our boundaries have to be set way before the end zone. Your boundary may need to be no heavy kissing or not being alone with the opposite sex. It's much easier to manage a boundary like this than it is to fight temptation with the prevent defense.

One of my defensive tools is not to have closed-door meetings alone with women. I usually explain that when I meet with women, and most understand and do not have a problem. I was meeting with one lady who was asking for my advice. She closed the door of her office behind us. I asked her to keep the door open and explained why. She got defensive and said, "Do you think I'm going to jump you or something?" She seemed offended that I would make such a statement. I told her it had nothing to do with her; it was just a commitment I have made. She insisted it would be okay. I finally told her, "Either you open the door or I'm leaving."

You can't play around with temptation. You have to respect it without surrendering to it. Whatever your temptation is, you have to cut it off. It may seem radical to some, but don't worry about that. They will get over it.

Playing Good Offense

There is a saying in sports, "The best defense is a good offense." We also have to play aggressive offense to defend against temptation. We do this by replacing worldly pleasures with godly pleasures.

In the situation where I was being tempted by the cookie, I could have played good offense by eating the fruit. This would have replaced my desire for a sweet snack and filled me up so I wouldn't be hungry.

I encourage single men I mentor to get connected with other spiritually mature men to hang out with and have fun. Being a Christian has to be fun; it shouldn't be boring. If they are married, I tell them to make sure they are having a healthy sex life with their spouse. You may have heard the old saying, "Don't go to the grocery store hungry." Well, the same can be said about a healthy sex life, especially for men. I may have a filet mignon at home waiting for me, but if I hadn't eaten all day and I'm starving, I am more likely to stop at McDonald's to eat a fast-food burger. Having a healthy sex life keeps you from starving and gives you more strength to fight the temptation to stop before you get home.

The decision for temptation is often a choice of immediate gratification verses delayed gratification, pleasure now versus pleasure later. The enemy would like you to believe that it's pleasure now or pleasure never.

The enemy says, "God is trying to limit and suppress you. God doesn't have your best interest at heart. I know a faster way." We get suckered just like Eve into taking a bite of the forbidden fruit, not understanding that more hangs in the balance of temptation than we realize. We gamble on the consequences, thinking that it's not that big of a deal. We have to be careful not to trade what's important for what is immediate. It's true that you can be forgiven immediately, but consequences can last a lifetime.

Defriend Temptation

When we were in debt, I got a letter in the mail from Citibank. They decided to increase my interest rate even though I had faithfully made my payment to them every month. I called to speak with them about it and was told that my credit rating had changed because of a late payment to another card. It was their policy to increase my interest rate. I was furious and asked to speak with the manager. That person told me the same thing and said it was in my agreement. They were right. I had put myself in this position, and I hated how it felt. I got so mad that I decided, "I will never use this card again." It was this anger that propelled us to get out of debt once and for all. In our experience with helping people get out of debt, most people stop short. They get a little room, and they think, *We aren't so bad off.* You can't get out of debt this way. You have to get mad at debt.

You can't be friends with temptation. My wife was just as mad at debt as I was. Carol said, "We don't need to go to a restaurant or hair salon unless we work there." She got mad at the debt, and debt was no longer her friend.

When we defriend temptation, we start to see it as our enemy. We don't invite the enemy over for coffee. A guy I coached who had an affair with a lady wanted to continue being friends with her after he had come clean with his wife and worked through a very difficult situation. I advised him to delete her from his phone. Don't worry about hurting her feelings. She will get over it, and not hurting your wife is more important than not hurting the other lady's feeling.

Defriending temptation means we have to cut any ties with the thing or people who tempt us to a life short of what God has for us. We can't try to do it gradually. We have to make a drastic break for it.

When Joseph was being tempted by his boss's wife, he quickly ran from the situation. He didn't try to stay and rationalize with the lady. He sprinted up out of there. That's what we have to do. Make a run for it. Don't worry about what the tempter thinks; just get away and don't look back.

We have to remember that mastering sin is a journey and not a destination. You will battle temptation the rest of your life. You will sometimes lose the battle. But you have already won the war. Your objective in mastering sin is not to make God happy with you. Remember God does not love you more or less because of your sin. He loves you, and there is nothing you or anyone else can do about it.

He wants you to master sin so that you can experience His peace not just in heaven but here on earth. Remember sin is crouching around our door and wants to master us. We have to squash it before it masters us. This requires a desire and a decision to master it. We must understand the vision God has for us and put our hope in Him. Because only God knows what's best for us, we can faithfully submit to His teaching and accountability. Through Him, we can master any temptation we face.

I master sin when I:

1. recognize my biggest temptations to sin,
2. understand God's vision for me in that area of my life,
3. make a commitment to pursue God's vision,
4. create and faithfully follow a plan to defeat temptation, and
5. share the plan with and follow advice from spiritually mature accountability partners.

In the following space, list your three biggest areas of temptation, and beside each, list God's vision, how you can play good defense and offense to master it, and whom you will share it with for accountability.

Temptation	God's Vision	Defense	Offense	Accountability
Example: doughnuts	enjoy doughnuts as an occasional treat	no doughnuts in the house	buy one serving of favorite doughnut once a week	Joe Bryant
1.				
2.				
3.				

It's Never Too Late to Repent

Sometimes even when you are mastering sin, you fall to it. You may lose some battles, but if you stick to the plan discussed in this book, you will win the war against your temptations to sin.

In the meeting when I was tempted by the cookie, I eventually fell to the temptation and ate a cookie. When I bit into the cookie, I realized the actual cookie wasn't as good as I had imagined it to be. It was okay but not better than the desserts I had available at home. Remember this is one of Satan's tricks. He has us so focused on the forbidden fruit that we are blinded to all the fruit God has for us.

One of Satan's tricks is once we sin, he says you may as well sin more since you have already messed up. He keeps encouraging us to take a step away from God until we look back and can't even see the trail back to God. We wonder, "How did I even get here?"

Jesus told a story of a son who asked his father for his share of the inheritance. He went away and squandered his wealth with wild living. When he was at the bottom, he came to his senses and returned to his father (Luke 15:11–32).

When I bit the cookie, I could have decided to stop there and throw it away. Instead I thought to myself, *I've already messed up so I may as well keep going.* That's another lie from the enemy. It's never too late to repent. It may seem awkward or stupid, but just throw that cookie away and start again fresh.

When you come to your senses, return to the Father like the prodigal son. There is no condemnation with God. He is always there. He doesn't leave us or get mad at us when we fail. There is nothing we can do to make Him not love us. Just recommit to following His way.

When naysayers tried to trap Jesus into discussion about following the law concerning the Sabbath, Jesus responded, "The Sabbath was made for men not men for the Sabbath." God's direction is not for His benefit but for ours. His direction is not because He's a mean God and just doesn't want us to have any fun. His direction is because He knows what's best for us and He wants us to live the best life possible. It's never too late to get back on track. There is no need for condemnation. Jesus took away any reason we have to be condemned.

In golf, there is something called a mulligan. A mulligan is a shot that doesn't count. You get to take another swing. At my church, we call it making a *fresh start*. Just start over again. It's never too late for a fresh start with God.

CHAPTER 7

OBEDIENCE

It bothers me when someone asks me for advice and then doesn't follow it. A single mom asked for help paying her bills. When we looked at her situation, she really needed to just reduce her lifestyle. We advised her to cancel her cable, for which she was paying $180 per month. When I told her this, she looked at me like I was an alien from another planet and decided not to follow my advice.

Six months later, she came back with even a bigger emergency. She was about to be evicted if she didn't get some financial help. We told her the same thing. She refused to take our advice and was upset that we didn't just help her. It was just as frustrating to me. We wanted to help her, but giving her money was not the best way to help her. It was frustrating that she refused to follow our advice.

The highest form of flattery to me is to follow my advice. I'm sure God feels the same way. He wants to help us, but we must obey His Word. Obedience to God's Word is the highest form of worship. Disobedience prevents God from working in our lives as He wants to.

King Saul

Saul is a perfect example of how God sees disobedience. Samuel had anointed Saul Israel's first king.

"Samuel said to Saul, 'This is what the LORD Almighty says …
Now go, attack the Amalekites and totally destroy all that belongs
to them. Do not spare them; put to death men and women, children
and infants, cattle and sheep, camels and donkeys'" (1 Samuel
15:3).

I love how God is specific. There was no room for misinterpretation.

So Saul attacked and defeated the Amalekites. He killed all his
people but …

> Saul and the army spared [King] Agag and the best of the
> sheep and cattle, the fat calves and lambs—everything that
> was good. These they were unwilling to destroy completely,
> but everything that was despised and weak they totally
> destroyed.
>
> Samuel went down the next day and confronted Saul.
> He asked, "What have you done? Didn't God tell you to
> destroy everything?"
>
> Saul responded, "But I did obey the Lord, but I just
> brought back the King and the soldiers took some things
> for themselves, and a few of their best things so that we can
> sacrifice to God."
>
> But Samuel replied: "Does the LORD delight in burnt
> offerings and sacrifices as much as in obeying the LORD?
> To obey is better than sacrifice, and to heed is better than
> the fat of rams. For rebellion is like the sin of divination,
> and arrogance like the evil of idolatry. Because you have
> rejected the word of the LORD, he has rejected you as king.
> (1 Samuel 15:4-23)

We know how the story goes. Instead of Saul having a great legacy
as king, David was chosen to replace him and would go on to be
the great king that God wanted Saul to be. His lack of obedience
cost him everything.

There are five things about obedience we can learn from Saul's tragic story. In order to walk in obedience, we must BOAST:

B - Be willing to do whatever God ask of us
O - Obey even when we don't feel like it
A - Allow God to change our thoughts
S - Stay humble
T - Take responsibility for our actions

B - Be Willing to Do Whatever God Asks of Us

In 1 Samuel 15:9, it says, "These they were unwilling to destroy."

Are there things in your life that you are just unwilling to give up for God? Some of us aren't willing to give up our lifestyles or a relationship. We are just not willing to do it. Maybe we are not willing to be inconvenienced, not willing to cancel cable, or not willing to give up a career.

It grieves God when we are simply unwilling to follow Him. The things we are unwilling to give up for God are the very things He wants from us. Obedience requires a willingness to do whatever God asks us to do.

O - Obey Even When We Don't Feel Like It

I got a call from one of the most spiritually mature men I know on an occasion when he was having problems with his wife. He was so frustrated by his wife's behavior that he was about to divorce her. There was no other woman or man. Neither was there any physical abuse. They were just not happy and not getting along. He said, "I'm tired of it." After I let him talk to get his emotions and thoughts out, I suggested that they seek counseling. He said, "You know what? I don't even feel like trying anymore." I was not sure what to say, but I knew I had to help my friend. Just when I was at a loss for words, these words came out of my mouth: "Faith is doing what God wants us to do even when we don't feel like it."

I don't feel like forgiving her. I don't feel like getting up and reading my Bible. I don't feel like giving. I don't feel like exercising.

Will you trust God even though you don't see Him? Will you trust Him when you don't feel Him?

"Jesus said, 'Why do you call me, "Lord, Lord," and do not do what I say?'" (Luke 6:46).

God is looking for those who will not only hear His word but obey it even when we don't feel like it.

A - Allow God to Change Our Thoughts

Romans 12:2 says, "Do not conform to the pattern of this world, but be transformed by the renewing of your mind. Then you will be able to test and approve what God's will is — his good, pleasing and perfect will."

Our actions are determined by our thoughts. We have to let God change our thoughts.

Saul lacked wisdom. Wisdom comes from God. We get wisdom when we spend time with God. The scripture says Saul had gotten up early to go worship the statue of himself. Instead of worshipping himself, he should have been getting up early to spend time with God. Only by spending time with God and mature godly advisers will we truly understand what to do.

S - Stay Humble

Saul started off very humble. Saul was so timid that when it was time to anoint him king, they couldn't find him; he was hidden with the baggage (1 Samuel 10:20–23). But look how that changed. When Samuel came to meet with Saul, his men told Samuel, "Saul has gone to Carmel. There he has set up a monument in his own honor." The same man who was hiding only a few years earlier was now erecting monuments of himself. We have to stay humble.

T - Take Responsibility for Our Actions

When Samuel confronted Saul, Saul sounded like my kids when they are caught doing wrong. They make excuses for why they did wrong. In their attempt to convince me in wasn't their fault, they say something like, "You remember when you had said ..." or "What had happened was ..." This was Saul's attempt to explain. "What had happened was ... we were going to sacrifice ..." But it all unraveled. I believe that if Saul had taken responsibility for his actions, it's possible that God would have saved his kingdom. Instead, Saul never took responsibility and ended up losing everything.

Don't make excuses. Take responsibility for and learn from your actions. Obeying God is better than any good thing we can do.

CHAPTER 8

SUBMIT TO EVERY CHANGE GOD WANTS TO MAKE IN YOUR LIFE

We have to continuously learn and grow in obedience to God. This is a process we will go through our whole lives. We will undoubtedly make mistakes, but the question is, "Are we submitted to the changes God wants to make in us?"

"If you keep My commandments, you will abide in My love, just as I have kept My Father's commandments and abide in His love" (John 15:10).

We all have character flaws that God wants to change in us. The change is for us not God. It's so we can live the best life possible.

I got stuck on a part of the scripture. I had read this many times. In Romans 10:9, Paul said if you confess with your mouth Jesus is Lord and believe in your heart He was raised from the dead, then you will be saved. But then I read in Luke 6:46–49 that there are a lot of people who will call Jesus Lord who will not enter heaven. Jesus made it clear by saying, "Those who hear my words and put them into practice will be blessed."

> Whoever says, "I know him," but does not do what he commands is a liar, and the truth is not in that person. But if anyone obeys his word, love for God is truly made complete

in them. This is how we know we are in him: Whoever claims to live in him must live as Jesus did. (1 John 2:4–6)

When reading this, you may question, "Does my willingness to obey have anything to do with me going to heaven?"

Clearly, it's not our works that get us into heaven, but a true indication of our heart's decision to believe and accept Jesus as Lord is our openness to follow His leadings.

There is a difference between believing Jesus is Lord and accepting Jesus as your Lord. Even Satan believes in Jesus. If our recognition of Jesus doesn't give us a desire to put into practice what we know He says, then maybe we don't really believe in our hearts that He is Lord. Simply put, if I really believed in my heart that Jesus is who He said He is, then I would desire to practice what he teaches. Conversely, if I don't desire to practice what He teaches, then I really don't believe and accept who He is.

I listened as a pastor friend Amy Matheny in Nairobi, Kenya, shared her testimony of making a choice to follow God. She said, "I wanted to feel better about what I was doing, but I wasn't ready to commit or change my life."

There is a point in every believer's life where we make a choice to commit to following God. I'm not talking about just believing He is God but actually following Him. If we don't make this choice, we don't grow and develop as God intends for us. Either we are snapped back by the enemy or we grow with some deformation that God didn't intend for us to have. Making a choice to follow God enables us to achieve the fruit in life we were intended to produce.

It's not to say that we will always be successful in putting God's teachings into practice. Our ability to successfully apply His teachings depend more on our spiritual maturing, but it starts with our willingness to submit to every change God wants to make in our lives.

King David was a called a man after God's own heart. It certainly wasn't because he didn't make mistakes; many of his mistakes are shared in scripture. But he clearly had a heart to follow God's ways.

"Search me, God, and know my heart; test me and know my anxious thoughts. See if there is any offensive way in me, and lead me in the way everlasting" (Psalm 139:23–24).

Going through the peace assessment process, which I discuss later in this book, only works if we are honestly asking God to show us where we are falling short of His expectations.

We must submit to every change God wants to make in our lives and humbly ask Him to remove our character defects. Evidence of our submission to God is our willingness to practice God's teachings.

List two or three changes you believe God wants to make in your life. Later we will revisit these as you set your goals. Commit now that you are submitting these changes to God, and pray for Him to remove these defects from your character.

1. _____
2. _____
3. _____

CHAPTER 9

TEST GOD

We are faced with many major decisions, and we don't want to make a bad decision that could have a drastic impact on our lives for years to come. As a stewardship pastor, I regularly get asked, "Should I ... buy this house? Sell this house? Sell my business? Start this business? Marry this person? Leave this person? Move to another state? Send my kids to private school? Take the lump-sum offer? Accept the job offer? Leave my current job?"

It is important that we get these answers right. To get to the correct answer, we have to test our desires against God's filter to make sure we are headed in the right direction. Gideon was a man who did just that. Gideon felt God was calling him to lead his people out of the oppression of the Midianites. This was a huge task not only because the Midianites were an enormously large army of men but also because Gideon was battling his own insecurities as a leader. Gideon wanted to make certain he was being led by God so he tested God not only once but three times. God passed each test, and Gideon went on to lead his people to win a triumphant battle over the Midianites (Judges 6, 7, and 8).

God wants us to test our desires as well. Any desire that we have that comes from God will certainly pass the scrutiny of these four tests (Exley 1993, 134).

1. The Bible Test

The first test is the Bible test. The Bible is the inspired, inerrant, and authoritative Word of God. When God gives us a desire, it will always align with His word.

God can never lead us in a way that contradicts His word. That's not possible. If God says it, then it has to be truth because it is impossible for God to lie (Hebrews 6:18; Numbers 23:19).

This is first because if it doesn't pass this test, there is no need to continue. If your desire contradicts the Bible, then stop here and know that it is not from God.

2. Test of Time

The second test is the test of time. Many times, we can test our desires by simply letting some time pass before we pursue the desire. God doesn't give us a desire one day, and then it goes away the next. If we don't pursue our God-given desires, then we feel a void in our lives and over time the desire gets stronger and stronger. The time test is a good check to see if this thing may be worth pursuing. In many cases, the test of time will reveal foolish thoughts and save us from unnecessary trouble. But if the desire gets stronger over time, then we should move on to the third test.

3. The Door Test

Revelation 3:7 says, "What he opens no one can shut, and what he shuts no one can open."

If God gives us a desire, then He also has to open the door for it to happen. If He doesn't open the door, then it's not His desire. This takes the pressure off of us to make things happen and places the responsibility solely on God. Every desire from God has to pass the door test.

4. Accountability Test

The final test is the accountability test. I suggest having at least one wise man or woman of God with whom you regularly and openly share details of your life for the purpose of guidance and accountability.

Even Michael Jordan Needed a Coach

You might believe as many others that you can get there on your own, but everyone needs a coach. Every great athlete understands this point.

Michael Jordan is considered by many as the best basketball player to have ever lived, but even he had a coach. Muhammad Ali is thought of as the greatest boxer ever, but he had a person in his corner, coaching him through every fight. Great athletes understand the value of having good coaching in their lives. They understand that the game is played, won, and lost by them as the player, but it could not be won without good coaching.

I was watching a documentary on former boxing heavyweight champion Mike Tyson. He was on top of the world. He seemed unbeatable. The key to his success was who he had in his corner. It turns out Mike had people in his corner who helped keep his life moving forward. Everything was going fine until his trainer died and he replaced other good coaches in his corner with people who were not looking out for his best interests. He had no one to provide direction and no one to hold him accountable when he was doing wrong. His life quickly unraveled until he found himself broke and in a jail cell.

Sometimes when we are in the heat of the battle, it can be hard to assess our game plan. What am I doing well? Where am I failing? What should be my focus and next step? Other times, we simply need someone to give us a nice swift kick in the rear end.

Even those who have achieved a level of success in life would benefit from coaching. Athletes understand this key principle. We need coaching no matter how good or experienced we are.

When Michael Jordan first came into the NBA, he was an immediate superstar. But he didn't become a champion until his coach Phil Jackson told him he needed to pass the ball to others and rebound better in order to win championships (Huffingtonpost. com, September 23, 2015). If you followed Jordan throughout his career, you would remember how many game-winning shots were made by his teammates because Michael listened to his coach and passed the ball.

Scripture says, "Two are better than one, because they have a good return for their labor. If either of them falls down, one can help the other up" (Ecclesiastes 4:9).

Coaches bring accountability. They cannot set your goals for you, but they can help you get there. Good coaches have a winning game plan. They are responsible for directing and preparing the player to win the game. They keep the big vision in mind as they guide the player to make the next move. A big reason why coaches are needed is that they have a sideline view. They are not playing the game so they can see things the player cannot see.

I benefited from good coaches during my high school and college athletic days, but more important, I have benefited from good coaching in life. It started with my dad and continued with other men who have helped me along the way.

One of the men who function in this role in my life is Jeff. Jeff started mentoring me when I was fresh out of college and working my first job. He worked with me and would later become my boss. He was a few years older, married, and had started his family. I admired his commitment to his faith, family, and career. I thought there couldn't be a better person to mentor me. I would go to Jeff for advice on any major decisions. I found myself becoming a lot like Jeff. He coached me through buying my first home and doing repairs. I basically just did what I saw him do. I watched how he treated his wife, and that was how I treated mine. I started banking where he banked. It might seem like I was giving him too much control over my life, but I figured if I followed his steps, it would have to lead me to where he was and I was okay with that.

Jeff was never controlling or judgmental. He would always listen and only gave advice when I asked him directly for it. He always made me feel valued and important. He provided encouragement when I needed it and correction when appropriate. He helped coach me through several difficult times in my life.

I have been fortunate to have a few men in my life like Jeff to help coach me through life. We all need good, mature people coaching us in order to find meaning and significance in life.

You have to give this person permission to speak life-giving rebuke into your life.

King David said, "Let a righteous man rebuke me and I will not refuse it" (Psalm 141:5).

David understood the value in giving a spiritually mature person permission to speak truth in his life. We need that too. We need a person who will say, "C'mon, man. You are messing up. What you are doing is not right." The person who does this becomes a valuable person in our lives.

Consistently seek his or her advice on major decisions by asking, "Do you think this is what God wants me to do?" and follow his or her advice.

Be open to his or her direction. When you ask for advice, be sure *not* to say, "This is what God told me to do. What do you think?" When people approach me this way, I respond, "If God told you, then it must be right." This way of asking doesn't give me much room to speak into these people's lives. They have already made their minds up and just want me to affirm what they have already decided in their hearts to do. Instead, say, "This is what I'm thinking God wants me to do. What do you think?" Listen to your mentor's advice and follow it. Having advice from people you trust does no good if you don't make a choice to follow it.

Listen to Your Older Self

Get advice from your older self. Many of the most important decisions I ever made were made in my teenage years or early twenties. Whom I would marry? Would I follow God? Where I would go to college? What I would major in? Where I would work? These were all key decisions. The hard part about it was that I was making these critical decisions with my twenty-year-old mind and experiences. That's why it is important to seek the wisdom of older people to help. I refer to them as my older self. The person has to be someone I want to emulate in a few years. He or she has already navigated through the issues I am facing. An older accountability partner can help you make decision from "your older self" perspective.

I have spoken with a lot of older people who looked back on some of these earlier decisions. No one looks back and thinks it was such a good decision to

- not go to church,
- start using drugs,
- spend every penny and borrow as much as possible,
- throw away an education, and
- not spend time with loved ones.

Those who didn't choose well look back and think

I wish I had ...

- trusted God more,
- been more selective on who I decided to let in my heart,
- spent more time with my family,
- taken better care of my body,
- managed money better,
- taken my education more seriously,
- followed my God-given dream, and
- worried less and enjoyed life more.

Having an older or more mature accountability partner gives you a step up in life. Instead of making critical decisions from your twenty-year-old mind, you make them from your older self. Your older self has a different perspective. Mark Twain said, "When I was a boy of fourteen, my father was so ignorant I could hardly stand to have the old man around. But when I got to be twenty-one, I was astonished at how much the old man had learned in seven years."

Think of someone in your life you feel could be a good spiritual accountability partner for you. Make sure this is a person who is at least a little further along than you spiritually. He or she should be living a life that pleases God and that you aspire to live. Don't have anyone with whom you would not trade places as your accountability partner.

Write the person's name here _____.
Contact him or her and ask if he or she would consider meeting with you periodically just for an update on your life and so he or she can give advice and provide input to your key decisions.

When we put our desires through each of these four tests (Bible, time, door, and accountability), it gives us a level of peace and confidence in our decisions. That peace is how we know we are headed in the right direction.

CHAPTER 10

HAVE A POSITIVE ATTITUDE

Peace begins when we possess the right attitude about our circumstances and ourselves. God made us as thinkers. Our lives consist of what we think about. Your thoughts will determine your action. Your action will determine your accomplishments. Therefore, our attitudes ultimately determine the level of success we achieve.

Jesus emphasized this principle by teaching that we must get our heart in order before we can get our life in order. He said out of the evil treasure of a man's heart come forth evil things. Out of the good treasure of a man's heart come forth good things (Matthew 12:34–36). It's all about what's inside. Real change occurs from the inside out.

In so many situations, the battle is won before it has begun. It all has to do with the frame of mind with which we enter the battle. Are we full of faith, hope, and optimism? Or are we negative and doubtful of getting results?

William James, a Harvard psychologist, said, "You are what you think about most of the time." Whatever you persistently allow to occupy your thoughts will manifest in your life. This is true whether these thoughts are good or bad. If you have a positive attitude then eventually good things will happen. If you have a negative attitude, then the bad thing you thought would happen eventually does.

This principle was illustrated when Moses sent the twelve spies into the Promised Land. Joshua and Caleb came back with a positive report. They said, "We should go up and take possession of the land, for we can certainly do it." The other ten spies returned with a negative report. They said, "We can't attack those people; they are stronger than we are." All of these men saw the same things so why were their reports so different? The difference is in their attitudes. Joshua and Caleb had positive attitudes. They saw the positive in the land promised to them by God, and more important they saw themselves in God's hand. The other ten spies saw themselves as small and weak. They were pessimistic and pointed out all the problems. Their negative attitude prevailed, and that generation of people never got to enter the Promised Land.

I am reminded of a story I heard of a shoe salesman who was sent to a faraway country, and after a few days, he sent back the message: "Coming home; nobody wears shoes here." Another salesman from the shoe company visited the same country. He wrote back to the home office after a few days: "Send more shoes! Nobody has them yet over here!" Same situation, different perspective.

Your attitude, not your achievements, will give you happiness and peace. The thoughts in your mind are more important than the things in your life. Too many people think if they could just move to a new place or have different circumstances, then they would be happy. At my church, we call this "destination disease." The problem with this is that wherever you go, there you are.

There are many things that we don't get to choose. We don't choose our parents or race or the part of the world we are born and raised in. But one thing we get to choose is our attitude. We have to decide daily that regardless of what comes our way, we will have a positive attitude.

When we have a bad attitude, it's up to us to change. My attitude will change only when I choose to change it. We have to choose our attitudes daily.

We don't know why sometimes life is tough. Only God knows. It doesn't make sense when we bury young people, have miscarriages, lose a job, get cancer, and so on. We have to choose our attitudes even when life is hard. We have to choose to have a positive spirit. This requires trust that God is still in control and is looking out for our best interests.

A few years ago, I was at a work meeting with my boss and several peers. During the meeting, I felt myself very frustrated with the direction of the organization and my boss. I didn't say anything negative in the meeting but was getting fed up. Later that evening, some of the guys went out to dinner. We were out when my boss called one of the guys and asked where we were and why we hadn't gone to dinner with the rest of the team. I thought to myself, *Can you just leave us alone for one minute?* I had a bad attitude, and I didn't like how I was feeling. The next morning, I read this scripture: "Finally, brothers and sisters, whatever is true, whatever is noble, whatever is right, whatever is pure, whatever is lovely, whatever is admirable — if anything is excellent or praiseworthy — think about such things" (Philippians 4:8).

These words changed my perspective. I started to take my thoughts away from the bad things associated with this organization and focused on what was good. I thought about how my boss had good intentions. She had never intentionally done anything to hurt me or the organization. In fact, she had done a lot of good things and had always been very pure in heart. Thinking about these things changed my attitude. It did not change the situation or my boss, but it changed me.

Our attitudes need continual adjustment. Our lives are like sailing a boat or flying a plane. We have a plan for our destination — but it is still critical that we make constant adjustments along the way. Here are some indicators you need an attitude adjustment:

- I haven't had enough time with God or myself.
- My family notices and tells me about my attitude.
- My relationships with coworkers become strained.
- My view of people begins to lower.
- My perspective becomes cynical.

If you change your attitude, you will change your life.

Your attitude is the one and only asset over which you have complete and unchallenged control.

Booker T. Washington was quoted, "The circumstances that surround a man's life are not important. How that man responds to those circumstances is important. His response is the ultimate determining factor between success and failure."

Having a Thankful Heart

Philippians 4:6–8 says, "Do not be anxious about anything, but in every situation, by prayer and petition, with thanksgiving, present your requests to God. And the peace of God, which transcends all understanding, will guard your hearts and your minds in Christ Jesus."

A key to having a positive attitude and dealing with the cares of our world is to have a thankful attitude. When we go to God with a thankful heart, the benefit to us is peace. I read a simple question once that asked, "What if you woke up today with only those things you thanked God for yesterday?" This certainly changed my perspective. I thought about what I had thanked God for yesterday. I had failed to thank Him for so many things. If I had answered this question honestly, today I wouldn't have my wife and kids and I wouldn't have good health. My job, investments, home, and cars would be gone. I wouldn't have any friends and would have no impact at all in people's lives. This question helped me to be more thankful, realizing God has done so much for me already.

Take the time to answer this question right now. Make a list of what you thanked God for this morning. Make another list of things you didn't thank Him for but if they were gone tomorrow, it would devastate your life. When you are done, look over both lists and be thankful for what you have and commit to reviewing this list whenever you find yourself with a negative attitude.

Small Group Discussion Questions

1. What interested you most in reading chapters 6 through 10?

2. If you feel comfortable doing so, share with the class one of your biggest temptations.

   a. In what way has your temptation followed the see-desire-take-hide pattern?

   b. How can you apply God's success pattern of vision, hope, take action, and be accountable to your situation?

3. What big things are you hoping God will do in your life currently?

   a. What scriptures give you confidence that what you are hoping for will happen?

   b. What can you do in faith as your part to show God you are serious about Him doing His part?

4. What change(s) do you believe God wants to make in your life?

5. Do you have a mature person in your life with whom you regularly and openly share details of your life for the purpose of guidance and accountability?

   a. If so, describe a time that person provided advice that benefited you.

   b. If you do not currently have someone, who do you think might be a good person for this and what's your plan to begin an accountability relationship with him or her?

6. If you woke up today with only those things you thanked God for yesterday, how would your life be different?

7. Share with the group something you are thankful for.

PART 2

PEACE IN RELATIONSHIPS

CHAPTER 11

PEACE IN RELATIONSHIPS

The second peace tier is peace in our relationships, which means being in relationship with people who love us and whom we love.

After peace with God, the relationship tier is the highest level of peace we can have. Consider this. If God told you that in seven days, you would die and go to live with Him in heaven how would you spend your last days on earth? I would bet that you wouldn't be thinking about finishing that project you've been working on at your job. You also wouldn't be thinking about going to the gym to lose that extra five pounds. The only thing that would be important to you at that moment is your relationships. You would likely spend your last days with your loved ones.

King Solomon tells this story to illustrate relationships are more important than money.

> There was a man all alone;
> he had neither son nor brother.
> There was no end to his toil,
> yet his eyes were not content with his wealth.
> "For whom am I toiling," he asked,
> "and why am I depriving myself of enjoyment?"
> This too is meaningless—
> a miserable business! (Ecclesiastes 4:8)

Many times, couples come to me for financial counseling only to find out that it's not a money issue but a relationship issue. Remember, water flows downward in the peace fountain. If there isn't water in the relational tier, then eventually the health, financial, and purpose tiers will dry up. Having healthy relationships is the key to experiencing true peace in your life.

Peace in our relationships involves:

- A devoted and happy marriage between a man and a woman
- Parents who are loving and children who are honoring
- Long-lasting, healthy friendships

Each of these adds to our level of peace, but you should understand that a person doesn't have to be married or a parent in order to have peace in relationships. I know many single people who have peace in their relationships. This is only to say that if a person is married or a parent, then having these relationships healthy becomes paramount to living a peaceful life. I discuss each of these in the following chapters.

Today's Families

Many families today look very different than God's original intent. Today we find divorce, unwed parents, promiscuous relationships, and same-sex relationships almost as often as we find monogamous, committed loving marriages between a husband and wife. Regardless of what is reality, scripture makes it clear what God's intentions are for relationships.

Marriage began with one man and one woman. Paul reiterates God's plan. When Paul talks about a husband, he uses the term *him*, and when he talks about a wife, he uses the term *her*. He specifically says each man should have his own wife. He didn't use a plural reference. There are many examples in the Bible where marriages were different than what God intended. For instance, Solomon and David both had many wives. But there isn't a case where the idea of anything other than sex in the context of marriage between one man and one woman was God's original intent. It's clear in scripture that anything else just isn't God's best.

A single mom who had never married asked me, "So if my family doesn't look like God's original intent, does that mean I can't have peace?" Fortunately for us all, Jesus is the Prince of Peace. His restoring power is big enough to move into any situation and provide restoration and peace. Our relational situation is never too hopeless for Jesus.

If you came to me and asked if you should get a divorce, enter into an unhealthy relationship, or have a baby out of wedlock, I would attempt to discourage you since that isn't God's best. But if you are currently in a family situation that isn't ideal, my first suggestion for you is to invite God into your life and relationships. Start by focusing on the activities discussed in the first peace tier and receive peace with God. Reread those chapters if necessary.

It's important to have peace in the first tier so that you can have peace in the second tier. Remember, water flows in one direction of the peace fountain. The following chapters provide you guidelines on receiving God's peace in the area of your relationships.

CHAPTER 12

FOUR NEEDS OF EVERY WIFE (RIBS)

The toughest job known to man is being a husband. I know wives think their job is tough, but our job is the toughest.

See, God set us husbands up in Ephesians 5:22. He started out by saying, "Wives submit to your husbands." We all said, "Yeah, that's right. I'm the man." But here is the setup.

"Husbands, love your wives, just as Christ loved the church and gave himself up for her" (Ephesians 5:25).

So in the husband-wife relationship, Paul compares the husband's role to the role of Jesus and the wife's role to that of the church. This sounded good until I thought about how the church treats Jesus.

- We think about Him once a week.
- We spend all His money.
- We don't do what He wants nor when He wants it. Then we expect Him to bless us and protect us in spite of it all.

And let's look at the husband's job description. Jesus says, "You treat the wife like I treat the church." How did Jesus treat the church?

He taught the church. He protected the church. He washed feet, provided healing, provided food. He served the church. But that's not all. I know how it ends for Jesus. Jesus ultimately had to die for the church. Every man reading this book collectively said, "Wait a minute. You are telling me I have to die? This isn't fair." You are right. Being a man is not fair. It's not easy. It takes guts. You have to be tough. Wimps need not apply for this position.

My dad always told me, "Son, you can have any woman you want if you are willing to be the man she needs." There are four basic needs of every woman that can be described with the acronym RIBS (Henley 2010, 87–91).

1. Relationship

Women are relational by nature. Being in a relationship with someone they love and who loves them is by far the greatest inward need for every woman. God designed her that way, and nothing else will do. Nothing else can compare to love. When a woman feels loved, it's as if she is in the very presence of God. And in fact, she is, because God is love.

Many times, we say we love someone, but our actions say different. Here is how God defines love.

> Love is patient, love is kind. It does not envy, it does not boast, it is not proud. It does not dishonor others, it is not self-seeking, it is not easily angered, it keeps no record of wrongs. Love does not delight in evil but rejoices with the truth. It always protects, always trusts, always hopes, always perseveres. (1 Corinthians 13:4–7)

How does this align with the behavior you display toward your wife?

In teaching me about women, my dad asked me, "Who is your dream woman?" I had this crush on pop star Janet Jackson so she was the first name out of my mouth. He thought for a minute and asked, "Who else would you consider a dream girl?" I said, "Vanessa Williams."

He said, "Yes, she is pretty, and what about that girl you like, Halle Berry?"

I said, "Yeah, she wouldn't be bad either."

He asked, "You know what they all have in common?"

I thought to myself, *Yes. Do you? They are all some of the finest women in the world.*

He told me, "Each of them has a man somewhere that ain't willing to put up with their [stuff]." (Note: I changed the word my dad used to be more appropriate.)

He said, "Women are looking for a man who sees her [stuff] and loves her anyway. She doesn't need a wimpy man. It takes a strong man that's willing to put up with her [stuff]." My dad told me, "You can have any woman you want, but you have to decide if you are willing to put up with her [stuff]." Loving unconditionally means you love her in spite of her [stuff].

2. Influence Authority

Where husbands have positon authority as head of their homes, wives need to have influence authority. Wives have to know that they are their husbands' number-one priority. The wife needs to know that she matters to him. Her words, thoughts, and feelings must influence him.

Every man wants his wife to respect him. This proverb tells us how to get respect. "Cherish her, and she will exalt you; embrace her, and she will honor you" (Proverbs 4:8).

Solomon was writing about wisdom as if she was a wife by referring to wisdom as "her." His advice about how to pursue wisdom is just as applicable for a husband in pursuing his wife. The word *cherish* means to appreciate her and make her your priority. *Embrace* means to hug, cuddle, or hold in one's arms. When we cherish and show affection to our wives, they naturally respond with respect.

Howard Dayton, cofounder of Crown Financial Ministries, shared this advice with me. "Consider every request by your wife as an opportunity to serve her." I may take it even further because I view every request from my wife as an opportunity to serve God. When we see our wives' requests as if they came from God, it changes the way we respond drastically.

Part of what makes my marriage work is the fact that Carol and I are both committed to serving each other. I see it as a part of my role as husband to serve her needs, and she sees her role as wife as the same. If you have ever been to a restaurant with excellent service, then you know exactly what I'm talking about. A great server will be kind and gracious to those he or she serves.

I was at a restaurant where the service was impeccable. It seemed the waiter anticipated my every need. Before I even noticed that my beverage was almost empty he was already bringing me a refill. He knew when I needed more napkins or needed plates removed. I felt valued, appreciated, and cared for.

This is also what makes a great marriage work. We have to serve each other with kindness and grace while anticipating what the other needs. We should submit to one another out of reverence for Christ (Ephesians 5:21).

A great waiter is never thinking about his needs. He's not thinking about what he wants to eat from the menu or where he wants to sit. His focus is on serving the other person. He trusts in the long run that if he puts his whole effort into serving his guest, then in the end, the guest will return the favor with appreciation for the server.

Husbands, serve your wife like the blessing from God that she is. Speak to her with kind words, ask about her desires, give her attention, provide her wants, make her feel like she is of the highest importance, anticipate her needs, and make them possible for her.

The way to know if you are doing your job is to look at her. Does she smile? Scripture says she should "radiate" (Ephesians 5:27). Our job is to figure out how to make her smile.

Ask your wife this question, "What are three things I can do weekly that would show you I love you and you are the most important person in the world to me?" I specify "three things" because most wives can likely think of twenty things we need to work on if we ask. We can't work on that many. Any more than three feels like nagging and fussing to us men. But focusing on three things is manageable. Listen to her answers. She may have a hard time articulating her wishes so you might have to ask for clarity. But be careful not to become defensive and don't rationalize it away with comments like "I already do that," "That's not true," or "That's not a big deal." It doesn't matter if you agree. Ask questions for clarity so you know exactly what she wants you to do, but don't minimize her wishes. The following are examples that will help you make sure her feedback to you is both actionable and measureable.

Bad Example	Better Example
I would like you to talk to me more.	Spend at least thirty minutes a day giving me your undivided attention to talk about our day and our relationship.
I would like to go out more.	I would like you to plan and take me on a date at least once a week.

I suggest hugging, kissing, and telling your wife, "I love you," every day. I also suggest taking your wife on a date at least weekly. You can never go wrong with these two suggestions. Commit to making your wife's "three things" a priority for you. Store this away for now. I will expand on this in a later chapter.

3. Beauty

Every woman needs to hear, "You are beautiful." If you don't tell her, then someone else will.

A recent study shows that women look in the mirror an average of eight times a day (Today.com 2012). Believe it or not, even the most beautiful women in the world likely look in the mirror, wishing something looked different.

Every true "playa" knows that the way to get a woman's attention is to compliment her on her looks. Women are so starved to hear this that they fall prey to any man who shows them some attention. Telling women that they are beautiful is so powerful that I purposely refrain from telling women other than my wife that they are beautiful.

Men are always hitting on my wife. That's the price you pay for having a beautiful wife. I wish I could be around when it happens so that I could have a chance to rearrange someone's face. I can see the headline now, "Memphis Pastor Arrested for Beating Up Man in the Grocery Store." The "playa playa" moves don't affect Carol because no one tells her she is beautiful more than I do. I don't just tell her but show her as well. I can't keep my hands off of her. I kiss, hug, and touch her every day. It grosses my kids out, and Carol calls me "manish," but deep down I think they like it. I think my kids also like to see me having adoration for their mom, and I know Carol loves feeling like she's the most beautiful woman ever.

One day, Carol was looking at some of her old pictures and saw a picture of herself when she was pregnant with our oldest daughter. She looked at the picture and said, "Why didn't you tell me I looked like a hog?"

Okay, how do I answer this question? I honestly thought she was cute pregnant. Sure, her body was different, but she was still beautiful.

When we truly love our wives, I think God gives us grace to see them more how He sees them. I can't explain it, but it's possible that I see her beauty when others don't. I remember being in a room full of couples and thinking to myself, *It's funny how my wife is always the best-looking wife at every church we attend.* Then it occurred to me that it's possible other husbands are thinking the same thing. *Naaah. That can't be true. My wife is actually the best-looking woman.*

I want her to know she is beautiful just the way God made her. She doesn't have to change one thing. He did not make a mistake when making her. Everything about her is beautiful just the way she is.

4. Security

Security is a basic need for women. Wives desire a peaceful home free of worries about how bills will be paid and how she will provide for the kids. She wants to choose whether to work or stay at home to raise her kids. She needs to feel secure and protected physically, financially, relationally, and spiritually.

Carol and I were walking one day. All of the sudden, she turned around to run. She turned so fast she stumbled and fell. I then saw the biggest dog I had ever seen running toward her. I didn't have time to think so I just got in between Carol and the dog and made a loud growling yell at the dog, "Aaaaaahhhhhhhhhh!" Fortunately the dog backed away, and the owner came out to get him. I don't know what I would have done if the dog had kept coming, but I do know if it comes to either her or me going down, then it's me.

That's our role as men. We have to fight for our families. We have to be willing to die. We have to die to our pride and egos. We have to die to our selfishness. Being a man means when the enemy is attacking your family, he's going to have to do it over your dead body.

One day, some knucklehead boys will want to marry my daughters. If some man wants to marry my baby girl, I need to know when Satan attacks and it comes down between him and her, that it's him. Our responsibility as husbands is to protect our wives even if it costs us our lives. I told you earlier that God gave us husbands the same role as Jesus had for the church. If you want to be the boss, you have to pay the cost. We have to be willing to die for her.

CHAPTER 13

THREE NEEDS OF EVERY HUSBAND (RAS)

There are three basic needs of every husband. They can be described with the acronym RAS (Henley 2010, 91–93).

1. Respect

In Ephesians 5:33, God commands husbands to love their wives and wives to respect their husbands. Respect is a key component in any great marriage. Respect is defined as a feeling of deep admiration for someone or something elicited by his or her abilities, qualities, or achievements.

Every husband longs for respect from his wife. Dr. Emerson Eggerichs, author of *Love & Respect*, writes "… without love, she reacts without respect. Without respect, he reacts without love" (Eggerichs, *Love & Respect*, 14–15).

Respecting a husband is not always easy. Quite honestly, people don't always behave in a respect-worthy manner. But the respect that is commanded here is not contingent on how the husband behaves. It's merely because of the position of authority God has given him as the head of the family.

It is similar to how we treat the president of the United States. Regardless of whether we voted for the president, agree with his or her views, or even like him or her, we still respect the position of president. If we were introduced to a current or past president, we would respectfully refer to him as "Mr. President" because of his position authority.

A husband is called to love a disrespectful wife and a wife is called to respect an unloving husband. There is no justification for a husband to say, "I will love her after she respects me," or for a wife to say, "I will respect my husband after he loves me" (Eggerichs, *Love & Respect*). Wives are commanded to respect their husbands simply because of the position God has given him as head of the family.

2. Admiration

One of the greatest needs of every husband is his wife's admiration. Where respect has more to do with the husband's position, admiration is more about what the husband does. Whether he understands it or not, he desperately desires her to admire him for who he is and for what he does. I have seen men fall into a trap of adulterous relationships simply because another woman admired them when they didn't feel their wives did. Men need to be admired by their wives.

One of the things that I love about Carol is that she truly admires me. This doesn't mean she thinks I walk on water. She knows I'm not good at a lot of things, but she appreciates me for the things I am good at and admires who I am as a man. She shows and communicates that she's glad I'm her husband. Her admiration drives me to be a better husband, father, and leader for my family.

Don't wait for big things to happen before showing and communicating admiration. Admire all the small things. Any sincere admiration will encourage husbands to be better men. It's important for a man to have a wife who has a sincere admiration and respect for him.

3. Sex

Husband and wives both possess sex drives. For women, sex drives can be as much about romance as about the physical act. But for most men, it's just about the physical act. I do not have another way of saying it. Husbands desire sex, pure and simple. There needs to be a healthy sex life in order to sustain the marriage relationship. Husbands and wives may mutually agree to temporarily abstain from sex for spiritual moments, but withholding sex from a husband is destructive in a marriage. Husbands and wives belong to each other. In order to have a healthy relationship, both spouses should desire to fulfill the sexual needs of the other.

CHAPTER 14

PEACE IN MARRIAGE TIPS

When Carol and I got married, it was the happiest time of my life. I would get off work and when I got to my street and saw that her car was there, a sense of joy would just come over me. Years after our wedding day, I still felt this joy. Then one day, I realized I didn't feel that same excitement. It was around the ten-year mark. We still had a good marriage, but I didn't feel that same excitement when I got home and saw her car in the driveway. I had lost some of my passion for our relationship. At that point, I made a decision that I would be intentional about rekindling the passion. I was intentional about showing her more affection and attention. We started taking regular dates. I would buy her gifts. The more I did these things, the more she occupied my thoughts and the more passion I had for her. I had to lead my feelings back to the love I had for my wife on our wedding day.

The enemy will have us believe a lie that, "You can't help what you feel. You just don't love her anymore. You should follow your heart."

God's truth is that love is a choice. We are commanded to continuously love our spouse. Love is not merely an emotion; otherwise it could not be commanded. We love our spouse because God says to. Love is not a feeling; it's a commitment. Love calls us to step up to the plate each day and give even when we don't feel like giving at all. Love acts and emotions follow. Oftentimes, marriage will require us to follow God even when we don't feel like it.

If a marriage has lost its passion, pull back from everything else like work, ministry, children's activities, and so on to make God and your marriage your top priorities. Then, strive to keep them at the top. Your marriage is your number-one ministry. I don't claim to know all there is about having a healthy marriage, but I do want to share a few tips that have helped us over the years.

Never Say No

Carol and I have an unwritten rule in our relationship. We never say no to each other. If she needs a hug, I always say yes. If she asks me to get her a glass of water, I always say yes. At my church, we have a saying, "Always carry a yes in your pocket."

Carol knows that if she says, "I want to get a new sofa or change the carpet," that eventually those things will happen. It may not happen right away because of finances, but she knows that her wants are a priority for me and I will begin planning to make them a reality. It may take years, but unless it's something that is not good for the health of our family, I will do all I can to make it happen.

Carol does the same for me. Neither of us takes advantage of this situation. We balance "never say no" by being thoughtful of the other so that we are not overly focused on ourselves. We cherish "never say no" and protect it by being considerate of one another.

Don't Make Divorce an Option

The popular thought today is that divorce is not that big of a deal. Many rationalize, "Plenty of godly people do it every day and do fine. Just cut your losses now and ask God for forgiveness. Then, you can just move on and start over."

The truth is you can be forgiven immediately, but consequences can last a lifetime. Divorce is not God's will for you. You can't violate the principles of God and expect the promises of God. God paints two pictures of marriage.

1. Husbands love your wives just as Christ loved the church (unconditionally, sacrificially, enduringly, patiently, and endearingly). It was not an option for Christ to divorce the church.
2. Husbands love your wives as you love your own body. Men don't hate or divorce their own bodies.

Both of these illustrate that divorce isn't God's best for us. Ruth Graham, wife of legendary evangelist Billy Graham, was once asked, "Did you ever consider a divorce?"

She responded, "Divorce no. Murder yes." If you commit to never make divorce an option, it will help you to work out a resolution for whatever you face.

This is not intended to provide condemnation for those who have gone through a divorce. These thoughts are intended to help the person who is still married and is considering a divorce. If you are divorced, you cannot undo what is done. God can heal your damaged spirit. Learn from your past, and commit yourself to God. He can and will provide healing and blessings to you going forward.

Learn How to Fight Fair

Conflict is inevitable in a marriage. Every couple has disagreements. Conflicts usually start when one of the spouses makes a complaint about the other. Complaining is not the problem. In fact, complaining is a healthy marital activity. The problem occurs when couples haven't learned or applied the rules to handling conflict constructively and complaining escalates into one of four toxic ways of interacting.

In a University of Washington study, Dr. John Gottman says there are four toxic ways of interacting in order of least to most dangerous (Parrot, *Saving Your Marriage before It Starts*, 121–124):

1. **Criticism**—attacking someone's personality rather than his or her behavior. Criticism entails blaming or making a personal attack or an accusation, while a complaint is a negative comment about something you wish were otherwise. Complaints usually begin with the word *I*, and criticisms usually begin with the word *you*.

2. **Contempt**—What separates contempt from criticism is the intent to insult and psychologically abuse your partner. When contempt appears, it overwhelms the marriage and blots out every positive feeling partners have for each other.

3. **Defensiveness**—Once a spouse acts in contempt, defensiveness enters the picture and makes things worse. The people being insulted respond defensively, not willing to take any responsibility or blame. They no longer are focused on the issue but rather on defending themselves.

4. **Stonewalling**—Feeling overwhelmed by emotions, they start withdrawing by presenting a "stone wall" response. Most are men (85 percent). They try to keep their faces immobile, avoid eye contact, hold their necks rigid, and avoid nodding their heads or making any indication that they are listening.

Nothing good can come from someone criticizing his or her spouse. In fact, only two results can occur from long-term criticism. Either you will turn your spouse into someone you hate or turn him or her into someone who hates you. We must learn to fight fairly in order to avoid toxic interactions and have healthy marital conflict.

The following list outlines seven suggested fair-fighting rules intended to help couples handle conflict without harming the relationship.

Rule #1: No Degrading Language

Avoid name-calling, insults, put-downs, or swearing. Putting your partner down or criticizing your partner's character shows disrespect for his or her dignity.

Rule #2: No Yelling

Yelling only escalates things. Chances are nothing will get resolved when your emotions are running so high. If you're mad and feel like yelling, then it's time to step away and cool down.

Rule #3: No Use of Force

Using physical force or threatening to use force (e.g., a raised fist or a verbal threat) in any way is unacceptable. Use of force includes pushing, shoving, grabbing, hitting, punching, slapping, or restraining. It includes punching a hole in a wall, throwing things, or breaking something in anger. Acting out your anger in these ways violates the other person's boundaries and sense of safety. Each of us has a right to be safe and free of abuse or physical danger in our relationships.

Rule #4: Choose Your Battles Carefully

You can't complain about everything. Ninety percent of issues couples fight over can probably be overlooked. Especially in the case for men, too much complaining from a wife feels like nagging. Before you complain about something, ask yourself if it's worth it.

Rule #5: Stay in the Present

Stay in the present and resist the temptation to use the situation as an occasion to bring up other issues from the past. Try to keep your focus on what can be done today to resolve the issue at hand and go forward from there. Don't pile on issues. Address one issue at a time.

Rule #6: Discuss Issues at the Appropriate Time

It is impossible to have a rational discussion in a climate of hostility and disrespect. Don't try to resolve issues in the heat of the moment. Also avoid times when you are tired, hungry, or under stress. Think of the appropriate time and place to have a constructive conversation.

Rule #7: Practice Assertive Communication and Active Listening

Let the one who has the complaint speak to express feelings and ask for what he or she wants in the relationship. When one speaks, the other should be listening—really listening, not just planning a rebuttal. Make a conscious effort not only to hear the words that another person is saying but, more important, try to understand the complete message being sent. You then let your partner know you understand him or her by restating his or her message. Once the complaint is given and the listener can restate the complaint, spend time discussing possible solutions.

Phrases to help air a complaint appropriately are as follows:

- When you do _____, it makes me feel _____.
- I would like you to do more of _____.
- I would like you to do less of _____.

Couple Mentors

It also helps for couples to have other spiritually mature couples to mentor them. Carol and I had Jeff and Joan Woodard to coach us when we first got married. They were just a little older than we were. We hung around them and learned from them. We did everything we could with them. I tease Jeff that he even went with us on our honeymoon. He came to my wedding. He coached us in buying our first home. He coached us through the decision for Carol to be a stay-at-home mom. Carol trusts the advice I get from Jeff, and I trust the advice she gets from Joan. The only time I disagreed with Joan's advice was when she told Carol to stop ironing all my clothes. That was just wrong. Joan really messed up a good thing. Seriously, having another mature couple to coach you through good and bad times can save you a lot of heartaches.

Couple's Getaway

Take a couple's getaway. I know many couples take family vacations with their kids, and these are good, but it has helped us to also take a getaway for just the two of us. We are committed to taking at least one family vacation a year, but we are just as committed to taking at least one couple getaway a year. Even better would be to get away as a couple once a quarter. I told a friend this recently, and he jokingly responded, "Great, so I can tell my wife you will keep our three kids so we can take a couple's vacation." Needless to say, I backpedaled out of that statement quickly. I know it can be tough when you have small kids, but it's important to make an effort to spend some time alone as a couple.

When couples don't spend time together, they find that they stop growing together. Their relationship may become all about the kids. Some of these couples wake up one day when the kids are gone, and they realize they live with a spouse with whom they don't have a relationship. The marriage relationship has to be the first priority in the family and not the children.

Taking time away will help you focus on building a healthy marriage relationship. It doesn't have to be an expensive trip. It can be an overnight stay at a local hotel. The important thing is to get away from your daily life to enjoy each other and spend some time thinking about your life and future together. A wise friend once shared some good questions for couples to ask themselves that might help generate discussion:

1. How are we doing?
2. How are the children doing?
3. What does our calendar look like the next three months?

Family Time

Just as scheduling time alone with your spouse is important, so is making time for your family. Put it on your calendar, and prioritize this time as you would anything else on the calendar.

A Healthy You

The best thing you can give your spouse is a healthy you. A phrase we use a lot at my church is "A healthy me makes a healthy we." In order to have a healthy marriage, we have to first have two healthy individuals.

One of my favorite things to do is to coach and mentor other men. I see it as not only a way to serve them but also as a way of serving their families. It's one of my greatest pleasures knowing that I'm helping to build healthy husbands and dads.

Work on being the healthiest individual you can be physically, mentally, and emotionally. I will speak more about this in the next peace tier.

Family Vision

When we got married, Carol and I didn't have any premarital counseling, but one of the things that really helped us was taking the time to write out our family vision. At the time, it was just the two of us, but we had a vision of a preferred future for our lives together.

Our plan included how we preferred to see the future for our work, church life, family, finances, and personal life. We dreamed about our future home and vacations. Obviously, this was written from the vantage point of twenty-five-year-olds so some of our hopes and dreams were somewhat superficial, but nevertheless it gave us direction for our lives.

The point is that we had a written document for how we envisioned our lives. Every year, we would tweak it and then consider our hopes and plans for the next twelve months. We didn't always reach every goal, but because we had something to aim at, it oftentimes kept us on track.

Whenever we needed to refocus our lives or make tough decisions, it helped to have the written vision to guide us.

One of the things we wrote in our vision was that I would go back to school to get my MBA at Duke. During this time, I was an engineer; I had been working for a great company for six years and was earning a great salary. Carol was a stay-at-home mom with our first child. I applied but didn't have the highest hopes since getting accepted was so competitive. My hopes were further decreased when I wasn't invited to a program that Duke had for their top minority candidates. I knew realistically that if I wasn't considered a top minority candidate that I had little chance of getting in the school.

After the news, I was offered a new position with my company, which would require that I move from South Carolina to Maryland. I went for a visit, loved the area, and decided to take the job. About the same time, we also received news that Carol was pregnant with our second child. I felt that maybe God was closing this door and opening another. I wouldn't be pursuing my dream of getting my MBA, but I felt we were still headed in a positive direction for our family.

After I had accepted the new job, I received a letter from Duke that I had been admitted into their business school. We couldn't believe it. We started jumping around, praising God right there in our living room. Our three-year-old was jumping too. She didn't know why she was jumping around, but she knew Mom and Dad were excited.

Then reality set in for me. "I can't quit my job and go back to school. How will I support my family with us expecting a second child soon?" I shared my doubts with Carol. "As much as I wanted to, there is no way I could quit my job now. What about the kids?"

Carol responded, "Travis, if those people at Duke are foolish enough to let you in that school, then you are going to be foolish enough to go. God will work it out."

We agreed to follow the plan. I left my comfortable job and went back to school full-time. Carol gave birth to our second child, Travis Jr., my first week of school at the Duke University Hospital. As I look back on it now, leaving my job to obtain an MBA was a great decision. We had a great experience at Duke. It was good for me personally and great for my family.

The fact that we had a written plan helped us make that very tough decision. It's not that we never deviate from the plan, but having a plan keeps us from just drifting through life. It helps us as a couple to stay focused and to dream together. Your plan doesn't have to be complex. It can be just one page, but it has to be written and cover each of the five tiers: spiritual, relationships, health, finances, and purpose.

Work on Your Marriage

Marriage is hard. We have to work at it. God uses issues in marriage to mold us into the people He wants us to be. When we give up on marriage, we give up on God's molding of us. Those who have the best marriages work at it by reading books, attending classes, and seeking counseling. We have to continuously work at having a healthy marriage.

It's never too late to work on your marriage. Nothing is impossible with God. God can fix your marriage and make it stronger than ever before, but you have to be willing to do your part. Every marriage goes through three or four tough phases. But when couples commit to working through it, they become stronger and happier in the end. Consider attending a marriage-enrichment workshop to work on your marriage.

CHAPTER 15

SINGLES, HOW DO YOU KNOW YOU ARE READY FOR MARRIAGE?

God says that it is not good for man to be alone (Genesis 2:18). This is the reason He created marriage in the first place. But we have to get married in His timing. So how do you know you are ready for marriage? There are four questions we can ask ourselves to clearly determine whether God wants us to get married. These four questions are in order. If there is a "no" answer to a question, then our answer is clearly "no" from God and there is no need to continue to the next question. Ask yourself these questions.

Question 1 — Do I have a God-given vision for my life to pursue?

You don't have to have your whole life figured out, but you must have some direction for your life. Vision comes from God. So we have to start with getting to know Him and allowing Him to give us a vision for our life. You have to have a vision for your life before you can partner with someone else in marriage.

Question 2 — Do I have the financial means to support a family?

By no means do I believe women shouldn't work or that their financial means aren't important, so please, ladies, don't get offended, but I'm convinced that a man must have a way to provide for his family before considering marriage. Before God gave Adam a wife, he gave him a job (Genesis 2:15). There is an old R&B song that said, "You have to have a J-O-B if you want to be with me." I think this is a reasonable expectation for every husband. If you don't have financial means to care for a family, then you can just stop here. Don't even bother considering the next couple of questions. God is clearly saying that this is not the right time for you to get married. You can proceed with this list of questions after you get a job.

Question 3 — Do I have a desire for sex?

Scripture tells us that one way we know God wants us to marry is that He gives us a desire to have sex (1 Corinthians 7:9). The desire for sex isn't bad. It lets us know that God wants us to get married. Marriage is the only legitimate way to fulfil your sexual needs. One of the many problems that come with having sex outside of marriage is that we miss out on seeing the desire as a cue for getting married. If we are already fulfilling the sexual desire outside of marriage, then there is nothing triggering a need to get married. We have to abstain from sex in order to clearly hear God's desire for us in terms of relationships. We rationalize that God hasn't brought the right person when in actuality we wouldn't know if He did because we have blocked God's way of communicating to us. It's like we have put blinders on and cannot see God's plan for us. Abstaining from sex outside of marriage takes the blinders off so we can clearly see the plans God has for us.

Question 4 — Has God given me a mate to love?

In the very beginning of time, as God was involved with creation, time and time again, He saw what He created and said, "It is good!" But after creating Adam and reflecting on His new creation of man for the first time, He said, "It is *not* good for man to be alone." This was the first problem known to man. Man had an "alone" problem. So God's solution was to cause man to go to sleep, and He took a rib out of man and created a woman and brought her to the man.

Adam responded, "I appreciate that, God, but can you make her a little taller or thinner or darker." No, I'm kidding. Adam responded,

"This is now bone of my bones and flesh of my flesh; she shall be called 'woman,' for she was taken out of man" (Genesis 2:23).

There is only one reason why Adam accepted Eve as his wife, and it's the only reason why any man should accept a woman as his wife. It's because God brought her to him. If you are single, it's important that you allow God to bring you a mate to love. You should have reasons to believe that the mate God has for you will fulfill the responsibilities of a husband or wife, discussed in the previous chapters. You should also follow the "Test God" steps discussed previously to confirm whether this is the person God would like you to marry.

Small Group Questions (Married)

1. Read Ephesians 5:25–33. How does God's view on the husband's and wife's roles in marriage differ from most people's view?

2. Provide a time when you felt or noticed the needs mentioned for husbands and wives.
   a. Wife
      ■ Relationship

      ■ Influence authority

      ■ Beauty

      ■ Security

   b. Husband
      ■ Respect

      ■ Admiration

      ■ Sex

3. Read Ephesians 5:21.
   a. What is this scripture commanding us to do?

   b. How can you demonstrate this in your marriage (be specific)?

4. Which of the needs discussed do you think your spouse would like you to improve on the most?

    a. Why?

    b. What can you do to better provide this need to your spouse?

5. Which marriage tip would make the biggest impact on your relationship? Why?

Small Group Questions (Single)

1. Read Ephesians 5:25–33. How does God's view on the husband's and wife's roles in marriage differ from most people's view?

2. Based on the four questions discussed, do you believe you might be ready for marriage?

   Why or why not?

3. What can you do to prepare yourself now for a successful marriage in the future?

CHAPTER 16

PEACE IN PARENTING

I realized something after our oldest daughter went off to college. When she would return home during a school break and I closed the door behind her and had everyone in the house, I felt a sense of peace that I hadn't felt before. All my kids were at home safe with me. There is nothing like this feeling for a dad. I'm sure this is what God will feel like on that great day in heaven when we are home to live eternally with Him.

I also have a sense of peace in the smallest things with my kids. One day, we were all riding in the car to church and the kids were debating over some senseless issue; I got the biggest joy out of it. I just enjoy being a family, doing regular stuff together. There is peace in having someone to love and someone who loves you.

Despite its joys, being a parent will challenge your ability to have peace more than any other thing in your life. In fact, parenting can be chaotic, messy, and very imperfect. It will test every inch of your being. There is no exact science to what and when to do what you need to do. Every child is different. As a parent, you find yourself saying and doing things you swore you would never say or do prior to having kids of your own.

A big challenge of parenting is that it requires a long-term perspective of success. In almost everything else we do, the results are seen in the short term. We eat better, and we lose weight; we study hard, and we get good grades; and we work hard and get a promotion. But parenting requires us to work hard for twenty-plus years before seeing our success pay off.

Our peace can't be in what we see or how we or our child feels. Our peace is not in the lack of conflict, having perfectly behaving children, or even always making them happy. In parenting, our peace has to come from the Spirit of God on the inside of us that confirms we are doing everything we can to accomplish our goal as parents.

Our goal as parents is to impress God's Word on our children, instruct them in God's way, and inspire them to leave our home and thrive on their own.

With four children ranging from thirteen to twenty-one, Carol and I are still very much in pursuit of this goal. Our parenting has not been perfect, and our children are not perfect, but we have peace in our family because of following God's direction as parents.

Our decisions and actions have to be made with this ultimate goal in mind. In the end, only pursuit of this goal will provide us peace in parenting. There are many roles parents play in meeting this goal, and here is just a short list of ten of these key responsibilities.

Ten Key Responsibilities Parents Have for Their Children

1. Teach them by example how to love God and love others
2. Provide protection, safety, and security
3. Provide love through abundant time, appropriate and loving touch, and encouraging words
4. Teach them the Word of God
5. Provide for them financially
6. Teach them life skills
7. Pray for them daily
8. Love Mom (Dad)
9. Provide or allow appropriate discipline or consequences (Psalm 23:4; Proverb 29:17)
10. Affirm who they are in Christ (Mark 1:11)

Spend Time with Your Kids

I heard it said that the way to spell love is T-I-M-E. I don't make it to every event my kids have, but I plan to spend some individual time each week with each child. For me, it doesn't have to be anything big. It could be attending a game or band performance. It could be going shopping or getting ice cream. Sometimes it's just me picking them up, taking them somewhere they need to be, or making a meal together. I just plan to spend some time where I can be alone with them. I try to make it doing something they enjoy. Donovan likes shooting baskets in the front yard. Gilana likes watching singing contests on TV. TJ loves to watch college football with me. I take Erica out to eat to spend time with her. Sometimes I spend time with them doing simple chores around the house. I may have them help me clean the car or fold clothes with me. The important thing is to spend time together.

Just spending time with our kids often provides us insight and opportunity to be the parent we need to be. When I'm around my kids, I get to see what they are good at and what they are not so good at. I get to see their personalities, likes, and dislikes. Just spend time with your kids. Find time to do things they like doing as well as time to show them how to do life. It doesn't have to be big. It just needs to be frequent.

When my sons were young, I volunteered to help coach their football teams. Travis Jr. played tight end as a twelve-year-old. He was a good player, but he happened to play a position where the boys playing the same position were really good so he didn't get to play as much.

He had gone almost the entire season without a catch when one game, the coach decided to call a play to him. I knew it was coming, and I was excited for him. He was wide open as the pass came to him. There was nothing between him and the goal line. All he had to do was catch the ball and run. The ball hit him right in the hands and then fell to the ground incomplete. He dropped the pass. He was disappointed. I hid my disappointment by telling him, "Just shake it off and play the next play. It's okay." I felt bad for him.

Silently I hoped the coach would give him another chance, but I didn't want to be one of those dads who interfered. A few plays later, to my surprise, the coach said, "Let's throw to Moody again." It was the same play, and he was wide open again. This time, he caught it. He was so shocked from catching the pass that he just paused for a second. I and everyone else on the sideline yelled, "Run!" He sprinted for the end zone. I ran down the sideline to the end zone as well. I think I was more excited than he was. I played college football in front of thousands of fans, and I have never been that excited about a touchdown in my life. I told him that I was proud that he didn't get down after the first mistake. It gave me a chance to speak a lesson over his life about getting back up after bad things happen. I was glad that I was just there spending time with him.

Teach them the Word of God

It's great to have formal ways of teaching God's Word to our kids through Bible studies and memory verses, but scripture suggests we also teach God's Word in casual ways (Deuteronomy 6:5–7).

One day, I was taking my daughter Gilana to school and she asked me this random question about heaven. She wanted to know if her favorite singing group would be in heaven. It gave me a chance to explain how all of us have an opportunity to go to heaven if we accept Jesus. She said, "I'm going to pray they all accept Jesus because heaven won't be the same without them." I told her that's exactly how God feels. He wants us all there too.

Use normal life situations to teach children the Word of God.

Provide Financially

Providing financially for our children doesn't mean we just buy them everything they ask for. I have seen too many parents get into financial trouble because they wanted their children to live the dream life. They wanted their child to have the best shoes and go to the most expensive private schools. There is nothing wrong with these things unless they sabotage the family budget or hurt the children's ability to succeed in life on their own one day. Parents have to decide what is best for their kids.

Today, many families are separated with Mom and Dad not married. In most cases, this requires one of the parents to have a responsibility to provide financially to help the other parent. I've talked to many dads who complained about the amount of child support they are required to pay. I've found in most cases that the amounts legally required are reasonable, but even if they are not, it's the responsibility of the parent to pay it. We have a financial responsibility to provide for our children. This doesn't mean you give them everything they ask for or want, but we have to make sure they have the basic needs met so they can thrive in life. These include shelter, food, and clothing.

Teach Life Skills

A part of our role as parents is to teach our kids life skills, such as selecting friends, managing money, working hard, taking care of a home and possessions, treating people right, and living healthily. They learn how to do life by observing us and through our instructions to them. We have to take this responsibility to teach seriously. One lesson I enjoyed teaching my kids was how to purchase a car.

When our oldest daughter was fourteen years old, Carol and I laid the ground rules for purchasing her car. We would match whatever she saved to buy her a car. We had previously opened a bank account for all of our children. When she wanted to spend her money frivolously, we would remind her that one day she was going to want a car. On her sixteenth birthday, she was surprised to find that there was no new car waiting for her. She asked, "Where is my car?" She had only saved $400. I told her, "I have my $400 ready, but there's not much you can get for $800." Erica was disappointed. She thought surely Mommy and Daddy would drop their foolish financial lessons and buy her a car. She begged and pleaded with us for the next eight months. She said, "Why can't you be like normal parents and just buy me a car? You *have* the money."

I have to admit I almost broke down on more than one occasion. She was wearing Daddy down. I started rationalizing why I should buy her a car—"My parents bought me a car" and "She could help us out more." But Carol stayed firm. She said, "Erica knew the deal. Now she needs to find a job and save her money." After several months of begging to no avail, Erica found a job working at a pizza parlor and began aggressively saving for her car. When she had enough saved, we started the car-shopping process. I was excited about this. Not because I was thrilled about buying a car, but I thought this might be my only chance to teach Erica how to buy a car. We want Erica to avoid the car-buying mistakes that get many people into financial trouble. We discussed our checklist and agreed that the car must meet these requirements:

- cost less than $4,000
- features include A/C, Automatic, 4-door Sedan, and >25 mpg
- less than 130,000 miles
- reliable model according to *Consumer Reports*
- no mechanical problems or oil leaks
- clean title and CARFAX report
- price less than *Kelly Blue Book* value for private sale

Armed with her checklist, Erica started looking for a car. By the end of the process, Erica had actually learned some things. Carol and I would find a car, and Erica would ask all the right critical questions. It took a while, but we found a car on eBay that met our requirements and that we all liked.

The day we went to get the car, Erica was smiling ear to ear. We went to the bank to take out her money only to find that she could not withdraw it without Carol's permission. I could see the disappointment on Erica's face because Carol was at work. Erica was relieved to find that I had enough in our account to get the car anyway and that we could get her money out later. I think this taught her the value of living with surplus rather than never having enough.

We paid $3,000 cash for a 2002 Mazda Protégé with seventy-eight thousand miles and in good condition. Erica was excited to finally have her own car and I think happy that we didn't let her choose some of the clunkers that she wanted to get throughout the process. She said, "Thank you, Daddy," more than once. I told her, "You got a job and saved your money. It's our pleasure to help you when you do your part." I think I may have enjoyed the process as much as Erica. I enjoyed making my little girl happy, and I was thrilled to teach her a lesson for a lifetime. As we drove home, I wondered if this is what God feels toward me when I do my part and allow Him to do His part.

Love Mom (or Dad)

One of the best things I can do for my kids is to love their mom. It gives children a sense of security and peace knowing that Mom and Dad love each other and that their family situation is healthy. By loving their mom, I also show them how to be a loving spouse themselves one day.

This is more difficult in today's family environment because there are so many variations of families. There is no perfect family. There are a lot of families where Mom and Dad are not a couple in love, but that doesn't mean you cannot have peace in parenting. The important thing is to commit to the responsibilities of parenting listed above.

Mom and Dad not being together also doesn't free Mom and Dad from showing love to the other parent. Even dads who are not married to their child's mother should have a love for her. I'm not talking about a romantic love. I'm talking about showing a love that Christians are encouraged to show toward others. That means being loving with words toward and about the other parent. You still must use good judgment when dealing with the other parent, but make an effort to parent in peace. You don't have to be best friends, but extend the love you would to anyone else you meet. Also, make sure the child loves and honors Mom or Dad. For instance, you can ask, "Did you honor your mom or dad for Mother's or Father's Day?" Regardless of how you feel about the person and what he or she has done, he or she is the parent of your child and for the sake of your peace, you need to give grace and respect for him or her.

Discipline Appropriately

"No discipline seems pleasant at the time, but painful. Later on, however, it produces a harvest of righteousness and peace for those who have been trained by it" (Hebrews 12:11).

Disciplining kids is a key responsibility of parenting. We find that this is a lot easier when they are toddlers and becomes more complicated as they get older. There are two ways to learn: by the wisdom of others or through the consequences of our own behaviors. You can tell a person not to touch the pot because it's hot. Some will listen to your wisdom and understand the pot is hot, and others will have to touch the pot themselves before they truly believe it is hot. It's less painful to learn by wisdom, but sometimes the consequences of a scar from the burning leaves a long-lasting reminder of the appropriate behavior. Sometimes parents make the mistake of rescuing children from consequences. This can only last a short time. It's actually better to allow them to experience consequences when they are still under your influence. It's a safe but somewhat controlled environment. If they don't experience the consequences early on, the consequences can get much harder the further they go in life and the parent won't be around to rescue them.

Our oldest daughter moved into an apartment her second year of college and was responsible for paying her own rent. I was copied on an e-mail from her landlord, saying that if she didn't pay her rent by Friday, that she would be evicted. I called Erica and asked if she had received the e-mail. She said she had and planned to pay when she got her next check.

On Monday, the landlord called me and said, "Erica's rent is overdue, and if she doesn't pay by the end of the day, then we will have to evict her."

I asked the lady, "Why are you calling me? If Erica doesn't pay by the end of the day, then you should evict her." She was shocked by my response. She expected me to do like so many parents and jump in to save the day. It's not that we didn't have the money and not that we wouldn't ever come to rescue our kids. We just don't jump in to every situation. We give them opportunities to work it out. Sometimes that means they have to feel the consequences of their wrong behavior. In this case, Erica paid her overdue rent and wasn't evicted. We were prepared to help if needed, but because we have allowed her to work through some things on her own, Erica has learned to manage her finances and grow toward financial independence.

Disciplining kids is never fun, but if you are thoughtful about it, you can maintain your peace. With discipline, the key is to determine appropriate consequences beforehand and be consistent with follow-through. This helps parents to maintain their peace of mind while dealing with an unpleasant necessity of parenting.

For example, our son Donovan just started driving. New drivers in our state have an 11:00 p.m. curfew. He recently went out with a friend. I explained the curfew and told him if he was even a minute late, then he would not be allowed to drive for a week. I suggested that he be in the car headed home at least an hour before curfew so that there aren't any misunderstandings or excuses when curfew time comes. I also suggested that he explain this to his friend ahead of time. Nevertheless, he was home before curfew. But if he had missed curfew, there would not have been a need to argue or get upset. The consequences were set, and he would have to live with them.

Discipline has to be appropriate and consistent. It's not what you do to a child but what you do for them. We don't always get this right with our kids, but our goal with discipline is correction driven by love.

CHAPTER 17

DAD'S AFFIRMATION

I was fortunate in that I had people to affirm me as a child. My parents always talked about how smart I was. My teachers and coaches saw something in me. Even though I was always big and a good athlete, people around me always told me I was smart. I would hear, "You are good in math and science. You will make a good engineer." I didn't know what an engineer was, but because others said I would be a good one, my brain decided that they must be right.

I was recruited by many colleges to play football, but I quickly narrowed them down based on who could offer me a chance to both pursue a degree in engineering and play major college football. I accepted a scholarship to play football at Georgia Tech and major in engineering.

When I signed to play football at Georgia Tech, I called for a press conference to announce, "After careful thought and consideration, I have decided to continue my academic and athletic career at the Georgia Institute of Technology." The next day, the headline read, "Moody Chooses Books over Blocks."

Once at Georgia Tech, I felt I was as smart as everyone there. I registered for a basic computer class. At least I thought it was basic. On the first day of class, the professor asked, "How many people have written programs of a thousand lines?" A few people raised their hands. He then asked, "How many have written programs of five hundred lines?" A few more raised their hands. Then he asked "One hundred lines?" I kept waiting for a chance to raise my hand, but it never happened. I thought this was supposed to be a basic computer class. I had never seen a computer in my life. To me, basic meant they would start with, "Here is a computer. Here is how you turn it on, and this is what you can do with it." I knew then that I had my work cut out for me, but because my family, coaches, and teachers had always affirmed me as smart, it never occurred to me that I wasn't. After five years of working extremely hard, I graduated from Georgia Tech with a degree in industrial engineering. My reality became consistent with what had been affirmed in my life. Sometimes it's best to be too smart to realize how dumb you really are.

"Dad, What about Me?"

You may have heard the phrase, "God of Abraham, Isaac, and Jacob." These are the fathers of our faith. Three major religions point to Abraham as the father of their faith: Judaism, Christianity, and Islam.

Abraham had Isaac, and Isaac had twin sons, Jacob and Esau. When Isaac was old and blind, Jacob, the younger son, tricked their father into giving him the blessing that rightfully belonged to Esau as the older brother. He dressed up like Esau, went in to his blind father, and asked for Esau's blessing.

After Isaac finished blessing Jacob, Esau came in and asked his dad for his blessing.

Isaac realized now he had been tricked and that he had given the blessing intended for Esau to his brother Jacob. There was nothing he could do about it now.

We all can identify with the people in this story. Isaac represents all of us because each of us has the ability and responsibility to give a blessing or words of affirmation to another.

Throughout the Bible, you see story after story of fathers speaking blessings or affirmations over their children. In Bible days, the blessing or words that dads spoke over their children meant everything. It was as if it was already done. They put great value on these words. They knew that once their father said these words, it was as good as done.

True fathers exist to affirm their children. It remains one of Dad's most important responsibilities.

Esau and Jacob represent those of us who desire to hear words of affirmation from Dad. All children want to hear their parents speak positive words over their life.

Esau, in particular, represents the person who never received affirmation of who he is and may be suffering the consequences because of it.

Scripture says, "When Esau heard his father's words, he let out a loud and bitter cry. 'Oh my father, what about me? Bless me, too!' he begged" (Genesis 27:34).

Isaac couldn't take his words back. Esau was devastated. Esau wanted so desperately to hear his dad speak a word of blessing over his life. He wanted his dad's affirmation.

I believe these are the same words that many of us are declaring with a loud and bitter cry. "Daddy, what about me? Bless me too."

Many of the problems in society today result from the lack of affirmation from dads. When there is no affirmation, sons and daughters act out in destructive ways.

Here are some statistics to back that up (*The Fatherless Generation*, 2014):

- 85 percent of youths in prison grew up without a father

- 85 percent of all children who show behavior disorders come from fatherless homes
- 71 percent of all high school dropouts come from fatherless homes

We are a society searching for Dad's affirmation. It seems everywhere people—not just children—are asking, "Dad, what about me? Bless me too."

The father's blessing is so important that God Himself affirms Jesus prior to Him beginning His ministry.

"And suddenly a voice *came* from heaven, saying, You are my Son, whom I love; with you I am well pleased'" (Mark 1:11).

Notice the next verse says, "The Spirit immediately drove Jesus out in the wilderness to be tempted by Satan." We know Jesus refuted Satan's temptations. He was able to do this because He knew who He was. He had been affirmed by His Father. We will have the same ability when we are affirmed. God knows we are better prepared for the world when we have affirmation of who we are.

Life is tough even when a person has Dad's affirmation, but having our Father's affirmation better prepares us for the battles ahead.

So why does affirmation work? Science tells us that there is a part of our brain that filters information for us. If we didn't have this system, we would be bombarded with so much information that our senses would overload. Instead, our brain registers what matters to us based on our goals, needs, interests, and desires. (Hogan, *Affirmations: Why They Work & How To Use Them*, 2011).

Most of us have had this experience when a friend shows us their new car and it's a make and model we have never seen before. Then, we suddenly begin to see that particular make and model everywhere we look. Your filter recognized what was important to you and allowed the information in.

When you hear positive affirmations spoken over your life, it sends a very clear message to your brain that this is important to you. You begin to think this is who you are so you start to behave consistently with the words that were affirmed. It's important to understand that this works whether the words are positive or negative. If you are told you are stupid, eventually you will act stupid. If you are told you are intelligent, then eventually you will act more and more intelligent.

You will eventually become that which is dominantly affirmed in your life. You will become who you believe you are. This is why it is so important to guard our hearts. We have to be careful whom we allow to speak into our lives.

One of my favorite photos from football is one with me running off the field with Coach Bill Curry shaking my hand and saying, "Good job, big man!"

That's one reason why we men love sports so much. It puts us in a position for other men to say, "Good job. You are good at that."

Affirmation is not just for our children. It's for us and all of those in our world. We should speak words of encouragement or affirmation to those around us.

Let's go back to Mark 1:11 to learn three ways God expressed affirmation to Jesus. With each expression, I will give you a phrase you can use to express affirmation to others regardless of whether you are affirming a son or daughter or spouse or friend.

I want you to use these phrases every day so you will need to write them down. Say it just like I give it to you. Don't worry if it sounds weird. It will still have the same affect if you just say it.

And suddenly a voice *came* from heaven, saying, "You are my Son, whom I love; with you I am well pleased" (Mark 1:11).

Three Ways God Expressed Affirmation

1. God expressed validity. "You are my Son."

Affirmation is not based on the person's behavior. It's solely based on who he or she is.

God is not a thermometer. He is a thermostat. A thermometer just tells you what temperature it is right now. But a thermostat sets the temperature.

God affirmed Jesus before He did anything. He didn't wait until after Jesus had done great miracles and made great sacrifices. Before all of this, He said to Jesus, "You are my Son." You are good because you come from good stock.

We have to speak validation over others.

Some of you are similar to me in terms of being skilled at seeing what's wrong. You are gifted at it. I could spend all day telling people what they are bad at. I have to work at seeing the good. Paul tells us that we should look for the good in others.

"Finally, brothers and sisters, whatever is true, whatever is noble, whatever is right, whatever is pure, whatever is lovely, whatever is admirable—if anything is excellent or praiseworthy—think about such things" (Philippians 4:8).

One of the guys I mentor serves weekly in our kids' ministry at church. This young man is an accountant and business guy. I couldn't really imagine him working with kids, but I wanted to provide support. One day, I decided to pop in to his class to say hello. When I saw him with the kids, I was really surprised. He was an outstanding teacher. He was funny and loving. It was like he had transformed in this class. He is always so stoic when I see him. I told him afterward, "Man, you are an amazing teacher. You are never this fun around me. God had anointed you to do this. And you are good at it."

People need to know what they are good at and not so good at. It helps to guide people to the will of God. I'm not one of the parents who believes everyone should get a trophy, but I'm also not one of those who puts pressure on my kids to be great at everything. I see it as my job to affirm their unique gifts and strengths.

My son Donovan played on his high school basketball team. I tried to attend as many games as possible so that I could affirm him. I intentionally looked for things he did well so I could say, "You did good at _____." If he didn't score but gave good assist, then that was what I would comment on. Whatever he did well was what I focused on. He didn't need me to tell him what he did wrong. That was what his coach was for. My job as a dad is to affirm what he did well.

Make a habit of telling people what they do well.

Your validity phrase is "You are good at _____."

2.   God expressed love.

God affirmed Jesus by saying, "[You are the one] whom I love."

We can't tell people we love them too much. Love can be shown in other ways, but we also need to hear it.

It's important to know that God affirmed Jesus through an audible voice. Affirmations must be communicated through words verbally or written. It's not enough to just think it in our heads. Our loved ones need to hear us say how we feel.

After Carol and I were married for just a short while, she told me, "You never tell me you love me anymore." I thought, *Really, I never tell you I love you?* but the wiser me refrained from that. Obviously I loved my wife and wanted her to know that. I asked her, "What would help you to realize that I love you the way that I do?"

She said, "You can tell me at least once a day."

So at least once a day since then, I've told my wife, "I love you." People need to hear how we feel even when they know it.

I don't want my wife and kids to doubt that I love them. I want them to know there's nothing they can do to make me love them any more or any less.

Your love phrase is simply: "I love you."

3. God expressed pride. "With you I am well pleased."

God expressed that He was proud of Jesus. We should affirm people in the same way.

I coached my sons' football teams when they were young. When my oldest son started playing, he wasn't keen about getting hit hard by the other boys, especially those a lot bigger than he was. Our team had this football drill to get the boys used to getting hit. It was called "bull in the ring." The boys would line up in a circle with one boy in the middle. The coach would call a number, and the boy wearing that number would run to give the boy in the middle a hit. The boy in the middle had to stay aware so that he could hit back. Usually the coach would call on a similar-sized boy, but on this particular day, he decided to call on all the large boys to hit TJ. One after another, he would call on these boys. The first one hit TJ really good. The second one even harder and almost knocked him down. The third boy hit him the hardest and did knock him down. I would have stopped there, but the coach called on another boy, who again hit him very hard. TJ got back up even though he was exhausted. The coach finally stopped and gave the boys a water break. As TJ dragged his tired body over to get water, I whispered to him, "Son, I'm proud of you." I was so proud of him—not because he was the greatest athlete. I wasn't sure if he heard me or even if he knew why I was proud of him, so later that night, I went to his room to say good night. I asked him, "Do you know why Daddy was proud of you today?"

He said, "Yes. Because I got back up." That was exactly right. I was proud of him because he got back up. I can't wait until he becomes successful in life to tell him I'm proud. I need to do it now.

There will be times in his life when he's going to get knocked down. He needs to know that he has what it takes to get back on his feet.

You are never too old to hear that someone is proud of you. Early on, for me, preaching was intimidating. It seemed everyone had an opinion and for some reason, those who had negative ones felt it was their duty to share theirs. The thing that kept me encouraged was that regardless of how it went, I could count on Mr. Curtis, my spiritual dad, to provide encouragement. He always said the same thing. "Son, you did good. I'm proud of you, and I love you." I'm forty-seven years old, and I still look forward to hearing those words.

Jesus was thirty years old when God affirmed Him.

We don't outgrow needing Dad's affirmation.

I tell my kids that I'm proud to be their dad.

When Gilana was three or four, the whole family attended her preschool year-ending program. They had read many stories during the school year and had been given an assignment to pick out a career from the story that they wanted to be when they grew up. Each took a turn coming up to the mic to share his or her career choice, and as each child shared, the parents so proudly applauded their little angel. One kid wanted to be a police officer, and another wanted to be a nurse. When it was Gilana's turn, she went up to the mic and proudly said, "I want to be a mermaid when I grow up." Carol and I applauded like she had said she wanted to be the president of the United States.

Our oldest daughter leaned over to me and said, "This is embarrassing."

I smiled and told her, "There is nothing you can do that will make Dad ashamed of you. We are just proud to be your parents."

Your pride phrase is "I'm proud of you."

And One

In basketball, they have this term called "and one." It's when you get fouled and get to take an extra shot. I have an "and one" phrase to add for affirming girls and women.

God affirmed Jesus in three ways, but if Jesus had been a girl, I believe He would have had a fourth affirmation. I know Jesus couldn't have been a girl, but go with me on this one. If Jesus had been a girl, I think God would have added one more phrase because girls are always more complicated.

My "and one" affirmation phrase is ...

4. You are beautiful.

My dad would wake me every Sunday making a loud noise and saying this Ben Franklin quote: "Early to bed early to rise makes a boy healthy, wealthy, and wise." I hated it growing up, so what do I do as a dad? I gladly torture my kids with the same saying. But when I wake the girls, I change it just a little. I say, "Early to bed and early to rise makes a princess beautiful, wealthy, and wise."

Every girl needs to hear "You are beautiful." We can't say this enough to our daughters. If you don't tell them, someone else will. It only takes one knucklehead boy to tear down her confidence.

I remind my daughters that they are beautiful just the way God made them. God is saying to women, "You don't have to change one thing. You don't have to lose or gain five pounds. You don't need to be taller or shorter. Your skin doesn't need to be lighter or darker. You are beautiful just the way I made you. I did not make a mistake when making you."

Many of us have never received Dad's affirmation. You may feel like Esau. You never heard "I love you," "You are good at that," "I'm proud of you," or "You are beautiful."

A friend called me recently wanting my advice on a job offer. This friend had grown up impoverished under some really bad conditions. He didn't have a dad, and his mom wasn't very supportive. In spite of his humble beginnings, he had made it to a very high-level position in a huge company.

He told me the new job wouldn't impact his family at all. He wouldn't have to relocate, but his income would increase a quarter of a million dollars annually. Yes, this got my attention too.

People come to me for wise advice so I wanted to think carefully before I answered. I confirmed what he had told me. "It's not illegal or immoral, doesn't negatively impact your family or church, and your income increases a quarter of a million dollars a year?" My response was something like this.

"Man, you better take that job. Why are you even talking to me?"

As I reflected on my friend's situation, I realized he wasn't supposed to be in his position. Statistically, he should have been in prison. He should have behavior problems. He should have dropped out of high school. But here he was running a major corporation.

He was having this level of success because he chose to listen to the affirmations of his heavenly Father instead of what the world said about him. God is a game changer. God wants you to know that He is your ultimate Father. Whether you have been affirmed by an earthly dad or not, God wants to be your dad and affirm you. He wants to be the game changer in your life.

You and I have a choice to make. Will we believe we are who God says we are? God loves you so much, He created you to do great things, and He is so proud that you are His child. He wants you to receive His affirmation of you and for you to share these same affirmations with others. Take time today to practice telling people these three things:

1. You are good at _____.
2. I love you.
3. I'm proud of you.

CHAPTER 18

FRIENDS

I have heard it said often, "Everyone needs to always have three people in his or her life: a Paul, a Silas, and a Timothy." Paul was a spiritual father. Like I discussed earlier, we need someone who provides direction and accountability. Timothy was a disciple of Paul. We all need someone in our lives like Timothy, whom we are mentoring and coaching. This person is likely a few steps behind us in life. We are serving as a spiritual father to him or her. But we also need a Silas. Silas was a friend and person who did life with Paul.

Proverbs 18:24 says, "One who has unreliable friends soon comes to ruin, but there is a friend who sticks closer than a brother."

You may know a lot of people, but how many of them really know you? It's better to have a few close friends than to have a lot of superficial acquaintances. These close friendships must be healthy friendships. Healthy friendships add value to your life while unhealthy friendships take away from your life. The friends you have or want may not always be the friends you need.

My healthy friendships are with the guys who know all the details of my life. They are whom I do life with. When I need encouragement, I can share with these guys. They celebrate successes and mourn losses with me. I can talk to them about my struggles without worrying about how they will take it. You can't have a hundred friends like this, but you need at least a few.

Be intentional about nourishing healthy relationships with close friends. You don't have to see them or talk to them every day, but these are people you know you can talk to when you need them.

Some of my closest friends happen to live in other cities around the country. In fact, I may not get to see them every year. Just because you don't hang out with them every day doesn't mean you can't have deep friendships with them. I maintain a relationship with my lifelong friends by talking on the phone periodically and making an effort to see them face-to-face whenever possible. We have such a close bond that when we do see each other it feels like it was just yesterday when we last saw each other. We have to nourish these relationships.

If you don't have a small group of long-term friends, then it's likely that you are the problem. We must show ourselves friendly in order to have friends.

CHAPTER 19

PRAY FOR LOVED ONES

For those who are in difficult relational situations or lack the relationships you desire, it's important to understand that your peace in relationships is not determined by others. It's all about what you do and how you treat others. It does not depend on you having the perfect spouse or kids or you having a spouse or kids at all.

Too many parents' lives revolve around their children. If their kids are doing well, then they have peace. If the kids are doing poorly, then there is no peace. Also, some who are single feel a lack of peace because they are not in a relationship. Our peace can't be controlled by others. Others can't give you peace or take it away. Only God and you can impact your peace.

Philippians 4:7 (NIV) says, "And the peace of God, which transcends all understanding, will guard your hearts and your minds in Christ Jesus."

Even when our relationships are lacking, God can provide peace. Your circumstances only impact your peace when you allow it.

All of my children don't always do what I want them to do. The older they get, the less control I have over their decisions.

And certainly you can't control the behaviors of a spouse or any adult family member or friend. It's not up to us to change people.

Only God can change hearts. We have to trust God can and will do His part. Knowing that God did the same thing for me gives me peace even when I don't see the behaviors I hope for in others.

My role is to continue to love them, pray for them, and provide coaching and support when appropriate.

We can't control how others behave. Sure, when your kids are young, you have more control, but even then, there's only so much control you have. The one thing we do have total control over when it comes to others is praying for them. Even when things are going the way we hope with people, we can still pray. We can pray for those loved ones in our life. Make a habit of praying for each individual loved one daily.

Small Group Questions

1. If God told you that in seven days you would die and go to live with Him in heaven, whom would you want to spend time with during your last days on earth?

2. Whom do you need to spend more time with, and how can you begin doing that?

3. If you are a parent, which responsibility of parenting is the most challenging to you?

4. Are you consistent at affirming others? Which of the four affirmations are the most difficult for you to share with others ("You are good," "I love you," "I'm proud of you," or "You are beautiful")? Why?

5. List names of your friends or family members who would possibly carry your casket or speak at your funeral. What can you do to be more intentional about nourishing these relationships?

PART 3

PEACE IN HEALTH

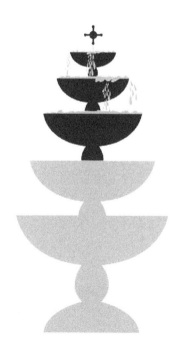

CHAPTER 20

PEACE IN HEALTH

The third peace tier is peace in our health. More specifically, God wants us to have peace in our physical, mental, and emotional health.

The hardest peace tier for me personally is this section that deals with my physical health. I have always been a big guy. Weight doesn't bother me. I have a big frame. I started my college football career as a three-hundred-pound defensive lineman. Post football, I have done okay keeping my weight down. My best weight was around 250 and highest post-football weight is around 285. The thing that bothered me most about my health was the feeling that my eating was controlling me; I was not controlling it. Poor eating habits, especially when it came to overeating desserts, was mastering me instead of me mastering them. I know from scripture that God expects us to be good stewards over our bodies.

"Do you not know that your bodies are temples of the Holy Spirit, who is in you, whom you have received from God? You are not your own; you were bought at a price. Therefore honor God with your bodies" (1 Corinthians 6:19–20).

This scripture tells us that our bodies are God's temples and we should honor Him by taking care of our physical health.

Since this is an obvious area of weakness for me, I thought I would use my own personal battle with healthy living as my own personal science experiment. My focus is not on losing weight but living a healthy lifestyle.

It's been a long time since I've done a science experiment, so I asked my twelve-year-old daughter what the components of her science experiment at school were. She rattled off the top of her head these five components:

1. Ask a question.
2. Make a prediction or hypothesis.
3. Have a plan and follow it.
4. Observe and record data.
5. Draw a conclusion.

So this is the format I will use for my healthy-living personal experience.

Ask a Question

I started my experimental health/fitness journey with the following questions.

- What is God's health expectation of me?

There are people who have all these tips for living healthy and avoiding things that are bad for you. One person told me, "You shouldn't drink carbonated drinks since it deteriorates the bones." Another guy said, "You have to drink this special water. It's known to cure cancer." People at the gym are always telling others that they have to work out this way or that way or eat this or that to see results. My thought is that it can't be that complicated to live physically healthy. Everyone has opinions on healthy living, but what does God say?

- Can I be healthy without committing an unreasonable amount of time and money on gym memberships and exercise equipment?

On December 31, I went into my gym and cancelled my membership. The gym manager seemed surprised. This is a time of year when people rush to join the gym. He was even more puzzled when I told him I was cancelling my membership to focus on my fitness. I wanted to see if I could live a healthy lifestyle without paying a lot of money for a gym membership or workout equipment.

- Does good health require giving up all foods that I enjoy eating?

I like food. I know eating foods that don't taste good is not a long-term, sustainable solution for me. During this experiment, I would seek to find a balance with eating healthy and enjoying good foods.

- Can I be both healthy and happy?

I'm bothered somewhat by those who think you have to look a certain way to be happy. I don't think this is what God has for us. Some people are so focused on the way they look that all they do is starve themselves and work out for hours each day. This doesn't sound like a life of freedom to me. There has to be a balanced approach to living healthy. How do I get that balance and be both healthy and happy?

Chapter 21

MY HEALTH SCIENCE PROJECT

My first step was to get a physical from my doctor. I was in fairly good health, but according to the doctor, I was overweight. My starting weight was 275 pounds. My doctor thought a weight in the 230–240 range would be a healthy weight for me. I also had a high cholesterol level at 225. The doctor suggested lowering this to under 200.

I made a list of the things I was hoping for (my requests to God):

- consistent, healthy eating habits
- improved endurance, energy, and strength
- lower weight to between 230 and 240 pounds
- lower cholesterol to under 200

Then I formed my hypothesis.

Hypothesis 1 — By eating healthier and exercising regularly, I will drop and maintain my weight to a healthier weight significantly less than what I weigh now.

Hypothesis 2 — I can be healthy without paying a lot of money for expensive gym memberships, fitness equipment, and personal trainers.

Hypothesis 3 — I can be healthy while still eating foods I enjoy.

Plan

So here was my plan.

- I will limit processed food, sugars, flour, and pasta and see those things as treats rather than part of my everyday eating. I will limit these treats to one day a week. I plan to incorporate more lean meats, fruits, and vegetables cooked at home into my diet and substitute water for sugar beverages.
- "For overall cardiovascular health, the American Heart Association recommends at least 30 minutes of moderate-intensity aerobic activity at least 5 days per week for a total of 150 minutes and muscle-strengthening activity at least 2 days per week for additional health benefits" (American Heart Association, May 2014). I plan to get my heart rate up to 125 to 145 BPM for at least 150 but no more than 300 minutes weekly with various types of aerobic and strength-building exercise.
- I will share my plan with others for accountability, encouragement, and support.

Observe and Record Data

Fitness Results

	Day 1	2 Months	9 Months
Run/walk 2 miles	24 min	22 Min	18 min 25 sec
# of push-ups in 1 min	22	33	50
Weight	275 lbs	250 lbs	241 lbs
Cholesterol	225	------	175

Chapter 22

HEALTH LESSONS LEARNED

During my initial doctor visit, my doctor asked me to return later in the year to recheck my cholesterol level. I went in after several months for my check. I was anxious to get my results. I knew I had lost weight and hoped that it would also result in a lower cholesterol level.

The nurse took me back to draw my blood, but instead of weighing me first like she had done on all my previous visits, she walked me right past the scale to an area to get my blood drawn. I asked, "Aren't you going to weigh me?"

She said, "No. You don't have to get a weight today."

That was when the South Memphis in me came out. I said, "No. Y'all gon' weigh me today. You weigh me every other time and write down how fat I am so you gon' weigh me today. In fact, everybody in here gon' get weighed. You, the doctor, everybody up in here gon' to get weighed today."

She laughed but realized I was serious, and she weighed me and said, "You've lost significantly."

"That's right. Y'all better recognize."

The plan was simple, and the results were significant. I lost thirty-four pounds. I was able to run two miles in under 18.5 minutes.

I increased my strength, energy level, and endurance. More important, I was able to reduce my cholesterol to a healthier level.

I was proud of the results. I was also happy that I was able to do this and still enjoy good foods. This experiment validates that weight loss can occur without paying a lot of money or spending an unreasonable amount of time. I proved to myself that I could be both happy and healthy.

Healthy living is not about being perfect. In fact, I only met my exercise and eating goals about 80 percent of the time. It's about progress more than it is about perfection. It is about making a decision to live healthily and making good choices more often than bad choices.

The bottom line is that there is no easy way to better health. We have to commit to eating healthy foods and getting our heart rate up by moving our bodies. I don't feel confident enough yet to say food is not a problem for me anymore because it is something that I continue to battle daily. But my experiment confirmed that if we follow this simple plan, we will live the healthy lifestyle God intends for us to have. Here are some of the lessons I learned during my fitness experiment.

Seek a Godly Vision

If we want to make a significant change in any area of our lives, we should start with seeking godly wisdom on that subject. So, my journey started with me seeking knowledge on living a healthy lifestyle. I wanted to know God's view of healthy living when it comes to my physical body.

I heard about this book from Rick Warren called *The Daniel Plan*. This got my interest. I have a respect for Rick Warren, and besides, he's a big guy like me. Rick and his team of health experts wrote this book to help people look at health and fitness from a Christian viewpoint.

I learned how to eat healthily. *The Daniel Plan* book helped me to articulate a godly vision for my healthy lifestyle. My godly vision is for a healthier me. My goal is to look and feel the way God intends for me to look and feel. I want to live without physical limits and have energy to do what I'm called to do. I want to look and feel healthy. I want to be healthy not only now but also when I'm old. I want to be free from all self-imposed sickness and illnesses. This is the vision I believe God has for my life and yours as well.

Renew Your Mind

Having a vision alone is not enough. We have to both understand and apply the knowledge we learn to our situation. When we start applying wisdom, it modifies the way we think.

One day, I was taking my car to have some work done not far from my home. As I headed out, I thought to myself, *How am I going to get home?* Then an idea came. *This auto repair shop is only about three miles from the house. I have on my running clothes. If they are going to take a while, I can just jog home and Carol can bring me back later.* This thought had never occurred to me before. But after several months of running three miles, my thinking had changed. It's the doing that changed the way that I thought.

Eating Healthily Doesn't Mean Eating Tasteless Foods and Vice Versa

Eating fewer processed foods meant that we were cooking more dinners at home. I was amazed at how tasteful some of the healthy home-cooked meals were. Carol had gotten recipes for lean meats and vegetables. It meant being more planful and creative, but the meals cooked at home were some of the best meals I've eaten. I've gotten use to eating fruits for dessert. I snack on fruits and nuts. I substitute water for sugary beverages. A friend asked if I got tired of drinking water. He said, "That seems so boring." For me, it seems like my taste buds have awakened to so many more tasteful things. I enjoy eating, and I don't have to give up tasteful foods to eat healthily.

Carol and I decided we would spend our anniversary weekend eating out at a lot of restaurants we had not tried. It was a way to celebrate our anniversary. Friday, we ate at a chic café. It was okay. I bought a bag of doughnuts to eat later. Friday night, we ate at a fancy restaurant. It was okay. Saturday, we finished off the doughnuts and bought Girl Scout cookies, and we ate lunch at a barbecue joint. Afterward we went to a museum. I felt a little sick to my stomach. The food I had been eating upset my stomach. I had to sit down but felt better after a few minutes of sitting. I realized I hadn't been missing much by eating healthily. The foods I thought I'd miss didn't taste any better, and they made me feel bad.

Exercise

I found that there are several health benefits to cardiovascular exercise. Not only has exercise helped manage my weight loss, but it is also having a positive impact on the long-term health of both my heart and lungs. According to the American Heart Association, being physically active is important to prevent heart disease and stroke, the nation's number-one and number-four killers.

To improve overall cardiovascular health, the AHA suggests at least 150 minutes per week of moderate exercise or 75 minutes per week of vigorous exercise (or a combination of moderate and vigorous activity). The key to cardiovascular exercise is to increase the heart rate.

The AHA also recommends adding weightlifting to the exercise routine at least twice a week. Weightlifting builds muscles and changes your body. During this fitness experiment, I'm starting to see muscles where I haven't had muscles before. I've also stopped having knee and back pains, which I have struggled with for several years. Regular exercise is also a way to reduce stress and improve emotional health. Overall, I just feel a lot stronger and more energetic.

Health Living Is a Choice

Being healthy starts with a decision. It's not enough to want to be healthy. We have to decide that we will live healthily. Not only does it start with a choice but it continues to be a choice daily.

On a recent trip to Dallas, I got stuck in the Memphis airport for several hours. I had planned to work out after we landed in Dallas. Now with the delay, I knew I wouldn't have time. So I had a choice. If I was going to exercise, I had to do it in the airport. So I decided to get my exercise by walking in the airport. I walked the whole airport in thirty-five minutes.

Another time, a family member was in the hospital having an emergency surgery. It was a critical situation, and I wanted to be there. I got the call late at night. I visited my family member until he was ready to sleep and told him I would be back in the morning early. I realized I had a choice. If I was going to work out that day, I needed to get it done at four in the morning. That was tough, but I decided that working out had to be a priority for me. Living healthily means making good decisions daily. We are not always going to make the right decisions, but we have to make more good ones than bad if we want to have peace in our health.

It's a Treat Not a Cheat

I realize that there is an emotion connected with eating. We have always used food as a way to celebrate. We do it at our special holidays and every big social event. There is a joy that comes with sharing your favorite meal in celebration with others. Jesus even did it six days before His death. John 12:2 says, "Here a dinner was given in Jesus's honor," and Jesus reclined around the table with his disciples and friends. This is normal. Having special occasions is not what makes us unfit. It's when we eat this way every day.

I met Omari, who was a personal trainer on the poplar show *The Biggest Loser*. I told him about my experiment and the plan I was following. I mentioned that I cheated once a week to have my favorite dessert. He responded, "It's not a cheat. It's a treat." He explained how psychologically it's much better to think of it this way to take away the negative connotations with cheating. This made sense to me and changed my perspective.

I schedule one day off a week to have my treat. I just don't think you can go forever without having some of those unhealthy things you love. The problem is when we are eating those things every day. Having a treat periodically is playing good offense against your temptation. It quenches the need and reminds you that you aren't missing anything. Sometimes when I'm presented a dessert, but it's not my off day, I wrap it well and put it in the freezer until my day off. This does two things. It gives me something to look forward to, and it helps me to avoid the desserts that aren't better options than what I have in the freezer.

We Can't Do It Alone

"Though one may be overpowered, two can defend themselves. A cord of three strands is not quickly broken" (Ecclesiastes 4:12).

I realized that it was so much easier having others help in my desire to live healthily. A big part of my success came from changing how I eat at home. This means that my family had to make changes as well and support my choices. My wife in particular supported me by buying and preparing healthier foods. Having my loved ones' support meant everything to me.

I also had friends who helped me. I went on a business trip with my friend Joe. I shared my fitness plan with Joe and gave him authority to hold me accountable. Joe took this role seriously and helped me stick to my fitness plan. He encouraged me to get up early in the morning to run. It was cold and rainy. If he hadn't pushed me, I would have easily got back in the bed. But because he was there with me, I endured running two miles. During the conference we attended, I avoided the things that are problems for me, like cookies and muffins. And they had a lot. It seems the more I try to eat right, the more I'm bombarded with temptation. I appreciated having Joe there to hold me accountable. The next morning, I got up on my own and ran on a treadmill at the hotel. At least this time, I wasn't running in the cold rain.

When I knew others were making healthy decisions along with me, it motivated me to stay with it. A friend at church said she was participating in "no-sugar September" and invited me to join her. I accepted since desserts are always a weakness for me. Every time I was tempted to eat a dessert, I thought about my friend and how she was counting on me to refrain from eating sugar. That thought motivated me to hold out. We all need others to support us, encourage us, and hold us accountable.

Weight Loss Is 75 Percent What You Eat

Last year, I decided that I would focus on having a healthier lifestyle. I did some research and found a website that advised exercise 150 to 300 minutes a week for good health while eating 2,000 to 2,600 calories a day of a balanced diet. I thought, *Okay, this sounds reasonable.* So I tried it. I did well in meeting my exercise targets all year but struggled with the diet goals. The result was that I started the year and ended the year at the same weight. Since I was exercising regularly, I thought, *Either this is the weight God wants me, or I'm not doing something right.*

One thing I learned from my experiment was that it was not the amount of calories I was eating but the types of food that impacted my weight. My weakness is desserts. I was eating desserts every day. In addition to desserts, I found that I was consuming a high amount of processed foods, flour, and sugars as well. These things were the main culprits to my weight gain.

As a rule of thumb, weight loss is generally 75 percent diet and 25 percent exercise (Huffington Post, 2014).

Too Much of Sugar, Flour, and Processed Foods Is Bad

The human body isn't designed to eat the amount of sugar we consume. So it hits the liver. The liver says, "I don't know what to do with all this sugar," so it starts to metabolize it in unusual ways, and it gets turned into what are known as low-density lipoprotein particles. And that's the worst kind of cholesterol. And for the body, a slice of white bread and a packet of sugar are essentially indistinguishable. The body receives them as the same (CNN.com, "Why Sugar Is Worse Than Fat," 2014).

Sugar also causes excess weight gain around the midsection. Prior to my fitness experiment, most of what I overate was sugar or turning into sugar. It shouldn't have been a surprise that by changing my diet, I was able to lower my cholesterol by 51 points as well as my midsection by four inches.

Expensive Gym Membership and Personal Trainers Are Not Needed

I dread cold weather. I'm a wimp when it comes to running outside in the cold. I thought maybe there was a workout video online. We cancelled our satellite TV but bought a device that allows us to watch the Internet on our TV. I searched for workouts, and all kinds of shows popped up. I found a routine that worked for me and did a forty-minute workout at the house. I realized that I had no excuse for not working out.

You can get in shape without going to the gym or buying expensive equipment. You can use your own body weight, but you have to move your body.

If joining a gym works for you, there are inexpensive options. After proving to myself that I could lose weight without being a member of the gym, we joined an inexpensive gym. It gives me the option to run on a treadmill the days I can't go outside and a chance to do more strength building with weights. Regardless of whether we prefer to join a gym or not, the point is that being healthy doesn't have to be expensive.

Start Again Each Week / No Condemnation

It is so easy for me to slip back into bad habits even though I know that it's not good for me. The last week of March was one of my worst weeks of eating during this experiment. I decided to recommit to the success pattern I discussed earlier of vision, hope, faith, patience, and accountability and got back on track.

It occurred to me that I didn't feel the usual condemnation. I just decided I hadn't met my expectations so I would get back on track.

I wasn't feeling like God was mad at me or worried about how I had let Him down. I had messed up. I knew what I needed to do and recommitted to doing it. I shared this with my accountability partners and asked them to hold me accountable for doing better. To me, it felt like the beginning of each week brought a fresh start and a clean slate.

I believe this is exactly how God wants us to respond when we fall short of His expectations. We are not saved because we meet those expectations. We are saved by grace because we can never meet those expectations. Thank God for Jesus and His grace. I don't have to meet any expectations to please God. He's already pleased with me. It's only so I can live a better life. When I follow God's plan, it leads me to a better life.

When I fall short, it leads me to a lesser life than God has for me. My eating right is for me, not for God. God is not displeased with you. There is nothing you can do to make Him love you more or less. He already loves you with all He has. When you mess up, just get back on track. Don't wallow in self-pity. God is not condemning you. Regardless of how you did last week, begin each week with a new sense of excitement. Each week is a fresh start with God.

Stop Comparing — We Are Not All Alike

One day in April, I touched my belt and realized I was wearing the belt in the last notch. When I looked at my belt, I could see how my belt was worn four holes from the hole I was using now. I had lost weight and needed to tighten my belt more to keep my pants up.

I was looking in the mirror and thought to myself, *I have a long ways to go.* My progress seemed to be very slow. I have a friend who is about my age and height who has a muscular, slim, and fit physique. When envisioning what the healthier Travis would look like, I imagined myself looking more like my friend.

Here I was losing weight and getting fit yet discouraged because I didn't look like the picture of fit I had conjured up in my mind.

One day, I was in the gym and I saw a slim guy with muscles, and I started to think, *Why can't I look like that?* Then I overheard his conversation about how he was trying to get his body to look like one of the other guys in the gym. The same day, I was talking to a guy at the gym who admired my weight loss and said if only he could look like me. That's the problem with comparisons. It never stops. While I was wanting to be like someone else who wanted to look like someone else, here was a guy wanting to look like me. Comparisons keep us from enjoying our own progress. It either makes us insecure or prideful.

I reminded myself of how much better I felt and how much better I looked in my new body. Yes, my body. It's not someone else's body but mine. I came to a realization that God did not make us all with the same body shape or give us the same capabilities. A lot of it has to do with your genetics. There are parts of my body that develop faster and others parts that develop little at all. I see muscles developing in my body in places that I didn't have before. But parts, like my biceps, aren't developing as much, no matter how hard I try. Comparing ourselves to others is counterproductive. I can only be the best me God created me to be. We have to resolve not to let comparisons discourage us or determine whether we are healthy or not. Just commit to being the healthiest you you can be. This will please God and give you peace.

Doctor Visits

It's important to have regular doctor visits to monitor overall health and fitness. It's not okay to go to the doctor only when something is wrong or hurting. Regular checkups will help to prevent illnesses and ensure you are on track to live the healthiest lifestyle you can possibly live. Just as important as going to the doctor is following through on whatever your physician tells you to do. It does no good to simply know what to do to become healthier; you must commit to doing it. We have to see our physicians as trusted advisers and do what they recommend we do.

CHAPTER 23

MENTAL AND EMOTIONAL HEALTH

"Above all else, guard your heart, for everything you do flows from it" (Proverb 4:23).

Some people call mental health *emotional health* or *well-being*, and it's just as important as good physical health. This book is not designed to help those who have severe mental or emotional health problems. Those individuals should seek professional counseling. However, there are some steps we can take to increase our peace by improving our mental and emotional health. Being mentally and emotionally healthy means you are able to cope with and manage the changes and uncertainties of life. It also means you are able to form and maintain good relationships with others in your family, workplace, and community, and among friends.

Steps you can take to increase peace in your mental and emotional health are as follows:

1. Take time to rest.
2. Refrain from abusing drugs or alcohol.
3. Deal with any unaddressed heart wounds.
4. Talk with someone.

Time to Rest

"By the seventh day God had finished the work he had been doing; so on the seventh day he rested from all his work. Then God blessed the seventh day and made it holy, because on it he rested from all the work of creating that he had done" (Genesis 2:2).

There are at least three types of rests that are important for healthy living.

1. Daily rest—sleep, breaks throughout the day, personal time

"The Centers for Disease Control and Prevention (CDC) recommends seven to nine hours per night for adults," which "has been associated with a number of other health benefits, including improved memory, lower levels of inflammation, and healthy weight" (CDC.gov, 2014).

Listen to your body. When you're tired, give yourself time for sleep. We need proper sleep. Without good sleep, our mental health suffers and our concentration goes downhill. Sometimes the things of this world can wait. If the world waited for God as He rested, then certainly it can wait for you to rest.

2. Weekly Rest—Sabbath

"Six days you shall labor and do all your work, but the seventh day is a Sabbath to the LORD your God. On it you shall not do any work ... the LORD blessed the Sabbath day and made it holy" (Exodus 20:9–11).

For knowing Him more intimately, God ordained one day in seven for us to unite without the usual daily distractions. The Sabbath provides a time of spiritual rest. In essence, God is saying to us something like this:

> This is My Holy Day—set apart for our special time together. I will cause you to forget all the things that Satan is doing to 'steal, kill, and destroy you.' Come apart from your earthly concerns. Come rest in Me. Join Me in this special day so that we may celebrate our relationship. As you abide in My Presence, your depression and discouragement will vanish. I will lift you this day to spiritual heights that look beyond

this world. I will restore you with joy. I will fill you to overflowing with hope. I will cause a peace that transcends all understanding to wash over you. Come, My child, for I love you and I want to spend this time with you. (Shelton and Quinn, *Ten Commandments Twice Removed*, 86–87)

How can you turn down this invitation? But every week people say, "Naw, I'm good. I don't have the time to spend with you, God. I'm too busy." When in reality, it's only when we choose to spend this time with God that our other time is blessed. I get more done when I take time with God then when I don't. It's the same principle as the tithe. When I give to God first, He multiplies what I have left to make it more than what I had before.

I schedule one day off a week as a Sabbath Day. I'm very protective of this day. On this day, I don't do any work. I jokingly say, "I don't wash a cloth or a dish on the Sabbath." Truth is I only do what I feel like doing. Sure, I pray and read my Bible and journal this day, but I don't feel pressured to spend hours studying the Bible. The purpose of this day is to rest. I stay away from things that sap my energy and do things that provide rest and relaxation. I spend time with my family and do all my favorite things like watch football, read, and listen to jazz. I stick to things that bring me peace and joy. I also dream on this day. One of my favorite things to do on my Sabbath day is take a nap. In fact, I may take two naps. The Sabbath is just my day to relax with God. I totally unplug—no work meetings or checking e-mails. I'm like a different person on these days. I'm so relaxed that coworkers who happen to see or talk to me on these days say that I don't seem like myself.

It's actually tougher for me as a minister, because when others are having a day off, I'm working. We have services at our church on Saturday and Sunday, and our offices are open Monday through Thursday. I often feel internal pressure not to take my Sabbath day off.

One particular week, I had a rough week and didn't get as much done as I needed to before my upcoming Friday Sabbath day. I was scheduled to teach a class on Saturday. I had a choice to do some work to get ready for the Saturday class or take my Sabbath day as planned. I hesitated, thinking, *I really need to get ready for it.* I finally decided I would just prepare as much as I can the next day and trust God would make it all work out. I did just that. The class went well. It seemed God multiplied my efforts and gave me grace where I needed it. I realized that I get more done when I honor God with the Sabbath day. Things will fall into place when we take time with God.

Another reason taking a Sabbath is important is that God designed our bodies with the physical and mental need to rest one day out of seven from ordinary labor. Our bodies aren't designed to go more than a week without rest. Sure, we may be able to maintain for a while, but eventually our bodies and minds will give out. My pastor, John Siebeling, likes to say, "Unobserved Sabbaths accumulate."

God created us with a built-in need to rest. To function correctly, we need proper rest. Rest rejuvenates our bodies and minds. It helps us to better cope with life and reduces stress.

A study by the Harvard Business School provides scientific support for the Sabbath day. The study found that people are more productive with a day off than they are if they work every day (*Harvard Business Review*, 2009).

My rules for a Sabbath day:

- don't do anything that I do during my normal workday
- do what gives energy and avoid what takes away energy
- no heavy lifting
- do what I enjoy
- it's okay to be selfish
- enjoy loved ones
- spend time with God
- spend time thinking
- allow time for emotions (laugh and cry) — I watch a funny movie or an inspirational movie that brings me to tears, such as *Courageous* or *Fireproof*. My favorite is *Facing the*

Giants. It's funny, has football, and makes me cry. You can't get any better than that.

3. Vacation Rest

A vacation is taking multiple days at a time away from work for rest and relaxation. We need to make vacations a regular part of our lives.

> As far as vacations go, the more the merrier. A study done at Erasmus University in Rotterdam found that among about 1,500 Dutch adults in which 974 of them took a vacation, those who took time off were happier than those who did not, mostly because they were excited in anticipation for their vacation. They also showed signs of slightly increased happiness for two weeks after they returned from vacation. So, the trick for success, says the study's leader, Jeroen Nawijn, seems to be taking two or more short breaks spread out in the year rather than one massive vacation. Spread out that happiness! ("9 Reasons to Take a Vacation ASAP, According to Science," *Huffington Post*, 2014).

One of the things I enjoy the most is our family vacation. This is especially true now that my kids are older and not all of them live in our home. We commit to taking a family vacation at least once a year and a Mom-and-Dad vacation alone at least once a year. Throughout the year, we take extended time off as needed. We try to do something at least quarterly.

Recently I took a look at my upcoming schedule and realized I was about to go into a very busy season. I decided that to prepare for this, I needed to be well rested so I scheduled a week-long vacation. I didn't have anything in particular planned. I didn't go out of town or stay at a local hotel. I just stayed at home doing nothing. According to the *Merriam-Webster Dictionary*, the official term for this is now *staycation*. I enjoyed the week doing nothing. I caught up on all the little things I'd been wanting to do but didn't have time to do. I took a lot of naps and basically did nothing. It was fun but seemed much too short. But at the end, I was well rested and ready to take on the expected challenges in the season ahead.

When I don't have enough rest, I can tell the difference. I am less patient with people and become more cynical. It's like when I was a small child and I got cranky, my mom used to say, "You are just tired. Go take some time to rest." I hated when she said that. I used to think, *I'm not tired. I'm just upset with what's going on!* But I would go take a nap like my mom said and afterward whatever I was upset about wouldn't be such a big deal. The situation didn't change while I slept. But proper rest gave me a brand-new perspective. It's no different for us as adults. When we are tired, we have a hard time dealing with the smallest of life's situations. We need to rest our minds, bodies, and emotions in order to deal with the ups and downs of life. We need to just heed the advice my mom gave to me as a child. "You are tired. Take some time to rest."

Believe it or not, your work will be there when you get back. Don't fall into believing that your work can't go on without you, therefore you can't take a day off. If something happened to you, the world and your job or business would continue just fine without you. Take time for yourself every day, every week, and several longer periods throughout the year.

Drugs and Alcohol

"Do not get drunk on wine, which leads to debauchery. Instead, be filled with the Spirit" (Ephesians 5:18).

I'm not a drinker, but I'm also not totally against drinking alcoholic beverages.

The Bible never says drinking alcohol is a sin. It clearly states that drunkenness is a sin. Drunkenness is using alcohol to the point where it negatively impacts your judgment.

In fact, studies show that occasional light drinking has some health benefits (Mental Health Foundation, 2014).

But some people drink alcohol to change their mood. Alcohol gives a temporary feeling of peace, but the effect is short-lived. When the alcohol wears off, you feel worse because of the way alcohol withdrawal symptoms affect your brain and the rest of your body. Drinking is not a good way to manage difficult feelings.

Apart from the damage too much alcohol can do to your body, you would need more and more alcohol each time to feel the same short-term boost.

Many people also smoke or use drugs or other substances to change how they feel. But, again, the effects are short-lived. Just like alcohol, the more you use, the more you crave. Nicotine and drugs don't deal with the causes of difficult feelings. They don't solve problems; they create them. In order to live healthily, it's important that we address the root issues that cause us to be emotionally unhealthy.

Small Group Questions

1. Which of the lessons learned on my fitness experience stood out to you most and why?

2. Do you have regular visits with your doctor? If no, why not?

3. What is the vision you have for your health?

4. What is one thing you would like to improve in your health?

5. What small step could you make that if done consistently would make the biggest impact on your health?

6. What adjustments in your life are needed to make this step a priority for you?

7. Do you take time to rest? If no, why not? If yes, describe the impacts proper rest has had on you.

CHAPTER 24

DEAL WITH UNADDRESSED HEART WOUNDS

"May God himself, the God of peace, sanctify you through and through. May your whole spirit, soul and body be kept blameless at the coming of our Lord Jesus Christ. The one who calls you is faithful, and he will do it" (I Thessalonians 5:23–24).

At some point, we all have areas in our lives where we are wounded and need healing from God. These wounds typically fall into one of three categories: body (physical), soul (heart), and spirit (eternal).

Complete healing consists of healing in all three of these areas. John 9 tells a story of Jesus healing a physical wound. This man was blind, and Jesus gave him his sight. It's easier for us to assess when we have physical wounds. Everyone can see he was blind. It's hard to deny or escape that reality. Spiritual wounds are a little harder, but every true Jesus follower, at some point, recognizes that he or she has a spiritual wound. Our sins create a spiritual wound that separates us from God (Romans 3:23). This wound left unattended leads us to an eternity living without God. Jesus healed this wound on the cross (Isaiah 53:5), and because of Him, we will live eternity with Him (Romans 6:23).

Physical health issues are easy to diagnose and rarely go unaddressed. People don't just walk around with broken arms. If we have a broken arm, we put a cast on it. If we have a bruised knee, we put a Band-Aid on it. But it is just as important to have a healthy heart. In 3 John 1:2, it says, "Dear friend, I pray that you may enjoy good health and that all may go well with you, even as your soul is getting along well."

It is much harder to detect when we have a wounded heart. Unlike the physical wound, the wounded heart often goes undetected and unaddressed. There is no cast for a wounded heart.

Lots of things can cause these emotional wounds. Disappointments or bad situations, such as the loss of a job, a failed business, or a failed marriage, can also leave us wounded. Even though we can't see these wounds, they affect us just as much as physical wounds. Our hearts are often wounded by what others may have done or said to us. When we are subject to verbal or emotional abuse, it leaves a wound.

There are entire industries dedicated to the brokenhearted. Bars, casinos, drug dealers, divorce courts, strip clubs, and jails thrive on unaddressed heart wounds. It is imperative as a society that we deal with this hurt. I am convinced God wants to heal these wounds.

You've heard that "time heals all wounds." Unfortunately this is not true for emotional wounds. People carry hurts from thirty and forty years ago. Time only makes it worse. We can try to hide, bury, or deny our hurts, but eventually they reveal themselves.

Suppressing these emotional wounds is especially common with men. It's not manly to show hurtful emotions. We can't cry or show any signs of "weakness." We don't talk about it and just go through life never dealing with our hurts.

Wounds left unattended fester and spread infection throughout your body. Not only does this keep us from experiencing the peace of God, but it hurts our relationships with others and our effectiveness as Jesus followers. We have to address these wounds in order to have freedom.

I discovered a wound that I didn't know I had several years ago when I was a general manager in a large Fortune 500 company.

There was a complaint from one of our corporate partners that possibly financial fraud was happening in the business unit I managed. This was a time when several high-profile corporate fraud cases were in the media so our company took this accusation seriously. Our company sent in an internal auditor to work with me and my team to investigate the issue. Since I was the general manager, the investigation was focused on whether I had done something inappropriate.

I gathered my team in my office for a conference call with the chief financial officer from the company who made the complaint. Discussion between the two companies was heated but remained professional. Then out of nowhere, the CFO from the other company said these words, "I'm not some [n-word] from South Memphis ..." I thought to myself, *He couldn't have said what I thought I heard.* But from the looks on all the white faces gathered in my office, I knew I had heard him correctly.

I was furious. I didn't hear another word said. I was so mad I could hardly think. I wanted to attack back but had enough sense to know that wasn't wise at the time. I knew I had to get off the phone before I said or did something I would regret. It took everything in me to just end the conversation.

I later realized that this guy didn't know I was black and from South Memphis. I worked in an industry that at the time was typically all white, so he assumed everyone in the room was white as well.

After the call, my staff left my office at a loss for words. I sat there quietly in my office an emotional wreck. I was angry and mad. I wanted to hit someone. I'm sure if that guy had been in Memphis at the time, there would have been a fight. I was so mad, but all I could do was sit in my office alone and cry. I couldn't believe this was happening in the twenty-first century. I thought about everything my parents had gone through so that I could have the life I have. I'm sure they believed if I was educated, worked hard, and made money, then things would be different for me and I would never have to be referred to by that word. I thought about my children and how I couldn't protect them from feeling this same pain. I just sat there crying. I couldn't explain exactly what I was feeling. I sort of felt numb. It was as if some part of me that I didn't know even existed had just died.

The CFO must have later realized that I was black and that his words were offensive, because he called to apologize. The company and I were cleared of any wrongdoing, and everybody went back to his or her normal life—everybody but me. I was left with a wounded heart. I tried to fake it on the outside, but on the inside, I was wounded.

The fact that this word was used so casually by a leader in a major corporation left me carrying around a bitterness, distrust, and anger for all white people. This wound was having a negative impact on my life.

We may not realize the effects of these wounds, but they affect how we behave or react to life circumstances. Our wounds prevent us from responding to normal issues of life rationally. It may cause us to lose our temper, shrink in fear, feel overwhelmed with anxiety, burst out in tears, or lash out in anger rather than deal with the issue appropriately.

I knew I needed God's power to heal my emotional wound, and He did just that. Because He has healed this wound in me, today I enjoy healthy, loving, and trusted relationships with friends who are white as well as friends from other ethnic backgrounds.

Maybe your wounds are different from mine, but you have them. If you don't address them, they will have a negative impact on your life.

I think back on how my life would have been so drastically different if I had not addressed this heart wound. I would not have some of my closest friends; I would not have written my first book, which was suggested by a white friend; and I would not be in ministry in a multicultural church. I would have missed out on so much if I had allowed myself to remain wounded. Not only would I have missed out on so much, but you would have too. I wouldn't be here in order to give you this message. So much is riding on the healing of your heart wounds.

There are five simple steps I follow to heal my heart wounds. These same five steps brought sight to a blind man in John 9, and they can help bring healing to your wounds as well.

> As [Jesus] went along, he saw a man blind from birth. His disciples asked him, "Rabbi, who sinned, this man or his parents, that he was born blind?" "Neither this man nor his parents sinned," said Jesus, "but this happened so that the works of God might be displayed in him.... After saying this, he spit on the ground, made some mud with the saliva, and put it on the man's eyes. "Go," he told him, "wash in the Pool of Siloam" (this word means "Sent"). So the man went and washed, and came home seeing. (John 9:1–3, 6–7)

Step 1. Admit I Am Wounded

The first step in the healing process is to admit I am wounded. We often deny that heart wounds are even there. When our wounds are physical, like the blind man's, they are harder to deny. The physical wounds are outwardly visible to everyone so it's fruitless for the blind man to deny he is blind. But heart wounds are different. We can hide, deny, and suppress it so no one knows they are there. We can even fool ourselves for a period of time.

You May Have Emotional Wounds If ...

Here are a few indicators that you might have some unaddressed emotional wounds:

1. You often feel like a victim.
2. You have a hard time building happy and committed relationships.
3. You become critical and judgmental of yourself or others.
4. You continue to fall into the same harmful habits.

5. You hurt other people physically or emotionally.
6. You are driven by gaining the approval of others.
7. You often lose your temper.
8. You hold grudges against others.
9. You are bothered by the success of others.
10. You can't take criticism.
11. You often feel hurt, down, or depressed.
12. You struggle making the progress you desire in life.

My dad used to say, "Only a hit dog will holla." He later explained that if you throw a rock into a pack of dogs, only the one that was hit by the rock will respond. When we lose our temper, lash out in anger, or feel a high level of anxiety, we have to ask ourselves what's really causing it. Here are some questions that may help you better understand your wounds.

1. Think about recent times when you lost your temper, became fearful, or overreacted emotionally to a situation.
   a. What caused this behavior?

   b. Would you have reacted differently if you were emotionally secure?

2. What wrongs, resentments, past situations, or secret sins are affecting your emotional health?

3. Is there anyone in your heart that you resent, fear, or refuse to forgive?
   a. If your friends were giving you a party, are there people you would not want invited?

   b. Who and why?

In order to begin the healing process, we must first admit that we are wounded. Healing begins when we openly confess our wounds to ourselves, to God, and to someone we trust.

Step 2. Stop the Blame

The second step is to stop blaming others. The disciples wanted to know who was to blame for this man's wound. We spend too much time focusing on who is to blame. We have to get past who is at fault and address the wound. We can't truly receive healing if we are busy blaming. Jesus shut the blame down immediately. He said, "But this happened so that the works of God might be displayed in him." Romans 8:28 says, "All things work for the good of those who love God and are called according to His purpose." This means God will use both good and bad things for his purpose. It's hard for us to comprehend this, but our wound is for God's glory. This does not take away responsibility from those who hurt us. Some of our wounds are caused by people who intentionally or unintentionally caused us great pain. We have to stop blaming them and forgive. We have to take ownership of the responsibility to become healthy. No one else can own my emotional health but me. When we forgive, it is for us as much as it is for the one we forgive. We cannot find peace and serenity if we continue to blame ourselves or others. We have to forgive others and ourselves.

Step 3. Let Jesus Touch My Wound

The third step is to let Jesus touch my wound. In this particular case, Jesus healed this blind man by touching the man's eyes. Jesus also has to touch our heart wounds in order to heal us. It's only when someone touches that heart wound that we even realize it's there. This is why having a relationship with an accountability partner or spouse is so necessary and yet so difficult. The closer people get to us, the harder it is to hide the wounds, and they often touch them without much notice. Just like physical wounds, heart wounds often do not hurt until someone touches them. Before that person or we know what happened, we respond with some hurtful behavior to those who touched the wound (anger or verbal or physical attack). We rarely are even conscious of why we reacted the way we did. We need others in our lives whom we trust who can help us address these wounds.

God wants to heal this wound, but it's up to us invite God in to help us just as King David did.

"Search me, God, and know my heart; test me and know my anxious thoughts. See if there is any offensive way in me, and lead me in the way everlasting" (Psalm 139:23–24).

Although David had all kinds of problems, God called David a man after God's own heart (1 Samuel 13:14). It's only through the Holy Spirit that you can overcome your wounded heart. The Holy Spirit is a gentleman and must be invited in.

In order to continue the healing process, we have to follow David's model of inviting God to search our hearts and remove anything that is not like God.

God uses other people to help heal our wounded hearts. But they have to get close enough to touch it. This is why it is so important to be connected with other people in our journey. We can't do life alone. None of us are superhuman. We all sometimes get tired or overwhelmed by how we feel or when things go wrong. Jesus will heal your wound through other people if you let Him. Get around people you trust, whom you can allow close enough to touch your wounded heart.

If things are getting too much for you and you feel you can't cope, ask for help. Your family or friends may be able to offer practical help or a listening ear. You should seek professional help if your current mental or emotional health is stopping you from getting on with life, having a big impact on the people you live or work with, or affecting your mood over several weeks.

Step 4. Do My Part

After Jesus put mud on the blind man's eyes, he told him to "go" and "wash" his eyes. At this point, the blind man had a choice. He could stay where he was and think, *Why waste my time? I have been blind from birth. Why would it change now?*

Many times, we say we want healing, but when it comes down to doing some unpleasant work, we shrink back and don't follow through. When it comes to our deliverance, God has a part and we have a part.

Here was a blind man, and Jesus is telling him to go find some pool to wash his eyes. Can you imagine how hard this was? It was going to take some effort on his part to get there. Why couldn't Jesus just heal him right there?

We have a role to play when it comes to our healing, and we must be courageous in doing it. This man had to choose to believe Jesus could heal him, accept Jesus's help, and do his part in order to be healed.

Our part includes committing to a daily time with God for self-examination, Bible reading, and prayer in order to know God and His will for our lives and to gain the power to follow His will. During this time, we have to be diligent about following the steps directed in God's Word concerning healing our wound. Remember, we cannot violate the principles of God and receive the promise of God. Spending time with God will give us the strength to follow His principles.

In our story, the blind man's part meant a change in venue for him. Our part may also require changes in our lives. Doing our part involves finding healthy coping mechanisms to deal with emotional wounds. For example, spend time thinking positive thoughts about your future, hanging out with positive friends and family, and participating in activities that bring joy (e.g., listening to music, reading, watching funny movies, and so on). We have to find healthy ways to off-load anxieties. It was only after the blind man completed his part that he was healed. We have to be willing to do our part while trusting God to do His.

Step 5. Let My Wound Be My Testimony

The final step is to let my wound be my testimony. After this man was healed, he later shared his story with others even at the risk of his very life (verses 25–27) and confessed and worshipped Jesus (verse 38). Our wound is our story. When God delivered us from over $100,000 in debt, the last thing I wanted to do was tell others about it. I didn't want people to know how foolish I had been. But our wound is our testimony. The experience that hurt us the most is what God wants to use for His glory. We have to share our healed wounds with others. In fact, it is part of the healing process. It's not for our glory but for God's glory.

When Jesus wanted to prove His resurrection power to His disciples, He showed them His wounds. We have to do the same thing. A healed soul commits to being used by God to bring His good news to others by example and by words.

Influential Bible teacher Ron Dunn remarked, "If God subtracted one pain, one heartache, one disappointment from my life, I would be less than the person I am now, less the person God wants me to be, and my ministry would be less than He intends."

I was in a meeting when someone challenged the group to share their past secrets by finishing this sentence, "I will not allow _____ to keep me from achieving my destiny." One by one, people began to share their past hurts and wounds. Wounds that were shared included having an abortion, being in jail, being kicked out of the home as a teenage mom, and working as a stripper. People shared struggles with debt, drugs, alcohol, and sexual abuse. These were just a few of many wounds shared in the meeting. I thought I was the only one who had things in my past that I was ashamed of and that hurt me. I realized that it's not just me. The most telling thing about this meeting was that it was a meeting of my church leaders. If the people God has chosen as His leaders are dealing with wounds, then no one should be embarrassed that he or she is dealing with wounds of his or her own. We all have them. In order to have peace in our lives, we must address these wounds and let our wounds be a testimony to encourage others.

Small Group Questions

1. Most of us find it easier to confess our wounds to ourselves and to God. We seem to have a tougher time sharing them with another person.
   a. What is the hardest part for you? Why?

   b. What are benefits of admitting you have emotional wounds?

2. Psalm 139:23–24 suggests we ask God to search our hearts and remove anything not pleasing to Him.
   a. What does this scripture mean to you?

   b. If you prayed this prayer, how do you think God would respond?

   c. What is the most difficult part about asking God for help and allowing Him to help?

3. Do you consistently take responsibility for your emotional health or blame others?

4. What is the problem with blaming others?

5. Based on the chapter readings, what is your next step (e.g., your part) to improve your emotional health?

6. Have you allowed healings from emotional wounds or past mistakes to be a testimony to others? Share a brief testimony of healing from an emotional wound.

PART 4

PEACE IN FINANCES

CHAPTER 25

PEACE IN FINANCES

The fourth peace tier is peace in our finances. Financial peace means no worries about how we will live or pay our bills.

Experts report 80 percent of Americans worry about money all the time (Tracy, *Maximum Achievement*, 28). Conflict over money is one of the top causes of divorce. Even though we live in one of the wealthiest countries in the world, we are a society where many of us are living paycheck to paycheck and praying to God we don't lose our jobs because we don't know how we would make it a week without our income.

Jesus said, "The poor you will always have with you" (Matthew 26:11). A friend asked me, "Why would Jesus say this? And if that's true, why should we bother trying to help the poor out of their financial situation?" These questions stayed with me for some time until one day I read this scripture and had this thought: *We can't always control whether we are poor or wealthy.*

According to World Bank, a person living in sub-Saharan Africa has almost a 50 percent chance of living in poverty (web.WorldBank. org, 2015), whereas a person living in the United States has less than a 20 percent chance of living in extreme poverty (National Poverty Center, 2012).

Some people are fortunate enough to be born into situations where the path to wealth is an easier road, and others, for all kinds of reasons, find themselves in a situation where they never make a decent income.

We can't always control whether we are poor or rich, but both the poor and rich have the choice whether to live financially free or not.

As a financial coach, I see people make a decision every day to limit their ability to be financially free. They spend too much and make poor financial decisions. I also see people who don't make a lot of money and who would be considered poor live financially free. They don't have much more than their basic needs, but they don't owe anyone and are free to live, give, and even save.

My wife has an uncle who buys used cars with cash. He has never earned a high income or lived a luxury lifestyle, but he also has never had any debt.

The movie *Cadillac Records* tells the true stories of several blues singers from the 1950s. The movie title came about because the owner would pay the artists by purchasing them a Cadillac. In one scene, the owner signed on a new artist named Howlin' Wolf, who drove up in a beat-up truck. After signing the contract, the other artists said, "Now you can get rid of the truck and the owner can buy you a Cadillac." Wolf shocked them all by turning it down, preferring that he just be paid in salary for his work. He responded, "I own that truck. It don't own me."

In a later scene, when one of their fellow artists had died, none of the artists with Cadillacs had enough money to bury their friend. So they went to the record company owner to ask for the money. Since he was the only one of the artists who had any money to bury their friend, Wolf stepped in and provided the money needed. He showed them that high income or a fancy lifestyle doesn't make us financially free and encouraged them to live a life of financial freedom.

Financial freedom starts with our thoughts. I find people either have wealthy thoughts or poverty thoughts. Wealthy thoughts lead to wealthy behaviors and financial freedom. Poverty thoughts lead to poor behaviors and poor financial results. It does not matter how much money a person with poverty thoughts receives. A person with poverty thoughts could receive large sums of money that seemingly are the solution to his or her financial dilemma only to find that it doesn't fix the problem. It may even make it worse. That may account for why so many lottery winners and highly paid professional athletes file bankruptcy. If there is a sudden increase in wealth without a changing of the receiver's thoughts, then eventually they are likely to end up with the same poor financial results. Part of my objective in this section of the book is to help you develop wealthy thoughts.

Typical Mentalities of the Financially Free People

One of the things I enjoy most about being a money coach is having conversations with financially free people. After years of meeting with hundreds of wealthy financially free people, I started to notice some commonalities. Almost every one of them had these eight mentalities.

1. They always think of ways to reduce or minimize living expenses. I got a call from a man who wanted advice on

eliminating his cable movie channels. The odd thing about it was that he was the head of the cable company.

2. They maximize their fun. They know what they like and value and don't mind spending money on that. But they are not wasting money on things that aren't important to them.

3. They think in terms of net worth. They do not think in terms of how much they will earn but how it increases their net worth. Net worth takes into account the value of assets minus any debts. Most people never know what their net worth is and therefore never build wealth.

4. They believe it's better to have money than it is not to have money. Initially, I thought this was true of all people, but I have come to find out it's not. If people really felt that money was better to have, then they wouldn't spend so much of it. Instead, they would save and invest more of it. Most people ultimately believe it is better not to have money so they spend it thereby allowing money to eventually flow into the hands of those who believe it's better to have money. It follows the old saying, "The rich get richer, and the poor get poorer." Financially free people are focused on being wealthy and not looking wealthy. They are always scheming about ways to earn money. They earn interest instead of paying it. Interest works for the wealthy and against the poor. They typically have multiple streams of income. Their belief that it's better to have money perpetuates the existence of money in their lives and allows them to build wealth.

5. They avoid paying excessive taxes. They don't want to pay a penny over what they are legally required to pay. Where most people see a tax refund as a bonus, wealthy people see it as the government borrowing their money without paying interest.

6. They aren't attached to assets. They make decisions based on the value and use of assets. A single mom bought a new car. I asked, "Did you sell the used luxury car, which could sell for $15,000?" She said she hadn't because she wanted to keep it for her teenager who would drive it in a couple of years. Wealthy people don't think that way. They see the car as $15,000 and think, "There's no way I'm going

to let $15,000 sit in my garage for two years and then give $15,000 to my teenager." They might decide to sell it and help their kid buy a $5,000 car in two years.

7. They believe it is not about how much you earn, but about how much you save. Financial freedom has little to do with how much you earn. Contrary to many beliefs, financial freedom is not just making large sums of money. I have witnessed many people who are financially free and have never made more than $20,000 a year. Conversely, there are plenty of people who make over $200,000 a year and still have no financial freedom.

8. They are always learning when it comes to finances. I get more calls and questions from wealthy people than I do from people who are struggling financially. Wealthy people see the value in getting good advice from others.

Winning in your finances is a choice, and it's available to both the rich and the not-so-rich. It requires that we learn and apply these seven keys to true financial peace:

1. Recognizing ownership
2. Learning contentment
3. Setting priorities
4. Living with margin
5. Spending wisely
6. Maintaining honesty and integrity
7. Managing money responsibly

CHAPTER 26

RECOGNIZING OWNERSHIP

It is important to understand God's role when it comes to money. We have a part, and God has a part. Many of us are confused about our part and God's part. God's part is He owns everything (1 Chronicles 29:11–12). The money we earn, the car we drive, and the home we live in all belong to God. As Christians, we are taught to give 10 percent to God and the rest is ours. However, that is not true. One hundred percent of it is God's. He created it all and never transferred ownership to people.

When we acknowledge God's ownership, every spending decision becomes a spiritual decision. We stop asking, "Lord, what should I do with *my* money?" Our question becomes, "Lord, what should I do with *your* money?" When you believe you own a particular possession, then the circumstances surrounding that possession will affect your attitude. If it is a favorable situation, then you are happy. Conversely, if it is unfavorable, you are unhappy. In his book *Your Money Counts*, Howard Dayton shares a story about his friend Jim who had come to grips with the idea of God's ownership and then bought a new car. He had driven it only a few days when someone rammed into the side of it. Jim's first response was, "Lord, I don't know why you want a dent in your car, but now you've sure got a big one." Jim recognized God's ownership.

Trusting God with our possessions was a big step for me, especially concerning our home and car. At the time we were going through debt issues, our house and car both needed some significant repairs.

The roof was leaking, the carpet had stains, and the minivan had some mechanical issues. Trusting God meant I had to ask Him what repairs I should make and how He wanted me to maintain His possessions. Consistently recognizing God's ownership is difficult, but if we are to have financial freedom, we must change our thinking about money and material things and recognize that it all belongs to God.

CHAPTER 27

LEARNING CONTENTMENT

Many times, we rationalize going into debt because we are not content with what we have. In fact, we often envy or covet what others have. Paul writes in Philippians 4:11–13:

> ... for I have learned to be content whatever the circumstances. I know what it is to be in need, and I know what it is to have plenty. I have learned the secret of being content in any and every situation, whether well fed or hungry, whether living in plenty or in want. I can do everything through him who gives me strength.

Being content does not mean that we never want the best God has to offer, but it does mean we depend on God to provide it.

A few years ago, my wife and I struggled with a decision to replace a vehicle. We have six in our family, so for us to transport everyone, we need at least a six-passenger vehicle. At the time, we had no car payments. Her minivan was ten years old, had 150,000 miles, and was starting to have the cosmetic wear and tear of being a family vehicle for four kids. Overall, the car had few mechanical problems and worked fine.

Because I know nothing about cars, I spent months researching the best replacement vehicle. I came up with vehicle choices based on economics, reliability, and meeting our needs. Carol, on the other hand, said she wanted a car that looked good. We settled on a used, low-mileage, seven-passenger vehicle that Carol liked. We had enough money in our retirement and children's education funds to pay cash, but we both knew that taking money from those accounts to pay for a car was not a good decision. Since we did not have enough cash on hand to pay for the vehicle, we looked at our budget to see if we could afford financing the vehicle. We realized we had an extra several hundred dollars a month by making a few minor adjustments. Therefore, we determined we could finance the vehicle.

We started shopping around at local dealers, in the newspaper, and on the Internet for this particular vehicle. We found one that fit our criteria at a great price on the Internet. Before making a major purchase, I had to check the advice of my Christian accountability partners. I walked through the decision with them, and they agreed it seemed like a good decision. Just before making an offer, I said a little prayer. "God, I think this is a good decision, but if this is not Your will for me, then let me know and I'll stop right now."

So I made an offer and received an e-mail that the seller had accepted it. It was a great car at a great price. I called the seller to arrange to pick it up, and I was told, "I'm sorry, but I sold that vehicle to someone else." I could not believe it. Initially, I was mad. "What do you mean you sold my car?" Then I remembered my prayer and realized God had other plans. I started my search again. I also kept praying to God about it, but God just would not release me to buy a car. Instead, he was encouraging me to be content with what we had until He provided more. God revealed that He wanted me to put the money in a car savings account each month so when the time arrived, I would have the cash available to purchase the car, or at least to make a down payment to lower our monthly payments. There was no doubt that God would provide us the vehicle we desired at the right time. Our job is to be content with what we have and be disciplined about our savings until He changes our situation.

The problem many of us have is that we want everything now. That is what advertisers are marketing to us. "Why wait when you can have it now?" Advertisements are intended to make you discontent with what you have. You thought your thirty-six-inch TV was great until you saw a fifty-inch, high-definition, wall-mounted plasma TV advertised in the paper.

My brother told me a story about one of his tenants. The tenants were two months behind on their rent. As he went to collect the rent, he noticed the tenant had recently purchased a sixty-inch big-screen TV. The tenants talked about how they wished they could afford to own a home but they were having trouble paying the rent. My brother asked why they would purchase a sixty-inch TV for an eight-hundred-square-foot house when their goal was to one day own their own home. The tenant rationalized that they were getting the TV now so they would have it when they moved into their new home. Sadly, this is how many of us think. Our desire to have it now sabotages our ability to reach our goals in the future.

Discontentment causes us to spend our future earnings today so we are forever in a cycle of debt. Contentment is not something we are born with. Paul's statement, "I have learned to be content," suggests that contentment is something we all have to learn. It can only be learned through spiritual maturity and applying the biblical principles God provides in scriptures.

CHAPTER 28

SETTING PRIORITIES

"But seek first his kingdom and his righteousness, and all these things will be given to you as well" (Matthew 6:33).

The following chart contrasts how most people handle money versus God's way of handling money. It list five ways of handling money in order of priority for each.

The World's Priorities	God's Priorities
1. Pay taxes	1. Giving
2. Spend on lifestyle	2. Saving and investing
3. Pay debts	3. Pay taxes
4. Saving and investing	4. Pay debts
5. Giving	5. Spend on lifestyle
result: overspending, debt, wanting more, materialism, chaos, conflicts in relationships	result: contentment, peace

The World's Priorities

The first column represents the order in which most of us handle money. We spend on our lifestyles and pay our taxes. We then spend what we have left to pay on our debts. We tell ourselves, "If I had more money, I would save more and give to God, but I just don't have enough for that." The truth is when we have the world's priorities, we wouldn't save or give even if we had more.

I was watching this ESPN documentary called *Broke*. It was a story that featured professional athletes and their finances. The report said, "By the time they have been retired for two years, 78 percent of former NFL players file bankruptcy or are under financial stress." Their stories were incredible! How could so many highly paid athletes go broke within two years of retiring? It was not just a few but the overwhelming majority (*Sports Illustrated*, 2009).

Take a minute right now to think about how much money you would need to earn to feel at perfect peace about your financial situation. Go ahead and write down that number somewhere. I'm willing to bet that the number you wrote down is more than you are earning right now.

The problem with the world's priorities is that we will never have enough. Even if we had Bill Gates's income, if we followed the world's priorities, we would go broke. Our wants will always be bigger than our income. The world's priorities result in overspending, debt, wanting more, materialism, chaos, and conflicts in relationships.

God's Priorities

God wants us to flip this order of priority upside down. Scripture tells us to give to God first (Proverb 3:9), save (Proverb 21:20), pay your taxes (Matthew 22:21), and then pay your debts (Romans 13:7–8), and then you are free to spend the rest on your lifestyle. I know what you are thinking, *If I put me last, then I won't have enough. I won't be able to do what I want when I want. What about the latest high-tech gadgets that we just got to have? This isn't fair. It's not enough.*

The funny thing about calling ourselves "disciples" of Christ is we have to live with a level of discipline. We can't live like the rest of the world and expect to represent God. Sure, we are not going to have as much stuff as others with our same income, but when we follow God's financial priorities, it results in contentment and peace.

CHAPTER 29

LIVING WITH MARGIN

I counseled three individuals who had recently lost their jobs. Two of them had previously made the decision to live below their earnings. This is called choosing to "live with margin." Both of them have little to no debt. They are both regular savers and as a result have over six months of living expenses saved up for emergencies like this one. They have been and continue to be generous financial givers to kingdom-building activities.

Even though these two were experiencing some normal anxiety from losing their jobs, my coaching session with them was very different than the usual. The economic crisis caused them to wonder what God had in store for them now. They both were asking, "Okay, God. What is my purpose?" We spent our time thinking about the following questions: What is it you like doing? What are you passionate about? What has God gifted you to do? For them, the current economic challenge was not a time of panic but a time of self-reflection.

I was encouraged after my coaching sessions with the first two special individuals. I was excited about what God had in store for them. I was convinced that God had a greater purpose for them both that would further provide peace and fulfillment as well as bring glory to the kingdom of God.

The conversation with the third person went much differently. He was already overextended on his mortgage and had significant credit card and car debt. This is an example of choosing to live with leverage. Proverbs 21:20 reads, "The wise have wealth and luxury, but fools spend whatever they get."

We choose to live with leverage when we spend every penny we earn, and on top of that, we borrow as much as we can. We save little and give even less. Living with leverage allows us to increase our lifestyles through debt and get more stuff, but as many are experiencing now, this can be devastating when life happens.

My heart goes out to this family living deeply in debt. He wondered aloud, "How will I pay my bills? Where can I find a job in this market? How do I keep from the embarrassment of losing my home?" His recent misfortune in the wake of the economic crisis had caused panic and fear. Along with it came an opportunity for God to show Himself to be in control and a provider. My conversation with him was more typical of a money map coaching session. We looked at what he owned, what he owed, and his current spending habits. We addressed the most critical issues and considered several painful decisions necessary for his financial and family welfare.

Through this experience, I realized that those who live with margins are not as threatened by losing their jobs or by increases in gas prices. They do not sit around praying for an economic stimulus check from the government. Granted, they do not have as much stuff, but they have homes to live in, cars that operate, and food to eat. They also have plenty of what really matters to them, such as peace with God, loving relationships, better health (due to less stress), financial security for their families, and a meaningful purpose in life that serves others. In the midst of a storm, choosing to live with margin leads to peace.

Regardless of how you have managed money before, you have a choice to make today. "Will I live with margin (well below my income) or continue to live on leverage (debt)?" Yes, God has the power to get us out of tough financial situations, but we can avoid putting ourselves in that position by choosing to live well below our income.

CHAPTER 30

SPENDING WISELY

Philippians 4:11–13 says:

> I am not saying this because I am in need, for I have learned
> to be content whatever the circumstances. I know what
> it is to be in need, and I know what it is to have plenty. I
> have learned the secret of being content in any and every
> situation, whether well fed or hungry, whether living in
> plenty or in want. I can do everything through him who
> gives me strength.

Too many times, we spend money that we do not have trying to
impress other people. Instead of building wealth, we spend money
trying to keep up with the Joneses, not realizing the Joneses are
up to their eyeballs in debt and leading us down the same path.

Many wealthy people live well below their means. That is how they
became wealthy in the first place. *The Millionaire Next Door* describes
the typical millionaire as a person who lives well below his or her
means, wears inexpensive clothes, lives in the same home for over
twenty years, and drives inexpensive American-made cars. You
ask, "How could that be? Why wouldn't millionaires have the
finest clothes, most expensive homes, and luxury cars?" It's simple.
They became millionaires because they believe *being* wealthy is
more important than *looking* wealthy.

Dave Ramsey, author of *Financial Peace*, provides these secrets to living in financial peace. "Avoid the lifestyle of the rich when you are not rich. The best things in life, including good {stuff}, come only at the expense of personal discipline. You must limit your style of living. You must figure out how much your actual income is and then proceed to live well below that mark."

Clearly God intends for us to spend money wisely. Wise spending does not mean you only buy things that are basic needs. God wants you to enjoy life and things. In June 2005, I was overwhelmed with balancing yard work with many other activities. One day, a boy in the neighborhood offered to cut my grass for a small fee. I realized that spending money in this case would free up my time, allowing me to do more in ministry and spend more time with my family. Wealth should allow us to simplify and enjoy life, not make it more complicated.

We are always faced with how we should spend money. Should we buy a bigger house, a luxury car, or the latest technology? The key is to prayerfully submit our spending decisions to God.

I counseled a friend whose family was relocating to another state. He was questioning how much he should spend on his next home. We started with a review of his financial situation. My friend had been very diligent with investing and controlling his spending. He has no debt, earns a high income, gives freely to his local church, and lives well below his income. After prayerfully submitting his spending decision to God, he purchased a very nice and what most people would consider expensive new home. Within a few years, my friend has been very pleased with his decision. He has paid off his home mortgage as well as paid cash for a vacation home that he and his family are enjoying very much. Just like my friend, God wants us to freely enjoy possessions when we submit our spending decision to Him.

Purchasing a Home and Automobile You Can Afford

Over the last fourteen years, I've had a chance to counsel a lot of people concerning their finances. I have found that 90 percent of the financial problems are caused by two decisions—the choice of a home and of an automobile. Typically, if we can get these two decisions right, we are usually okay financially.

We get into trouble when we see how God blessed someone else and get anxious to see progress in our own lives. When it comes to making home and car purchasing decisions, I think it's smart to stick to these two basic guidelines.

No more than 20 percent of gross income on mortgage or rent.

No more than 7 percent of gross income on car financing.

Obviously, it would be best to pay cash for a car, but realistically not everyone will have resources for that option. These are just guidelines and not to be used as a religious law. I have formed these after coaching so many people over the years and observing those who live on a balanced budget. I found that following these guidelines provides the best environment to live on a balanced budget and be financially free.

CHAPTER 31

MAINTAINING HONESTY AND INTEGRITY

Leviticus 19:11–13 says:

Do not steal.

Do not lie.

Do not deceive one another.

Do not swear falsely by my name and so profane the name of your God. I am the Lord.

Do not defraud your neighbor or rob him.

Do not hold back the wages of a hired man overnight.

God requires us to be totally honest with others. If we want to be blessed with more, we have to deal with others honestly. We cannot cheat on our taxes or obtain illegal cable and expect God to bless us. Dishonesty stems from pride or greed. Dishonesty hurts our ability to witness to others. Non-Christians are discouraged when dealing with dishonest people who profess to know God. Many would rather deal with dishonest non-Christians. At least then they know to expect dishonesty. Proverbs 14:2 teaches us that you cannot practice dishonesty and still love God. If you love God, you will do those things that please Him. Honesty provides a platform for us to be a light to others and puts us in a position to be blessed by God.

Small Group Questions

1. Which keys to financial peace speak to you most? Why?

2. Read the parable of the talents in Matthew 25:14–30.
   a. What does this parable illustrate about our responsibilities as stewards?

   b. What other principles are illustrated in this parable?

3. Prayerfully evaluate your attitude of ownership toward possessions. Do you consistently recognize God as the true owner of possessions?

4. Why is it important to recognize God's ownership and control when it comes to money and possessions?

5. How do the world's priorities differ from God's financial priorities?

6. What are benefits of living with margin versus living with debt?

7. What was the worst financial spending decision you have ever made?

CHAPTER 32

MANAGING RESPONSIBLY

Genesis 1:26 says, "Then God said, 'Let us make man in our image, in our likeness, and let them rule over the fish of the sea and the birds of the air, over the livestock, over all the earth, and over all the creatures that move along the ground.'"

God made us to have authority over the world. We are stewards over all God created. A steward or manager is someone who has responsibility to take care of something that belongs to another. In Matthew 25:14–30, Jesus tells a story that illustrates the difference between good stewards and unfaithful stewards. In this story, a property owner prepares to go on a long journey so he gives his servants his property to manage while he is gone. He gave one servant five units of money, another two units, and another one unit. This is a great example of stewardship. The servants who were given five and two units both invested their units and gave the owner double the units on his return.

Their master replied, "Well done, good and faithful servant! You have been faithful with a few things; I will put you in charge of many things. Come and share your master's happiness!"

Conversely, the man who was given one unit did not invest what he was given so when the owner returned, he could only give him the one unit he had received.

His master replied, "You wicked, lazy servant! So you knew that I harvest where I have not sown and gather where I have not scattered seed? Well then, you should have put my money on deposit with the bankers, so that when I returned I would have received it back with interest.

"Take the talent from him and give it to the one who has the ten talents. For everyone who has will be given more, and he will have an abundance. Whoever does not have, even what he has will be taken from him. And throw that worthless servant outside, into the darkness, where there will be weeping and gnashing of teeth."

This scripture shows that as stewards, we have a responsibility to invest money wisely. It also illustrates that God does not provide us all with the same resources or potential. Neither does He expect us all to accumulate the same wealth. Because God is all-knowing and He provides as He sees fit, we have no reason to envy or covet what others have. It pleases God when we take what we have and multiply it. God wants us to be productive.

I had been driving my son's car while he was out of the country for the summer. I decided to clean it up really good before he came home. I went to the car wash and spent a lot of time detailing his car. Just like all the other people there that day, I took care and pride in making the car spotless. I paused for a moment to look at the other cars being cleaned. Every car was a newer model car. I was the only one detailing a seventeen-year-old car whose paint was partially faded. I could imagine others watching me sweat so hard to clean this car saying, "Why is he spending all that effort on that little car? It couldn't be worth much anyhow." Well, they are sort of right. The car only cost us $1,450. But I was reminded of a scripture when Jesus said, "Whoever is faithful with little will also be faithful with much." Jesus was letting us know that we have to take care of the small things to show Him we will be faithful with much more. We can't wallow around praying for a brand-new, shiny car that we promise to love, cherish, and care for while ignoring the car He has already given us. We have to act as if the car we have is the one we are praying for. Shine it up and take care of it. This shows God we are ready to be trusted with more and becomes good practice for handling the new car God will bless us with.

It is only when we can be faithful with the little things that God can trust us with more. One day, we all will come face-to-face with God, and He will hold us accountable for our actions. On that day, I want to hear God say, "Well done, my good and faithful servant." This desire keeps me committed to being a faithful steward.

It is impossible to become a fully developing follower of Jesus without also becoming a fully developing steward of financial resources.

Faithful stewards take the following steps in this order of priority to manage well what God has given them.

1. Put yourself on a written balanced budget.
2. Build an emergency fund.
3. Commit to no new debt and have an aggressive plan to pay off existing debt.
4. Invest for the future
5. Confirm a proper insurance and estate plan are in order.

CHAPTER 33

GET YOUR FINANCIAL FACTS

It starts with getting the facts about your financial situation. We have to think of ourselves as a corporation and God as an investor. Would God invest in you? God is an investor in our lives, and He's going to have the same questions any good investor would have:

- What's your income?
- What are your operating expenses?
- What's your profit margin?
- What is your debt ratio?

There are so many of us who cannot answer these questions. This is how most of us sound to God.

"Well, I don't know exactly how much I earn or where I spend it. I'm certainly not making a profit. I don't know how much debt I have, but I know it's a lot. I just know I don't have enough money so will you give me more?"

None of us would invest in a company like this, so why would God invest in a company knowing that there is no return on His investment? Jesus said, "Whoever can be trusted with very little can also be trusted with much, and whoever is dishonest with very little will also be dishonest with much. So if you have not been trustworthy in handling worldly wealth, who will trust you with true riches?" (Luke 16:10–11).

We have to be honest with ourselves and ask, "Would God buy my stock?"

Getting the facts about our financial situation starts with these four questions:

- How much do I earn (e.g., gross not just net)?
- How much and where do I spend?
- How much do I owe?
- How much do I own?

The answers to these questions will help you develop a budget or spending plan. You can't really make good financial decisions without answering these questions.

How Much Do I Earn and Spend?

It is important to know accurately how much you are earning and where you are currently spending money. I suggest you track all spending and income for at least thirty days. This is not difficult to do. Most of us only have at most three to five expenses a day. It shouldn't take more than five minutes to track daily.

Many times, we don't know where we spend our money. I had a couple I recently counseled come to me and say, "We didn't realize we were spending $300 a month on cigarettes." Another said, "We didn't realize we spent more at Starbucks than we gave to church." A couple whom I coached was spending $1,100 a month on bank fees. I can't stress enough how important it is to discover where you are spending money.

What Do I Owe and Own?

Believe me, it was hard for us to view on paper how bad our financial situation really was. Even though Carol and I were the only ones to see it, I was embarrassed that I had allowed our finances to get this way. It seems most of us don't do this step because we are afraid to learn how much we really owe. We prefer to be in the dark when it comes to our finances. We think if we ignore it, maybe the debt will go away. However, in reality, it is critical to see the total picture … no matter how bad it looks. In 1 John 1:5–10, Paul warns us about this very thing:

> This is the message we have heard from him and declare to you: God is light; in him there is no darkness at all. If we claim to have fellowship with him yet walk in the darkness, we lie and do not live by the truth. But if we walk in the light, as he is in the light, we have fellowship with one another, and the blood of Jesus, his Son, purifies us from all sin.
>
> If we claim to be without sin, we deceive ourselves and the truth is not in us. If we confess our sins, he is faithful and just and will forgive us our sins and purify us from all unrighteousness. If we claim we have not sinned, we make him out to be a liar and his word has no place in our lives.

Paul prefaced this statement by saying in verse four, "We write this to make {your} joy complete." Paul knows that when we try to keep our little mess a secret, we allow Satan to come into our lives. Earlier I mentioned that the number-one cause of divorce is financial difficulties. Many times, couples wait until it's too late to address their financial problems. Sometimes spouses even keep financial problems from each other. The enemy may not be able to affect your relationship with God directly, but walking in darkness allows Satan to affect your relationship with your spouse or others. The above scripture tells us that if we allow God to shine light on our situation, we will have fellowship with one another. Writing down everything you own and everyone you owe exposes your situation to yourself, your spouse, and symbolically to God. He already knows, but just as He did with Adam when he asked, "Where are you?" He wants you to expose your problems to Him. This scripture reminds us that only then will He change our situation and only then can we move toward a financial breakthrough.

A secondary benefit of listing what you own is that it could highlight items you can sell to accelerate debt repayment or to reduce monthly expenses. For instance, if you own a third vehicle that you only drive on special occasions, you could sell it to pay off other debt while reducing your cost of maintenance, vehicle taxes, and insurance.

Chapter 34

ESTABLISH A BUDGET

Now that you have the facts, you can establish a budget. Some people don't like budgets because they believe it takes away their freedom, but budgets actually provide freedom.

The following story may help explain this principle better. There was a group of kids playing on a playground next to a busy street. Some parents stopped letting their kids play there because of the danger. Then one day the city put up a fence. Now the kids had the freedom to play right up to the fence. The fence did not limit them; it only protected them and provided freedom to play and have fun without the worry of danger. That's what a budget does for us. It clearly sets our safety boundaries. It says to us, "As long as you play on this side of the fence, you are safe." The problem with some of us is that we jump the fence and play in the busy freeway and then wonder why we got hit by a semi. Budgeting is a critical step in becoming financially free.

Luke 14:28 says, "Suppose one of you wants to build a tower. Will he not first sit down and estimate the cost to see if he has enough money to complete it?"

Jesus reminds us that it is wise to start with a plan or budget before beginning to spend. A budget helps you plan how you will spend money.

Many of us spend more than we make, which results in a budget deficit. When we did this for the first time, we found that we were spending about $1,600 more each month than we were earning. When this happens, the hole of debt just gets deeper and deeper.

There are only two ways to balance a budget: make more money or spend less money. Most of the time, our earnings are sufficient. The problem occurs in our spending habits. You might be amazed at how we spend our hard-earned money on what we consider insignificant things. For instance, a person who stops at Starbucks to get a daily cup of coffee and an occasional muffin may be surprised that he or she is spending $140 a month on this small habit. David Bach calls this the "latte factor" in his book *The Automatic Millionaire*.

Look for ways to reduce your spending. Small adjustments can make a huge difference in achieving financial freedom. Some of the small changes we made included eliminating cable television; reducing options on our phone, such as call waiting, caller ID, and long distance; and brown-bagging my lunch instead of eating out.

Many people fail at budgeting because it becomes cumbersome to keep up with receipts and track expenses daily. Families that simplify the money-handling process are more likely to remain within their budget. There are several useful tips to simplify budgeting that we use and recommend to others.

- Stop using credit and debit cards. We are likely to spend 30 to 40 percent more when using a credit card than with cash.
- Maintain a balanced checkbook to minimize bank fees. Only write a check when you know you have cash in your account.
- Withdraw cash to use the "envelope system" for food, clothing, entertainment, and miscellaneous expenses. Stop spending when the money runs out.

CHAPTER 35

BUILD AN EMERGENCY FUND

One activity that is critical in this commitment to no new debt is to establish an emergency fund of at least $1,000. Emergency funds are there in case the car breaks down, the roof leaks, or you have a medical emergency. Remember that this fund is not intended for the new pair of shoes that you just have to have before the sale ends. My experience with emergency funds is that usage is very rare. If you use it more than once or twice a year, you may want to reconsider whether you are experiencing true emergencies.

A couple I recently counseled is a great example of the benefit of emergency funds. This couple had made significant improvement in their financial situation over only a few months. They went from considerably overspending their monthly budget to having a budget surplus and beginning their debt repayment plan. One change they made was creating an emergency fund.

I received a call from the husband one day, and he shared a recent event. The transmission on his wife's car needed major repair. They had accumulated $1,200 in their emergency fund, and the repairs would cost $900. He said a few months ago his attitude would have been, "Man, just when I get some money, something happens." Now he was praising God for providing the funds to take care of unplanned emergencies like this one. This couple was prepared for their little emergency because of their commitment to becoming more disciplined in their finances and to God's financial guidance.

Even before paying off debt, we suggest you put away at a minimum $1,000 for emergencies. Things will happen. If you don't have money set aside for emergencies, you cannot break the debt cycle.

Build up to at least $1,000 in the emergency fund before focusing on repaying debt. Continue to save a portion of all income for emergencies until your emergency fund is three to six months of living expenses.

CHAPTER 36

MANAGING DEBT

I was watching football during the Thanksgiving weekend, and I couldn't help but notice the numerous commercials that encouraged the use of debt to make all my dreams come true. They promised, "No payments, no down payment, no interest for two years, and no annual fees." One company even advertised, "You are actually rewarded for using our card." We cannot blame the companies for marketing the use of credit because it makes great business sense (for the companies). First, studies show that consumers are likely to spend 30 to 40 percent more when using credit cards than when spending cash. Also, most people who use credit cards carry a balance and therefore end up paying two to three times the amount of the original cost because of interest. Because they carry a balance month after month, they may end up paying ninety dollars for a thirty-dollar shirt.

Although the Bible does not say using debt is a sin, it clearly discourages the use of debt. Debt presumes on the future. When we go into debt without a guaranteed way of repayment, we assume we will earn enough in the future to pay the debt. We are presuming that our jobs or income will continue. James 4:13–15 warns us against presuming on the future:

> Now listen, you who say, "Today or tomorrow we will go to this or that city, spend a year there, carry on business and make money." Why, you do not even know what will happen tomorrow. What is your life? You are a mist that

appears for a little while and then vanishes. Instead, you ought to say, "If it is the Lord's will, we will live and do this or that."

When we go into debt, we spend our future earnings today so that we are forever in a cycle of debt.

Debt affects many areas of life spiritually, mentally, and physically. Debt prevents us from building real wealth, and it increases stress, which contributes to mental, physical, and emotional fatigue. In Proverbs 22:7, debt is described as a form of slavery or bondage: "The rich rule over the poor, and the borrower is servant to the lender."

One of Carol's favorite commercials is a Lending Tree commercial. A man comes on the screen and says, "I'm Stanley Johnson. I've got a great family. I've got a four-bedroom house in a great community. Like my car? It's new. I even belong to the local golf club. How do I do it? I'm in debt up to my eyeballs. I can barely pay my finance charges." The commercial finishes with Stanley pleading, "Somebody help me."

Today many of us live in financial chaos. Too often, we are living paycheck to paycheck and using one credit card to pay the minimum on another credit card. To those around us, we look like we really have it going on, but in reality, we are "in debt up to our eyeballs," and we have no real wealth. Although we have all the luxuries of life, we struggle to pay our bills, have no investments, and have no education fund for our children. We have improved our lifestyles through debt, only to discover the burden of debt then controls our lifestyle and we have become enslaved to our financial situation.

Financial freedom has little to do with how much money you earn. Financial freedom means being free of worries about how you will pay your bills, what will happen if you find yourself without a job for six months, or how you will take care of unforeseen emergencies. As a budget counselor, I have seen people who lack proper insurance for their family, yet their kids have $200 sneakers.

The average person in the United States has little or no money saved, regular obligations to support an excessive lifestyle, significant credit obligations, and a total dependence on next week's paycheck to stay afloat.

- According to Nerdwallet.com, the average American with credit card debt owes $16,140.
- *Jet* magazine reports a study conducted by Citibank that 57 percent of all divorces are a result of financial tension in the home.
- More and more check-cashing companies charging over 300 percent in interest are popping up in low-income neighborhoods.
- Lenders are preying on those caught up in wanting it all now, which is leading to an increase in bankruptcies and foreclosed homes.

Four Steps to Eliminating Debt

In the next few sections, I recommend practical steps you should take to get out of a problem debt situation. Living on a balanced budget and having at least $1,000 saved for emergencies are prerequisites for focusing on debt repayment. Only begin debt repayment when those steps are complete.

My wife and I know these steps work, because this is the path we took in getting out of debt. It is important that you wholeheartedly follow all the steps. The journey to becoming debt-free will require faith, hope, and discipline, but be encouraged that God will help you through it.

Step 1 — Create a Debt Repayment Plan

After developing your budget and determining how much you can pay each month against your debts, contact your lenders to work out the best repayment plan you can. You can only pay what you have, so don't get stressed out when you do not have enough to pay everything. If your creditors force you into bankruptcy, seek appropriate legal counseling. Nonetheless, you should make every reasonable attempt to negotiate a repayment before declaring bankruptcy.

Your monthly budget should include a reasonable amount to pay toward your debt. You may increase your monthly debt payment as you are able, but you should never decrease the amount over the repayment process. As you pay off one debt, you will take that amount and begin putting it toward the next debt. This is called the *snowball effect* and is recommended by many debt counselors. Before you begin paying off debts using the snowball effect, you must first identify which debts you should repay first.

List your debts from the lowest to the highest balance. Also list the interest rates for each debt. Pay off your debts in the order of lowest to highest balance. Paying off smaller debts first will motivate you on your way to becoming debt-free.

Step 2 — Make a Commitment to No New Debt

This step requires making a decision to be both disciplined and content. Committing to no new debt is our way of saying, "Okay, God, we are trusting you with our situation." It may mean you will have to perform *plastic surgery* on your credit cards to eliminate any temptation of using them. Be content with what you have until God provides more. As I mentioned earlier, Carol and I were tempted to finance a new car. Every day after work, I would check out the latest postings for this car on eBay. Every day, I became less and less content with our minivan. Finally, we made a commitment that we would save money in order to pay cash for our next car. Carol and I decided we would stop shopping on the Internet. If we had not done this, we certainly would have convinced ourselves to buy a car and finance it. I suggest you stop shopping, going to the mall, and looking through catalogs. You may even have to limit TV watching to avoid commercials. The less marketing and advertising you subject yourself to, the less temptation you will have to break your commitment to no new debt.

Step 3 — Consider a Radical Change in Lifestyle

Selling our home made a significant impact on our ability to be debt-free. In 2001, we sold our home and moved into a smaller home. This allowed us to reduce our budget by $1,000 a month. In

2004, we relocated with a career change. At this time, our income continued to increase, and we were doing well financially. After prayerful consideration, Carol and I decided that if we downsized our home again, we could eliminate all nonmortgage debt. We moved into a smaller home once again. This change helped us reduce our mortgage and eliminate all other debt by the end of 2004. Prayerfully considering a radical change in lifestyle shows God that we are committed to doing whatever is necessary to be in His perfect will.

At that time, our monthly expenses were about half of our monthly income. This provided us a lot of flexibility in our savings, investing, and giving. Carol and I felt that our adjustment in lifestyle was temporary. We believed God would provide a larger home for us one day, but until then, we had chosen to be content with our current home. When we moved in 2008, again we borrowed less than what we had previously. Our goal was to eventually pay off our home. But this time, God answered our prayers and we were able to get the larger home that we had hoped for. God reminded us that He is faithful and cares about what we care about.

Step 4 — Use Windfalls to Accelerate Debt Repayment

All of us have fantasized about what we would do if we won the lottery. We already know we would pay off all of our debts, buy our dream house, provide gifts for our friends and relatives, take a vacation around the world, and even give a little charitable gift to our church. Despite the unlikelihood of this happening, we are often faced with smaller fortunes that come our way, yet we fail to take advantage of them. Think about the tax refunds, overtime pay, cash gifts, payments from insurance or legal settlements, and annual bonuses from work. It is as though God is providing our million-dollar lottery payout one thousand dollars at a time. These unexpected bonuses are God's answers to your prayers and can be used to help you reach your financial goals faster. Instead, many of us either squander extra funds trying to upgrade our standard of living or allow these funds to be absorbed into everyday living and bills. We suggest a proactive approach to dealing with unexpected bonuses we call the 10-60-20-10 rule.

If you have debt to pay off, consider allotting

- 10 percent to charitable giving,
- 60 percent to your smallest debt(s),
- 20 percent to savings (emergency savings to keep from using credit), and
- 10 percent to enjoy.

Carol and I followed a similar strategy to accelerate our debt repayment. We prayed for God to perform miracles in our lives, and He did. We wrote a plan that included our financial goals, as well as our wish list of ways we would enjoy money. Time and time again, God blessed us with bonuses, big tax returns, gifts from friends and family, and unexpected extra funds. After honoring God with 10 percent, we were diligent in using the majority of these funds to accomplish our debt-free goal. However, we also made sure we used some of the unexpected money to enjoy. We took family vacations, bought some of the toys on our wish list, and just had some fun.

Every spring, millions of Americans receive a tax return, only to go out and spend it all. A few months later, we wonder where the money went. The amount of the extra income will not matter if you do not have a plan to use it. The key is to be prepared to handle God's blessing when it comes your way. Decide to use any windfall that comes your way to help you become debt-free and to build wealth.

CHAPTER 37

INVEST FOR THE FUTURE

It is wise for us to invest a portion of every income we receive. Also, it's best to make savings automatic. You do this by setting up automatic drafts into a savings or investment vehicle on a regular frequency. The benefit of this is that you make a decision once to begin accumulating wealth. It is way too tempting not to save if we are making this decision every week.

Long-term savings should consist of retirement investments to eliminate dependency on your current income, savings to operate a business if you so choose, and funds for children's education if you have kids, as well as other investments for long-term wealth building.

For the financially free, I suggest pursuing a diversified portfolio of assets or streams of passive income that provide the owner the ability to maintain a lifestyle in which, at a minimum, all basic needs are met without dependence on receiving income from actively working.

The Bible does not teach a certain percent to save or invest, but I agree with several Christian and non-Christian financial experts who suggest saving 10 to 15 percent of your monthly income. Crown Financial Ministry's fundamental principle is to spend less than you earn and invest the difference over a long period of time.

Invest 10 to 15 percent of your gross income in long-term investments, such as IRAs and pretax retirement (e.g., 401(k), 403(b), or SEP plans). If your company offers a matching 401(k) program, you should invest up to the portion the company matches if your current budget permits. This is like getting free money. It also lowers tax liabilities.

The Bible encourages us to avoid risky investments (Ecclesiastes 5:13–15) and to diversify our investment over seven or eight investments (Ecclesiastes 11:2). There are many investment vehicles, but my purpose is not to recommend specific investments. You can choose from many investment resources to help you figure out the best investment vehicles for you.

Funding Your Child's College Education

Our oldest daughter was about to graduate from high school and had begun the college search process. Initially, she wanted to go to a very expensive school in the Northeast. We supported her desire but reminded her that we were prepared to pay half the cost of going to a state school and she would have to make up the rest through scholarships and personal savings. She said, "Why can't you just pay for it or take out loans like everybody else?" I had to contain my wife from choking her. I convinced Carol that strangling our daughter would not be the best example as pastors. We were faced with helping her make a tough decision. How do you choose and fund a college education?

You may be facing the college decision now or anticipating this decision in a few years, so I thought I would share some of what we learned during this process. We now have two children in college. We are by no means experts. We realized we'd better learn quickly because with four kids, we will likely be contributing to one college or another for the next thirteen years.

Here are a few suggestions as you prepare to help fund your children's college education:

1. Begin saving for college today. Look into a college savings plan (e.g., 529 Plans) and invest in mutual funds that are allocated age appropriately. Don't panic that your child is getting close to college. Just start saving today and do the best you can.

2. Do college planning and selection early. Start the college search during your children's junior year of high school. Help your student focus on getting good grades and preparing for college entry exams. Visit schools and try to narrow choices down to four or five schools. It is important that you think about schools in terms of both "getting in" (academic fit) and "paying for" (financial fit). Make sure your list includes some schools that are "sure things" in terms of both academic and financial fits. Apply to each of the schools as early as possible during the student's senior year of high school.

3. Create a budget with your student. Be clear about what you can and cannot contribute to help fund your child's college education. Be realistic. Caution students to avoid credit cards altogether. They will have plenty of opportunities to build credit later.

4. Don't feel pressured to fund the whole thing. Give your children some responsibility. Require them to fund part of their education through working summer jobs and scholarships. Have them save money they received as graduation gifts for their college education.

5. Minimize the amount of student loans. Consider ways to reduce college cost. Is attending a state school a better option? Can they take classes at a local junior college and transfer later to a four-year college or stay at home while attending a local college? Think creatively about college funding. Set a goal to complete college with a degree in hand and minimal loans, if any, to repay. If you do take out loans, try to limit loans to federal subsidized loans. The US government pays interest on these loans while your child pursues a degree. All other loans begin accruing interest immediately, and this adds up quickly.

6. Don't sacrifice your retirement savings. Saving for your own retirement is more important than saving for college.

This is hard for most of us parents, but our children will have more sources of money for college than we will have for our golden years.

Begin Paying Off Your Home Early

I notice from talking with people that many Americans never even consider paying off their homes. We somehow always seem to have a thirty-year mortgage. That's fine when you are twenty-five, but I'm meeting people in their forties and fifties who are starting over with thirty-year mortgages.

There are various ways of paying off your home early. Some mortgages offer a bimonthly payment, which equates to one extra payment a year. This could reduce your mortgage by up to seven years. Some people opt just to make an extra payment every month. Whichever works for you is fine.

Carol and I have made several career moves across the country, and each time we did, we automatically got a thirty-year mortgage. We kept telling ourselves that we would pay a little extra in order to pay off our mortgage sooner, but we never did. We just weren't disciplined enough to do it. Finally a few years ago, we decided that we would refinance our home for lower time terms in order to repay our loan quicker. This made our mortgage payment higher without the flexibility of lowering it, but it forced us to pay it off earlier. If you are not making progress on paying off your mortgage, then maybe you will need to do what we did to make it happen. Your goal should be to pay off your home during your highest income earning years. For most Americans, that's prior to our sixties.

Life Insurance

In order to help provide for your family, you should have adequate insurance coverage and estate planning.

Life insurance provides protection for loss of income due to the insurer's death. Not everyone needs life insurance. The people who need life insurance are those who have others financially dependent on them. That would exclude children from needing life insurance or anyone else who doesn't have anyone dependent on their income to survive. Insurance is not an investment. Many insurance salespeople sell products that combine investments and insurance. They argue that a cash-value policy is a form of forced savings. This is true, but you'll probably earn more investment return if you invest the money yourself.

They sell you on many reasons why this is beneficial, but the only person who really benefits from whole life or universal life policies are the salespeople. Their commissions are much higher on this product than on term-life products. In most cases, a low-cost term policy is the best solution for life insurance coverage. When you have enough invested assets to cover the needs of those depending on your income after your death, then you become self-insured and no longer need life insurance. Your goal should be to get to a place financially where you are self-insured.

Estate Planning

Several years ago, Carol and I were talking to a friend, who happens to be an attorney, when she said, "Anyone with kids or a home who does not have a will is a fool."

Carol said, "Travis and I don't have a will."

Our friend responded, "Then you both are fools." Even though she had a brash way of saying it, she was right.

The majority of people who die do not have a current will for a number of reasons: they don't want to think about dying, they feel it's only for the rich, or they just don't realize the consequences of not having it. To die without a will can be expensive and time-consuming and can be heartbreaking for your loved ones.

A friend and church member lost his father recently. Although his dad had been sick for a while, he didn't have a will in place. When I asked how my friend was doing after the funeral, he shared how family members were fighting over who should get what. When we lose our loved ones, we are already hurt from their loss. The last thing we need is to have the added emotional pressure of deciding how to split up their possessions. The emotion of losing a family member can bring out the worst in the best of people. Hurt people hurt people.

Depending on your comfort level and the complexity of your estate, you can choose to consult with an attorney who specializes in estate planning or create your will on your own. If you choose to do your will yourself, you should have your draft documents reviewed by an estate planning attorney in the state you live in to make sure they will properly protect you and reflect your estate planning wishes.

Typical estate planning documents (which should include a will, a health-care power of attorney, a general and durable power of attorney, and a living will) done by an attorney could range from $300 to $1,500, but this cost is miniscule compared to the cost of dying without a will.

About thirty-six of one hundred people die before retirement age, so don't put it off because you are young. One of the greatest gifts you can leave your family for that emotional time will be an organized estate, a properly prepared will, and possibly even a revocable living trust.

Small Group Questions

1. Consider God as an investor and you as a company stock. Would it be a smart investment for God to invest in you? Why or why not?

2. Do you have a written budget or spending plan?

   a. What are your feelings toward budgeting?

   b. Is it possible to be a good financial manager or steward without a budget? Explain.

3. Do you know your net worth? Explain why it is important to know your net worth.

4. Read Romans 13:8, Proverbs 22:7, and 1 Corinthians 7:23.
   a. Is debt encouraged in scripture? Why?

   b. How does this apply to you personally?

  c. How would your life be different if you had no credit card debt, no car loan, no student loan, and no mortgage loan?

  d. Do you have a strategy to get out of debt? If so, please describe it.

5. What does scripture say concerning savings (Genesis 41:34–36; Proverbs 21:20; Proverbs 30:24–25)?

  a. On a scale of 1 to 10 with 10 being "Very Pleased," how pleased are you with money you have saved for emergencies?

  b. Why is it important to save for emergencies?

  c. If you are not saving, how do you propose to start?

6. Read Proverbs 21:5, Proverbs 24:27, Proverbs 27:23–24, Ecclesiastes 3:1, and Ecclesiastes 11:2. What principles do these scriptures communicate about investing?

7. On a scale of 1 to 10 with 1 being financially free and not needing to receive an income to continue your current lifestyle:

   a. How would you rate your level of financial peace?

   b. What could you do to move you closer to a 1?

   c. What is the first step that you can make now to become more financially free?

8. What financial mentalities of financially free people surprised you most?

PART 5

PEACE IN PURPOSE

CHAPTER 38

PEACE IN PURPOSE

When we achieve peace in relationships, health, and finances, we accomplish a level of success. But many people achieve this level of success in their lives and yet don't feel fulfilled. It's because they have yet to connect with their purpose in life. God wants to provide success in your life, but even better, God wants to provide significance in your life. Significance is a higher level than success, and it's found in the final peace tier. The final peace tier is peace in purpose.

We have to use our success to fulfil the purposes God created us to do. You are not alive right now on accident. God wants to use your life to do something big and great. God has a plan for your life. In order to move from success to significance, we have to realize success is not just for you.

Hebrews 6:7 reads, "Land that drinks in the rain often falling on it and that produces a crop useful to those for whom it is farmed receives the blessing of God."

In this scripture, we are referred to as the land and rain represents God's Spirit. This scripture tells me that when I build God's Spirit inside of me and let Him build success in my life that benefits others, then I will be blessed.

As I mentioned earlier, all of us want God's blessing. We all have a desire to have a significant life. This scripture reminds us that

God wants to bless us as well. But it also leaves us with a question to answer. This scripture says that the land (you) will produce a crop (have success) that is useful to someone else. If you are the land and your land is producing a successful crop (success in your relationships, health, and finances), whom is your crop for?

We get stuck in the financial tier. Water goes in, but it never comes out.

Our lifestyle becomes a big sponge and just keeps sucking up all God's resources.

We used to pray, "Lord if I could just make $30,000." So God gives us $30,000, and what happens? Our lifestyle goes up to $30,000. "Lord, if we can just make $100,000." Then our lifestyles go up to $100,000. When you are focused on yourself, you will never have enough.

That's one of Satan's biggest tricks. Keep your focus in the financial tier. Our lives become about having the right home, car, and retirement savings. The enemy wants to keep you occupied with things of the world. He wants you spending so much money that you have to spend every waking hour working. You work so much that you can't get involved in church. You owe so many people you can't possibly give more to the church. He wants you stuck in the financial tier. If life is only about filling the financial tier, then we miss out on what life truly is.

God made each of us with this big void, and we spend our whole lives trying to fill it. God knows it's there because He created us with it there. We do everything we can to fill that void, but nothing works. We think to ourselves, *Man, if I could just live here or drive that, then I would be happy.* But the truth is you wouldn't be happy if you had those things. Those things can't bring you happiness because there will always be a bigger house and a newer car. Worldly success alone will not make you happy.

Isaiah 55:2 speaks about this: "Why spend money on what is not bread, and your labor on what does not satisfy? Listen, listen to me, and eat what is good, and you will delight in the richest of fare."

God doesn't mind us having nice things. In fact, He loves to bless us with nice homes and cars. He just never intended for those things to be the object of our chase. He wants to be what we chase and what we thirst for. He is the only thing that can fill that empty void and bring us peace and happiness. He has a plan for you that is bigger than you, your family, and your success.

Earlier, I told you how Carol and I took a Crown Financial Small Group Study that helped us get out of debt. After we took the class, our pastor asked us to teach it. I thought to myself, *How am I going to teach the class when I still have over $100,000 in debt?* But nonetheless we agreed. During this class, the strangest feeling came over me. The only way I can explain it is that I thought I was going to burst. I had never felt God like I felt Him at this time.

Afterward, I prayed to God, saying, "I don't care if I ever get out of debt; if I can just feel You like I feel You now, then that's all I need."

I think that's when God snapped His fingers and said, "That's what I've been waiting on. Now I can use you." I believe then He put things in place to get us financially free. I'm so glad He didn't listen to my silly prayer. There was no way He could leave me in debt. He had bigger things in store for me. I finally realized that God knew He needed someone to take this message to hurting people. He knew I would be speaking to you through this book. He also knew you would not listen if I always had money and never had any huge amount of debt. He also knew I would have more compassion for others since God had shown compassion for me. It became so clear and simple. God allowed Carol and me to go through difficult financial times in order to give us a ministry that will help others do the same. My personal story of being delivered from what seemed to be an unwinnable battle with debt encourages others to begin their own journey to a life of financial peace. We learned that we are blessed by God to be a blessing to others.

God gives each of us skills, passions, and experiences to carry out the mission He has for us. It's quite possible that He will use the very thing that we are embarrassed about to serve His purpose.

The last thing I wanted to do was let my friends know that I had struggled financially, but that's part of my purpose.

God did not just free us from financial debt so that we can have a bigger house and car. He freed us so that we may have purpose in our lives. Over the years, we have helped thousands of people become financially free. Financial freedom had two parts. It's freedom *from* something and freedom *to* something. Most people get excited about being freed from debt or a job they don't like. But I get more excited about what God is freeing people to. My question is always "What is your to?" All of us have a "to." For some of us, our "to" is to be a missionary in Africa or to own a successful business that gives a lot of money to the kingdom. Perhaps your "to" is to be an elementary school teacher or to help feed hungry kids. Why in the world would God set you free from your situation? You should ask yourself, "What is He freeing me to?"

I believe God wants to bless your life. He wants to bless your relationships, your health, and your finances. But it's not just for you. Here is where the "prosperity gospel" goes wrong. The prosperity gospel says it's all about you and your success.

Water flows through each level of the fountain. The water is not intended to remain stagnant. When we realize it's not just about us, we make different choices in life. We realize then that we are blessed to be a blessing.

In 1993, Bill Gates, the founder of Microsoft and one of the richest men in the world, pledged to give more than 50 percent of his net worth away and hoped to eventually give away 95 percent of his net worth. He also encouraged other billionaires, such as Warren Buffet, to join him. In a March 2014 interview with Chris Anderson on Ted.com, Bill and Melinda Gates said, "It's the most fulfilling thing we've ever done." It's when we give of ourselves to something bigger than we are that we find true fulfillment.

When we understand this concept as believers, we begin to allow resources to flow through us and give our lives generously toward the greatest cause ever: spreading Christ's love and building His church. We then move from just having a successful life to living a life of significance.

The reason God gives us success in each tier is so we can be effective in reaching others for Him. God is about building His church, and He has given us each a purpose connected with building His church.

Jesus modeled what it means to live a life of significance. Everything He did contributed to the ultimate goal of redeeming the world to God. We are to follow His model and commit to the same six activities in order to fulfil our purpose on earth:

1. Make disciples.
2. Live a life others desire to have.
3. Show love to others who can't repay us.
4. Discover and pursue our big dream.
5. Work for God.
6. Build a generous spirit.

CHAPTER 39

MAKE DISCIPLES

When Jesus arrived on the scene, the people thought that He would establish an immediate earthly kingdom. Jesus wanted them to know that His kingdom would not be fully established until He returned and to be faithful until then. So, He told this story in Luke 19 that is referred to as the parable of the ten minas.

Jesus described himself as "a man of noble birth" and said that he would go back to heaven but would return again someday. While He was away, He gave three servants ten minas each and charged them to put the money to work until He came back. Some commentaries say these minas equaled a year's salary. Whether that amount is accurate or not, we can be certain that it was something of great value.

This story goes on to say that the enemies of God rejected Him. However, it doesn't change the fact that Jesus is Lord and He will come back for a final judgment. So the king comes back to find out what interest they had gained with what He had given them.

One servant had gained ten minas and another five minas. The king's response to them both was, "Well done, you good and faithful servant."

Then a third servant came who had been given something valuable but did nothing with it. He said, "Here is the mina you gave me."

The king responded, "Why didn't you put what I gave you to work so that when I returned, I would collect it with interest?"

There are two questions we have to ask ourselves to understand key messages in this story. The first is: what is it of great value God has given me?

If I asked most people to list those things of great value that God has given to them, the list may looked something like this: money, relationships, skills, experiences, passions, health, wisdom/biblical understanding, personalities, and so on.

The great value that God has given us can be summed up in one word —*grace*.

This free gift gives us the opportunity to live eternally with Him in heaven.

The second question is "How do I pay God interest on what He has given me?"

Interest is a financial term we are all familiar with. Interest either works for us or against us. If we have debts, then interest is working against us. If we have no debts and have investments, interest is working for us. None of us are neutral to the effects of interest. Even if you don't have debt but don't invest money, interest works against you simply because of the impact of inflation. Interest is either our friend or our enemy.

God is using this financial term to demonstrate a spiritual truth. We are either using our lives for God or against God. There is no neutral. Doing nothing is working against God.

There is only one thing I can do to gain interest on the salvation God gave me —that is participating in the salvation of others. We gain or pay interest to God by participating in the development of other Jesus followers or making disciples.

CHAPTER 40

THE GREAT COMMISSION

When I played football at Georgia Tech, I loved the moments right before the game started. We would go out and warm up and then go back into the locker room before going out to face our opponent. For me, there was no better feeling. Right before going out on the field, our coach, Bill Curry, would call us all together for his last words. We would be on the edge of our seats because we knew what he told us at this point was important. He would give us our final marching orders before game time.

Jesus had a moment like this with His disciples in Matthew 28:16-20. Jesus got them together and said, "Okay, boys, it's game time. All power and authority in heaven and earth has been given to me." I'm sure in their minds they had been waiting for this and they were on the edge of their seats because they knew the next words out of His mouth would be important. Jesus continues, "Therefore go and make disciples of all nations, baptizing them in the name of the Father and of the Son and of the Holy Spirit and teaching them to obey everything I have commanded you. And surely I am with you always, to the very end of the age." This is called the Great Commission.

The Great Commission has been referred to as "the marching orders of the church," which is a phrase coined by early church fathers. Some people think this is the responsibility of the church, but Jesus is talking to every believer or follower. The church wasn't even formed at the point of Him giving the Great Commission.

What is the Great Commission calling us to do? There are four verbs in this scripture: *go*, *make*, *baptize*, and *teach*. All of these are important in understanding what we are commissioned to do, but only one of these action verbs is the main command. The other verbs just help explain how to do the command. Most people think the command verb is to "go" but without the other verbs, you don't know what to go and do. The main command is to "make disciples." "Make disciples" means "to cause one to be a pupil or disciple" or to turn others into disciples. The other three verbs are participles, which help explain *how* we are to make disciples. This commission is our responsibility as believers. We are to disciple the whole world.

Such a daunting task could be depressing, but it isn't because Jesus rigged the process. His strategy was brilliant. One of my mentors, Soup Campbell, taught this strategy to me. It's simple. "See the masses through the man. Build and equip the man to reach the masses."

See the Masses ...

Everything Jesus did, He did with the big picture in view. Jesus came into the world as a man to save the entire world.

He is the atoning sacrifice for our sins, and not only for ours but also for the sins of the whole world (1 John 2:2).

... Through the Man
Though his vision was for the masses, it seemed Jesus focused very little time on the masses. His goal was not to build the biggest group of church followers in Jerusalem. In fact, He often said things that pushed the masses away. Jesus spent the vast majority of His time building into men who would reproduce themselves. Jesus begins His ministry in Matthew 4:18-19.

> And Jesus, walking by the Sea of Galilee, saw two brothers, Simon called Peter, and Andrew his brother, casting a net into the sea; for they were fishermen. Then He said to them, "Follow Me, and I will make you fishers of men."

Jesus didn't just call them to repent of their sins and find a church to sit in. He called them to repent and to *follow* and become *fishers* of men! We are called to do the same.

Build and Equip the Man ...

Jesus' plan to prepare the disciples was simple. The disciples were to *be with* Jesus (Mark 3:14). As they spent time with Him in the context of relationship, they were trained. So, when they got to Acts 2 and Jesus was gone, they didn't even skip a beat. They were ready! This is the same method Jesus wants us to use to train others.

One of the guys I get to do ministry with is Joe. I have known Joe and mentored him for several years. He and his wife took one of our financial classes. I saw that Joe had a passion for financial ministry and the ability to be a leader, so I asked him to lead a small group. Later I asked him to become a financial coach. Along the way, Joe has been coaching alongside me teaching. He has spent time with me and asked questions. I have progressively given him more and more responsibility. Now Joe leads our money coaching team and has developed other small group leaders and financial coaches. This is Jesus' simple method of discipleship.

In John 17:4, Jesus says, "I have brought you glory on earth by finishing the work you gave me to do." If we read this without noting the context, we would probably think of the cross where He exclaimed, "It is finished!" But in John 17, Jesus has not yet gone to the cross. Jesus twice says "It is finished"—on the cross (the work of redemption was finished) and here in John 17 in the garden of Gethsemane (the work of reproduction was finished). His strategy to evangelize the entire world was set in place. He had discipled eleven men, which would result in the entire world being evangelized.

The disciples seemed to instinctively know what was being asked of them. There was no Q&A after the commission because they had seen it modeled before them.

... To Reach the Masses

"But you shall receive power when the Holy Spirit has come upon you; and you shall be witnesses to Me in Jerusalem, and in all Judea and Samaria, and to the end of the earth" (Acts 1:8).

The standard of New Testament Christianity is reproduction. At some point in the discipleship process, there has to be a commissioning. "You do with other guys what I'm doing with you."

This had to seem like a daunting task. I'm sure they asked, "How can we reach the entire world when it's just us few?" Along with the eleven disciples were maybe another hundred or so believers.

The disciples were to be witnesses for Christ in Jerusalem, Judea, Samaria, and the ends of the earth at the same time! That seems impossible! The only way that Christ-through-you will impact all of these regions is prayerful, obedient multiplication.

Soup Campbell used to tell me, "Moody, you should be worth more to Christ when you're dead than when you're alive."

He explained that if I discipled one hundred men and died today, then I've impacted one hundred men for God. However, if I invest in one disciple for year one, then in year two, both me and my disciple start discipling someone else for a year, and so on, then in twenty years, I've gained 1,048,576 souls for God. Even after I'm dead, I continue to reach more people than I did while I was alive. Soup was right. I'm worth more to God dead than alive.

If we keep faithfully discipling men and women, there is no doubt reaching "all nations" will happen.

CHAPTER 41

HOW DO I MAKE MY LIFE COUNT?

As I mentioned before, Jesus gives us a perfect vision for discipleship (gain interest on what He has given us) and strategy (see the masses through the man, equip the man to reach the masses), but how do we actually carry it out and make our life count? Paul shows us in 1 Thessalonians how we are to actually carry it out and the results of us being obedient to the plan.

How would you finish this statement? My life really counts for the Lord if/because _____!

This question is not assessing your worth/value in being created and loved by God. Rather, it is a question of stewardship.

Most of us would say Paul's life counted because he wrote most of the New Testament. Paul might have answered this question in a number of different ways, but we have at least one example in scripture where he does give an answer.

Paul answered this question by saying, "For now we really live if you stand firm in the Lord" (1 Thessalonians 3:8). This was a bold statement.

What was so important about the Thessalonians standing firm? Paul had followed Jesus' strategy for reaching the world, but it depended on the people he had discipled to follow as well. If they did, Paul felt his life would have great meaning. If they did not, then Paul felt his life would have made very little impact for Christ. For Paul, everything hinged on them standing firm.

Paul and Silas were in Thessalonica at least three weeks but no more than six months (Acts 17:1–9). What did his time with them look like so such a tight relationship was formed?

In 1 Thessalonians 2:7–16, Paul highlights a model or plan for making disciples. Jesus himself modeled this plan with his disciples. He taught them the Word of God and shared his life with them. They learned how to live a Christian life by watching Jesus, asking Him questions, and hanging out with Him. We are to do the same.

In his writing to them, Paul demonstrates how discipleship is really spiritual parenthood.

- "We were like a mother" (2:7). What is a mother like? Loving, affectionate, nurturing, concerned, giving, etc.
- "We loved you so much we were delighted to share with you not only the gospel of God but our lives as well" (2:8). Paul didn't just preach to them. He spent time with them. He didn't just tell them what the Bible says, but showed them by allowing them to observe how to live. They saw Paul walk out a Christian life.
- "We were like a father" (2:11). What is a father like? Protector, leader, provider, teacher, disciplinarian, and so on.

What are some obvious goals when raising a child? Get them out of your house. Prepare them to take on the world. You want them ultimately to be able to marry well, have kids, and prepare them to do the same. That was Paul's hope for them, and the Thessalonians accepted it. They became imitators of Paul, Silas, and Timothy and became a model to all believers in Greece! In fact, their faith went out to the ends of the earth! (1:6–8).

The best thing a parent can do for his or her child is model how to live. When my boys do something to mistreat a young lady, I ask them, "Have you ever seen Daddy treat Mom that way?"

Fortunately, they can usually say no. As their dad, I naturally want them to imitate me. The best thing I can do for them is live how I want them to live, and then I can say, "You do what you see Daddy do." This keeps the pressure on me and forces me to work on being someone who is "imitable."

How I mentor other men is simple. I meet with two to four guys weekly for a couple of hours. Each of the mentees is required to spend time daily with God, reading scriptures and praying, memorizing a verse that he recites out loud at the beginning of each session, journaling what's happening in his life daily, and tracking progress against his goals weekly. After opening with prayer and their memory verses, we spend the first part of our meeting with me teaching a Bible truth from our reading. In the second part of the meeting, we each share from our journals the key happenings in our lives. I encourage them to be open and honest with their challenges. We encourage and support each other. We provide accountability without judgment. I also invite these guys to do life with me. I invite them to be a part of what I do in life and try to be a part of their lives outside of our meetings. Guys usually spend six months to a year in my group, and then they are released to mentor other men the way I mentored them. I continue to be available to them as a lifelong mentor even after we no longer meet weekly.

> Mentoring other men is one of the most impactful uses of my time on earth. I believe one day we will all go before God to account for our lives and that we had better have good answers to two questions: "What did you do with my son, Jesus?" and "What did you do with what I gave you?" (Rick Warren, *Purpose-Driven Life*, 34)

At that point, on Judgment Day, nothing else will matter. My college degrees and executive positions will not help me. The car I drive and the home I live in will mean absolutely nothing. It will not matter if I had the wealth of Bill Gates, Donald Trump, and Oprah combined. None of this will be enough to compensate for not having good answers to those two questions. My answer to the first question determines where I will spend eternity. None of the good things I have done will get me there. There won't be any reason for me to boast, because all I did was accept God's free gift of eternal life. But the second question I hope to respond as Paul did in 1 Thessalonians as he professes he would boast before Jesus. What was their hope/joy/crown in which they will boast before Christ Jesus? It was the Thessalonians! Paul will boast in the Thessalonians (1 Thessalonians 2:19–20). They are the fruit of his life for eternity.

When *you* stand before the Lord, in whom will you boast? To whom will you point? Will you merely say, "I went to church …?" If our lives really are to count for Christ, then there should be someone we can point to like Paul and say, "It's because of you my life counts for Christ."

When I stand in front of God, I hope to stand and boast about you. I will boast loudly, "Look at those men you gave me to mentor. Lord, you gave me ten minas. Look! I have earned you ten more." I yearn to hear His response. "Well done, you good and faithful servant." I know all of us would like to hear these words. The only way we can hear them is if we are intentionally involved in discipling others. Even after we no longer live, people will come to know Christ through our lives. Then, we are worth more to God dead than alive.

CHAPTER 42

BEING A MENTOR

We can't be intimidated to be a mentor just because we are not perfect. It does require that we prepare ourselves to have others follow us. Knowing that others are watching me inspires me to strive to be someone who is followable. One of my mentors made it clear to me that he was not Jesus and would not be perfect.

Mentoring others makes us vulnerable. When others are close to us, they get to see our many shortcomings. That's part of the coaching process. It didn't matter that he was imperfect. I saw how he handled shortcomings and how he readily confessed and overcame his sins. This is a valuable part of the process. It helped me to realize I wouldn't be perfect either and gave me confidence to share my own imperfections with others. Our weakness shouldn't keep us from discipling others when we have a sincere desire to follow Christ.

Choosing People to Mentor

An acronym one of my mentors taught me to help with choosing men to mentor is FAT.

F — Faithful

He warned me not to waste time with men who are not faithful. To test faithfulness, I give potential mentees assignments and check to make sure they are completed. I give them scriptures to memorize each week and require them to recite by memory prior to each meeting. To encourage faithfulness, I charge them five dollars for each word that they miss. It amazes me how few times I actually have to collect money. My having high expectations of them and inspecting what they do encourages them to maintain a high level of faithfulness.

A—Available

Mentees must commit time to being mentored. I have had weekly sessions at six in the morning at my home and three thirty in the afternoon. Regardless of when they are held, it will require mentees to make a commitment to be available. The only way to effectively mentor others is to spend time with them. That's what Jesus did with the disciples. They were discipled as they walked from city to city and as they sat around the dinner table. Mentees must take time to be with the person who is mentoring them. This time has to fit into the mentor's everyday life.

When Jeff was mentoring me, I would call him to talk about some issue I had. He would say something like, "Why don't you meet me at my house in the morning? I'm putting down mulch and could use your help." Soup once asked me to drive him to a prison where he would do ministry. I learned many valuable lessons on the three-hour drive there and back. Mentees have to make themselves available.

T—Teachable

Finally mentees have to be teachable. There is nothing you can do to help a person who isn't teachable. Some people feel they are full grown. You can't tell them anything. They spend all their time trying to tell you. These people are time wasters. If they aren't teachable, then don't allow them to waste your time. I had a guy who asked me to mentor him, but every time I coached him to do something he didn't like, he balked at it. He explained that I wasn't mentoring him the right way. I lovingly told him that he needed to find a coach he could receive teaching from because obviously I had nothing to teach him.

We have to be careful to use our time wisely. Time is the one thing we can never create more of. We can earn more money, but we can never get back lost time. It's important to make the best use of the time you spend discipling others.

CHAPTER 43

LIVE AND LOVE

One thing about social media that drives me crazy is how some people seem to brag about things that are going well in their lives. For instance, if someone has had success losing weight, then every conversation seems to be about their fitness success. Every Facebook post is another picture and another invitation to work out. It feels overwhelming to me. I'm like, "Is anything else going on in your world besides working out?" I especially hate it when these people constantly tell the rest of us what we are not doing right concerning our health. This bothers me more than it motivates me to become fit.

Many Christians do the same thing when it comes to trying to get others to follow their faith. It's not our jobs to make people see their wrongs. We can't make people get it by constantly telling them what they are doing wrong.

I have family members whom I love dearly but who do not believe in Jesus as their God. I do not allow this to affect our relationship. We don't get into religious debates. I don't see it as my role to save them and make them see who Jesus is. Revelation comes from God and not from us. We think we are attracting people to God by constantly talking about the Bible and telling them they need to know Jesus, when we may actually be pushing people away from God.

Jesus never forced Himself on people. He simply demonstrated how to live and showed them love. People were drawn to Him.

Robert Coleman shares this example in *The Master Plan of Evangelism*.

> Take, for example, his prayer life. It wasn't by accident that Jesus often let his disciples see him conversing with the Father. They could see the strength which it gave to his life, and though they could not understand fully what it was all about, they must have realized that this was part of his secret of life. Note that Jesus did not force the lesson on them, but rather he just kept praying until at last the disciples got so hungry that they asked him to teach them what he was doing. (Coleman, *The Master Plan of Evangelism*, 64)

People have to get their own revelations from God concerning what He wants them to work on. I hate it when some people have success in some area of their lives and then they want everyone to do the same. They make comments like, "You should do this," or "It's really easy."

After nine months of watching me lose weight on a fitness plan, Carol told me she had an epiphany. She said, "You have lost weight, but I haven't. I've been cooking meals for you, but I'm not watching what I eat. It just hit me that I can get healthier too." I had never communicated to Carol that she should eat differently. I didn't see that as my responsibility. On her own, she committed to eating better and improving her health. Everyone has to come to his or her own revelation.

It's not up to us to make people feel guilty or to tell people what they need to do. My motto in reaching others for Christ is "live and love." If we live the life we want them to live and show people love, then we will be effective in winning others for Christ. We have to teach people how to live instead of telling them how to live. We teach them by living it out in plain view of others.

CHAPTER 44

LIVE A LIFE OTHERS DESIRE TO HAVE

Matthew 5:14–16 says,

> You are the light of the world. A town built on a hill cannot
> be hidden. Neither do people light a lamp and put it under
> a bowl. Instead they put it on its stand, and it gives light
> to everyone in the house. In the same way, let your light
> shine before others, that they may see your good deeds and
> glorify your Father in heaven.

It's our mandate as Christians to live the best life we possibly can
live. This doesn't mean that we will all be rich, drive luxury cars,
and live in big homes. Sure, those things would be nice, but they
are far from guaranteed or even necessary to live the best life we
can live. This mandate to live our best life as Christians doesn't
require perfection, either. It simply means that you pursue a life
that models how God says we should live. The key is that we *pursue*
a godly life and success. We have a responsibility as Christians to
pursue success in life.

We are a light to the world. We need to live a life that others desire.
Who would take marriage advice from someone who doesn't have
a good marriage or financial advice from someone who is deep in
debt? We need to have success in order to draw others to God.
Our success attracts others to God because they long for what we
have. It's our duty as Christians to show others by the way we live
how to have success in life for themselves. You don't have to tell

people what to do. They are watching you. Just live it and do so impressively.

We do not have to put up a front that our lives are perfect and nothing ever goes wrong. In fact the opposite is true. People need to see how we handle adversity. Jesus said we will all have trouble in this world but to be of good courage because He has overcome the world. We are a model to others of how to handle all of life's problems — the good and the bad. Others want to know if we will still give when our finances are low, if we will still support our children when they disappoint us, and if we will still treat our boss with respect even when he or she chastises or corrects us. These are true tests of character.

How you handle life's challenges is what draws others to you and ultimately to Christ. A few years ago, my cousin Carolyn was in the hospital battling cancer. She was only a few years older than I, but we had not been close cousins. In fact, I didn't even know her married name. I was at the hospital anyway visiting another friend and thought I would visit her too since I was there. I had planned to just pop in to encourage her and not stay long.

I had known Carolyn all my life. I knew her to be nice but quiet. Quite honestly, she was very underwhelming. We had greeted and hugged each other at family functions, but I couldn't actually remember ever having a conversation with her.

In my visit with her, I sat and really talked with her for the first time in our lives. She was in a lot of pain but enjoyed having someone there to talk to. She wanted to know about my life and told me stories about her life. She discussed past mistakes and things she was proud of. She discussed her battle with cancer. I found out about her family and church, her hopes and dreams. Before I knew it, I had been with her for over an hour.

The strange thing about my visit was that I felt so encouraged by it. There was something uplifting about how she was dealing with this difficult time in her life. I asked her if she minded if I visited again next week. The next visit was the same, so my visits turned into weekly visits for the next several months. What began as a gesture by me to uplift my cousin became a way for me to be uplifted by the life she was living. Carolyn finally died of cancer after several months of treatments at the hospital. I would miss our weekly visits, but I wasn't sad about her death. I knew she was in a better place. I was so thankful that I had had this time to spend with her. She was an extraordinary woman who allowed God's light to shine through her life.

It's that light that people are drawn to. It's our job to let it shine. When we let God's light shine through us, we will not have to worry about having to witness to people. They will find us. Every man I have ever discipled has come to me and asked for my help. They each saw something in my life that attracted them to God. Once they come to me, then I have a free opportunity to speak into their lives. They are ready to hear the Word of God so I better know it and be ready to share it.

"But in your hearts revere Christ as Lord. Always be prepared to give an answer to everyone who asks you to give the reason for the hope that you have. But do this with gentleness and respect" (1 Peter 3:15 NIV).

Our responsibility is to live our lives in a way that others can see God in us and are drawn to Him.

CHAPTER 45

BE IMPRESSIVE

When I was younger, I was always impressed with the wrong things. I was impressed with people who wore certain clothes, drove certain cars, went on luxurious vacations, and lived in big houses. As I've gotten older, those things don't impress me anymore. The following is a list of ten things that impress me about people. I think these things will also impress people about you and draw others to desire to live a life like yours.

Ten Things That Impress Me

1. Dads involved in their kids' school activities (not just sports)
2. Couples married over twenty years who are affectionate and still in love
3. People exercising and taking care of their bodies
4. Families spending time together having fun
5. A person completing a college degree
6. Someone who pays off a home or car
7. Someone completing a race, any race (that person had to train for it and accomplish it)
8. A person doing something he or she loves and is good at
9. Someone happily serving someone else in need
10. People who live out their faith and do not just talk about it

Simply going to church alone isn't impressive. Many people who go to church are living the worst lives. We have all seen hypocrisy in churchgoers. It's not even about knowing the Bible. Plenty of churchgoers know the Bible front to back, but they never live it out. People aren't impressed with how much Bible you know or how often you go to church. People are impressed when you live out your faith and when you live with conviction. Even when someone has a different faith than mine, when he or she lives it out with conviction, I'm impressed.

Be impressive and live a life that others desire. As people are drawn to us, they will be drawn to God.

CHAPTER 46

LOVE

John 13:34–35 says, "A new command I give you: Love one another. As I have loved you, so you must love one another. By this everyone will know that you are my disciples, if you love one another."

Jesus commands us to love others as He loved us and said this is how others will know we are His disciples. Loving people means that we follow the model Jesus demonstrated during His ministry on earth. Jesus challenges us to show love in three ways.

1. Jesus challenges us to be loving and compassionate to those in need.

Matthew 25:35–36 says, "For I was hungry and you gave me something to eat, I was thirsty and you gave me something to drink, I was a stranger and you invited me in, I needed clothes and you clothed me, I was sick and you looked after me, I was in prison and you came to visit me."

Jesus healed those who were sick, fed those who were hungry, and freed people who were in bondage. It wasn't about preaching to them. He just loved them and served them. We need to do the same.

2. Jesus challenges us to show love without expecting those we show love to to repay us.

If you love those who love you, what credit is that to you? Even sinners love those who love them. And if you do good to those who are good to you, what credit is that to you? Even sinners do that. And if you lend to those from whom you expect repayment, what credit is that to you? Even sinners lend to sinners, expecting to be repaid in full. But love your enemies, do good to them, and lend to them without expecting to get anything back. Then your reward will be great, and you will be children of the Most High, because he is kind to the ungrateful and wicked. (Luke 6:32–35)

Our lives should include doing good things for people who can't repay us. We can't show love to only those who agree with us morally or spiritually. We should show love to both Christians and non-Christians. A pastor friend of mine caught a lot of flak because he and his congregants helped a Muslim congregation who was in need. It's amazing how religious some people can be. What they did was show love to them. Their love wasn't contingent on these people converting to Christianity. It was solely based on the challenge from God to show love to others who can't repay.

3. Jesus challenges us to speak hope, life, and freedom to those in bondage.

"The Spirit of the Lord is on me, because he has anointed me to proclaim good news to the poor. He has sent me to proclaim freedom for the prisoners and recovery of sight for the blind, to set the oppressed free" (Luke 4:18; Isaiah 61:1–2).

People around us may not be physically in prison, but many are bound nonetheless. Some are bound by addictions, habits, or hang-ups. We can love others by helping them to live a life of freedom. Our method has to be in a life-giving way. People respond to hope and life. It's our responsibility to love people by speaking life into their lives.

Again, this is not about saving people as much as it is about loving people. I get asked often, "How do you get guys to follow you as their mentor?" In truth, I never seek them out. They always find me. It's something about what they see in my life that draws them to wanting to know me more.

The combination of living and loving will open more doors to speak into people's lives than anything else you do. When you live and love, people are naturally drawn to you and want to hear what you have to say.

Small Group Questions

1. Do you regularly recognize that your life is not just about you? How so?

2. Read Matthew 28:16–20.
   a. What is the Great Commission calling us to do?

   b. What stands out to you the most about the strategy "See the masses through the man. Equip the man to reach the masses?"

   c. What do you think prevents more people from discipling others?

3. How would you finish this statement? My life really counts for the Lord if/because _____!

4. How does the thought of you mentoring others make you feel?

5. Who are the people in your world whom you believe you could mentor? List their names.

6. Read Matthew 5:14–16.
   a. What can you do to allow God's light to shine through your life?

   b. How does the fact that others are watching the way you live as a Christian make you feel?

   c. How can you better live a life that others would desire?

7. Read Luke 6:32–36, Matthew 25:35–36, and John 13:34–35.
   a. Do you consistently show love to others outside of those who love you? Explain.

   b. What can you do to show more love to those who cannot repay?

CHAPTER 47

WORKING FOR GOD

I have heard varied reports that anywhere from 60 to 70 percent of people dislike their work. We spend the majority of our lives working. It is heartbreaking that 70 percent of people spend the majority of their lives in a place where they are unhappy. God did not intend for man to despise work. God created work before sin entered the world. Therefore, God intended for us to work all along. God created work to build our character while enabling us to provide for our material well-being. Work also is a way of experiencing a more intimate relationship with God and with other people.

Dave Ramsey writes in *Financial Peace*, "Happy and effective people have found a vocation for which they have a natural aptitude and have committed themselves to excellence in that vocation. These are people who have a vacation for a vocation." God has given each of us natural abilities and passions. If we can identify those, we will not only be happier and perform better in that role, but we will also become well-paid for it. God gives us all unique skills and abilities. We should not be jealous of others' skills. Working where we are using our skills most effectively indicates that we are doing what God has called us to do.

It is time for you to work hard to excel at your vocation. Colossians 3:23–24 reminds us that we should perform our work as if God is watching because He is: "Whatever you do, work at it with all your heart, as working for the Lord, not for men, since you know that you will receive an inheritance from the Lord as a reward. It is the Lord Christ you are serving."

It does not matter that our employers cannot see that we are slacking off, because we are not working solely for them. We should always strive to work hard and do our best. As Christians, we are to set an example for others. We do not want others to associate Christianity with laziness. Martin Luther King Jr.'s famous street sweeper quote reminds us that God expects excellence in our work: "If a man is called to be a street sweeper, he should sweep streets even as Michelangelo painted, or Beethoven played music, or Shakespeare wrote poetry. He should sweep streets so well that all the hosts of heaven and earth will pause to say, here lived a great street sweeper who did his job well."

CHAPTER 48

WORK IS MY MINISTRY

As Christians, we are called to serve Christ with our lives. What if we viewed our work as an opportunity to worship God? Only a few of us will actually have careers as a pastor, a minister, or a missionary. Many more of us serve at our local churches every weekend by singing in the choir, teaching children, or serving as an usher or greeter. But when Sunday is over, most of us return to our jobs outside the church.

We often forget to connect our faith to our work. We don't consider the reason God has us at our jobs. We don't think about the purpose and meaning we can bring to our work. For most of us, our mission field is our workplace.

Whether you spend your nine to five in a cubicle, planting crops, nursing people, teaching, or running a business, most of life happens at work. We spend over half our lives at work.

A successful Christian businessman Stanley Tam said, "My business is my pulpit."

You may not be the type of missionary who moves to the far regions of Africa, but around the conference table, the water cooler, and the cubicle, you get to serve the God who created you.

I was talking to a military leader who had over 1,400 people reporting to him. He shared how people noticed every little thing he did. The fact that he said grace before he ate lunch did not go unnoticed. People are watching. You are impacting them whether you want to or not — good or bad.

God gave you a skill, a passion, and work to be used for ministry. It's not about handing out tracts and forcing the gospel on people. That would be weird. Seeing your work as a ministry is about becoming aware of those around you, loving them, and making a point to bring light into their lives.

You could be the closest thing to Jesus that your coworkers ever see. We have to create environments that lead to conversations that lead to transformations. When we do our work with excellence, integrity, and diligence, it's an act of worship. We are displaying God's craftsmanship to a nonbelieving world around us. We are earning the right to be heard.

Through you, we have been invited into parts of the city, country, and world that many of us as pastors will never see. You have conversations with people who may never set foot in a church.

Whether we love or hate our work doesn't matter. Choose to turn the focus away from you and to the mission God has for you. God has designed us and created us to work. Make your work your ministry.

Practical tips to earn the right to speak into people's lives:

1. Strive for excellence. If you do that, it will earn you the right to share, and it will give you credibility. If you have no credibility, you might as well stay home.
2. Work with integrity. You may not know what your employees are doing, but they always know what you are doing. People need to trust you first, before they trust and accept what you are saying.
3. Pay people accurately and on time.
4. Generate profits and success. There's absolutely nothing wrong with a profit; the problem comes when we make it our purpose instead of a function. Jesus said, "The poor

will be with you always," but you don't have to be one of them. Profits and success give you a platform from which to speak. Bill Gates has a platform to speak into people's lives. Whether he uses it or not, he has earned the right through his financial and business success. Your success in the business world will provide you a platform for God.

CHAPTER 49

HOW TO GET PROMOTED AT WORK

There are lots of things that figure into being promoted on the job. For Christians, we know all promotions come from God. Just like in every other area of life, God has a part and we have a part to play.

In 1 Samuel 16, we have a great example of how to get promoted. God anoints David as the future king of Israel and begins the process for promoting him. It begins with promoting David from a person who watches sheep to what was in essence an internship for King Saul.

God was working all sorts of activities behind the scenes to make this promotion happen. He caused an evil spirit to come on Saul, gave one of his attendants an idea to bring in a lyre (harp) player to ease Saul's stress, and made situations happen where one of Saul's servants happened to come across David and remembered he was a lyre player. God was busy behind the scenes when to David it may have seemed like nothing close to a promotion was happening.

But David had a part to play as well in order to get this promotion, and it was displayed when King Saul was looking for someone to add to his team as a harp player.

> One of the servants answered, "I have seen a son of Jesse of Bethlehem who knows how to play the lyre. He is a brave man and a warrior. He speaks well and is a fine-looking

man. And the LORD is with him." ... David came to Saul and entered his service. Saul liked him very much, and David became one of his armor-bearers (1 Samuel 16:18, 21).

This story highlights five key lessons we can learn from David in order to help us get promoted.

1. Be good at what we do — In 1 Samuel 18:5, it says, "Whatever Saul sent him to do, David did so successfully that Saul gave him a high rank in his army." Playing the harp doesn't sound like a prerequisite for being king. Yet, if he hadn't been good at playing the unimportant harp, then David would not have gotten the attention of Saul's servant and been recommended for the position. We never know what God is using in our lives to propel us to the next level. We have to be good at what we have in front of us to do now.

2. Have a good reputation — The servant said David was "a brave man and a warrior and the Lord is with him." We have to live in a way that our reputation speaks for us. Being a person of good character who is trustworthy makes a big difference when you are considered for promotion. Even people who do not have good character respect those who do.

3. Communicate well — "He speaks well." How we communicate makes a huge impact on whether we get promotions. We have to work on both oral and written communication. Reply to e-mails in a timely way, and communicate regularly with your boss. We also have to manage social media well. It is helpful to block out social media while at work and to make sure any social media communications are reflective of the image you would like your boss to see.

4. Look your best — "He ... is a fine-looking man." A Duke University study reveals that our physical appearance is a significant factor in hiring, compensation, and promotion at work (Williams, "Good Looks Can Get You That Job, Promotion and Raise," 2011). We can hope that wasn't the case, but studies show that attractive people are more likely to be promoted. There is an old saying that you never get a

second chance to make a first impression. Always look your best when it comes to your appearance. Looking sexy isn't the same as looking your best. Studies show that looking overly sexy may actually work against you (*Forbes*, "What Not to Wear to Work," 2009). Dress to impress, but dress appropriately for your workplace.

5. Be likeable—Verse 21 says, "Saul liked him very much." When all things are equal or close, people promote whom they like. Having a positive, can-do attitude is vital to being likeable. It also helps to have a sense of humor and a friendly good nature. Smiling and being courteous goes a long way. It is as simple as the old saying: "Treat people the way you want to be treated."

CHAPTER 50

WHEN I RETIRE, THEN I WILL HAVE PEACE

I talked with a guy who had retired from thirty years in the corporate world. I asked, "What are you going to do now that you've retired?"

He said, "I'm doing it. Nothing." He initially talked as if he had made it to some great level in life, to some final destination that we all must achieve. He said, "I just wake up and do whatever I want. I don't really do much at all." Then he went on to say how doing nothing has had a negative effect on him. His mind isn't as sharp. Things he used to remember now he doesn't. He lost weight and started to have more physical problems. I felt sad for him. He thought he had reached some final destination, but it turned out not to be what he had expected. For him, the pinnacle of life meant not having a clock to punch every morning and not having someone tell him what to do.

We were not built to retire. It's not biblical. The word *retirement* doesn't appear in the Bible. This guy's body and mind were breaking down. If we don't use it, we will lose it.

I understand how some people feel bad about their jobs. Most people go to work every day to a place they hate. I feel sorry for these people. I have been fortunate to work in jobs that I have enjoyed. I couldn't imagine going to work every day doing something I hated.

Sometimes you have to do what you don't like so one day you can do what you love to do. Someone said, "If you do what you love, you will never work a day in your life."

Obviously our work changes as we get older. Maybe we don't "punch a clock," but there are plenty of good things in store for us. Purpose continues to fulfill us all of our days.

To some extent, peace and freedom come when we can live life on our own terms. But when God frees us from something, there is a bigger purpose in life that He is freeing us to pursue. Why is God freeing you from thirty years of hard work? What is He freeing you to?

CHAPTER 51

MY JOB FEELS LIKE STEERING UPSTREAM

Jim Collins talks about how all great companies applied what he refers to as a *hedgehog concept*. He explains that this concept flows from the deep understanding of the intersection of the three circles asking these questions (Collins, *Good to Great*, 95–117):

1. What you can be the best in the world at?
2. What can you make money doing (paraphrased)?
3. What are you deeply passionate about?

He explains, "To have a fully developed Hedgehog Concept, you need all three circles. If you make a lot of money doing things at which you could never be the best, you'll only build a successful company, not a great one. If you become the best at something, you'll never remain on top if you don't have intrinsic passion for what you are doing. Finally, you can be passionate all you want, but if you can't be the best at it or it doesn't make economic sense, then you might have a lot of fun, but you won't produce great results" (Collins, *Good to Great*, 97).

I found that we can also apply this concept to our personal life. Unless we ask ourselves these same three questions and operate in the intersection of the answers, then we can never fulfil our potential to have peace in our work lives.

I was in the perfect job as an executive-level manager with the Target Corporation. It was the ideal job. It should have been a slam dunk, but it wasn't. For whatever reason, I never excelled at this job. I was trained and skilled to do it. I even wanted to be good at it. I had a great boss, and Target was the right culture for my personality. I tried hard, but at the end of each year, my reviews were just average.

I felt kind of like I was steering a speedboat upstream. Steering a speedboat upstream is certainly possible, but it takes so much energy. When we operate in the intersection of the three circles, it feels like we are steering the boat in the direction of the stream. This feels so much better, and the ride is much more enjoyable.

I learned an important lesson. No matter how comfortable the situation is, you won't fit anywhere but where God wants you. God had something else in mind for me. He had given me a big dream.

CHAPTER 52

DISCOVER AND PURSUE YOUR BIG DREAM

"And we know that in all things God works for the good of those who love him, who have been called according to his purpose" (Romans 8:28).

> Every person on earth was born with a purpose or dream for his or her life. You may not be able to describe it or may have even forgotten it. You may no longer believe in it, but it's there. Like the genetic code that describes your unique passions and abilities, your Big Dream has been woven into your being from birth. You are the only person with a Dream quite like yours. And you have it for a reason: to draw you toward the kind of life you were born to love! (Wilkerson, *The Dream Giver*).

When we are not pursuing our big dream, it feels like something big is missing from our lives or that we are missing from something big. It's because God has created us all to achieve great things. We can never have peace until we are pursuing our dream.

We all have a big dream. Maybe we have forgotten about it or rationalize why it's too risky to pursue. We have thought secretly, *I would be good at this and really like it. But it would take too long or cost too much or I might not be successful. It's probably better that I just play it safe and keep doing this job I hate. At least it pays the bills, and in thirty or forty years, I can retire and then do what I really love.*

It's sad that very few people embrace and pursue their dreams.

I was at the barbershop and listened to a man talking about retiring from a long career with a company. He had been retired for a few years. I was curious as to what he was doing now that his long-awaited retirement had happened. He said, "I keep myself busy doing things around the house."

I thought to myself, *Really! You waited forty years so you can plant flowers and change light bulbs?* I could tell this wasn't fulfilling to him by the tone of his voice, but he had lost sight of his big dream or maybe he thought it was too late.

There is a pattern followed by all dreamers whenever they reach for their dream and attempt great things for God (Wilkerson, *The Dream Giver*, 70).

1. Become aware of a personal dream or calling, then decide to [pursue it].
2. Face fear as they leave a place of comfort.
3. Encounter opposition from those around them.
4. Endure a season of difficulty that tests their faith.
5. Learn the importance of surrender and consecration to God.
6. Fight the giants that stand between them and the fulfillment of their dream.
7. Reach their full potential as they achieve their dream and bring honor to God.

Just like every other dreamer, I followed this same pattern in order to pursue my dream.

CHAPTER 53

I HAVE A DREAM

When I read Bruce Wilkerson's book *The Dream Giver*, it stirred up thoughts about the dream God had given me.

One day, I saw Dave Ramsey on *The Oprah Winfrey Show* and felt God was saying, "That is what I called you to do." I felt I was called to be in that chair helping to free people financially in order to pursue their God-given dream.

When Oprah retired from her show, I thought, *How dare she cancel this show before she had a chance to interview me!* I saw myself in that chair.

I wrote down my big dream: "To teach financial stewardship in order to help millions of people grow closer to Christ, live in peace, and fund God's great commission."

I shared my dream with Carol and a few close friends who encouraged me. I was excited to know God had given me this big dream.

Fear of Leaving What's Comfortable

But the more I considered it, the bigger it got and the scarier it became. How would I reach millions of people? How in the world could I pursue this when we were finally on level ground financially?

I was working as an executive with Target, making a nice six-figure income in a great working situation. It was a career that most people envied. Target was a great company, and I worked with great people. We lived in a nice home with a very comfortable lifestyle. Pursuing my big dream meant leaving what was comfortable.

Initially I thought maybe I could do both. I wrote my first book while working at Target. I would get up early every morning before work and write for a few hours until it was done. Then a pastor friend encouraged me to speak at his church. Soon I was speaking more often and being requested to help more pastors. One day, I received an e-mail from a pastor who wanted my help with one of his church members. I read this family's story and could feel their cry for help. They seemed discouraged and hopeless, and I knew that I could help bring hope to this family's situation. I wanted to help, but I couldn't because I had obligations at my job. I went home and told Carol that day, "I believe God is asking me to pursue my dream full-time."

Dream Champions

I wasn't sure where to start, but I shared my thoughts with a friend whom I had been working in ministry with at Crown Financial Ministry. He told me about an opportunity to serve in ministry in my hometown, Memphis. This opportunity gained my interest. I would have to develop my own plan and raise funds through donations to support my ministry. I would work as a missionary and receive a salary from the monies I raised. The maximum salary I could receive was less than half of my base salary with Target, and I wouldn't receive a bonus like I had at Target.

I shared my excitement with one of my friends, who said, "Only God can make you excited about taking a 50 percent pay cut."

Carol and I discussed it and felt since we didn't have any debts that we could live on half our income. It would be tight and definitely required changes in our lifestyles, but we could do it. But we still had the problem of raising the money needed for our ministry budget. We had to raise not only my salary but all monies needed for ministry.

I made an agreement with God. I said, "If this is from You, then You will provide the resources." Carol and I agreed and my accountability partner agreed that we would not commit to leaving my job until we had raised at least a half year's worth of financial resources.

I had a friend who knew a lot of people in Memphis who could provide financial support. He said he would help me by introducing me to these people and letting me share my ministry vision and financial needs. I had never done this before, but I put together my plan and agreed to take a day off of work to drive to Memphis to share my plan and raise money for our ministry.

The day before I was scheduled to go to Memphis, my friend called and said something major had come up with his business and that he might not be able to spend the day with me after all. He said I could come anyway, and he would still try to do it. I had already taken the day off so I decided to give it a try anyway.

I got up early the next day, put on my suit and tie, and headed to Memphis. About thirty miles before arriving in Memphis, I noticed my engine light was on. I noted to myself that I should get that looked at while I was in Memphis. A few minutes later, I heard a loud noise and the car started shaking. I pulled over and realized that I had a blown tire. So I got out of my car with my suit on to put on the spare tire and found the spare tire was flat as well. I called for a tire service and got back in my car to wait. I started talking to God. "Are You trying to tell me this is not the plan?" I didn't get frustrated. I was okay if God was not wanting this to happen, but I was committed to following through on my plans for the day.

Finally I got to my friend's office, and he was able to break free a little after lunchtime. He said, "I think we can still salvage the day and introduce you to a few people." We started going down the list of people he planned for me to meet. We went to each guy's office, but either he was gone or not available. Not one person he had scheduled was available to meet. I stayed calm, but I was disappointed. By the end of the workday, we started heading back to his office. My friend apologized for not being able to help me. I told him it was all right. As we headed back, he saw that his dad was in his office so we stopped in to say hello.

They chatted, and I waited patiently for them to catch up. Then his father asked me about what I did. I thought to myself, *I'm not going to come all the way to Memphis and not share my plan with somebody.* So I started sharing my big dream, the resources needed, and how I thought I could impact the city of Memphis. I could see my friend over his dad's shoulder, waving me off. He said, "Travis, maybe this is not a good idea."

But his dad said, "No, let him try to sell me if he thinks he can."

My confidence dropped, but I thought at worst case, this would be good practice. I put my pretty brochure on his desk and started talking. He put his hand over the brochure and said, "I don't need to see this; you just tell me why you think I should support you."

Now with only a tiny mustard seed of confidence left, I shared with him my story of coming out of debt and how I believed God could use me to help set other people financially free as well.

After hearing my story, he asked me, "What kind of donation would make you feel good about your trip?" Before I could answer, he pointed his finger at me and said, "And don't be greedy."

I was somewhat prepared for this question. I knew I needed at least $60,000 to take care of our ministry needs. I had hoped to meet with at least ten people who would commit $2,000 each so I responded, "$2,000."

He looked at me silently for what seemed like forever and finally said, "What about $20,000?"

I started praising God right then in his office. I had just met this man, but I started hugging him. He wrote me a check for $20,000.

There was no turning back now since I had taken his check. But I felt if God could provide this money in this way that I could trust Him to provide the rest. I started my plan to leave Target and go into full-time ministry with Crown.

I had a conversation with my boss to explain my plan, and surprisingly my boss and the company were very supportive. I was given several months to continue working while I was raising funds for ministry. In fact, some of my early donors were coworkers at Target.

Near the end of my tenure with Target, we received a visit from one of the high-level corporate execs. These visits are always political by nature. Each of my peers jockeyed for face time with the exec so they could propel their careers. I was okay with being in the background because I no longer cared about a career at Target. But on this particular visit, the exec wanted to spend time with me. He had heard about me following my big dream and had questions. He wanted to know how I found the courage to follow my dream. He said he had a dream as well. I thought this was odd. He had to be following his dream since he was a high-level executive at a great company making huge sums of money. He share that he had a dream of being a college professor. I was reminded that God has given all of us a big dream, and success doesn't necessary bring peace and happiness. He was happy I was following my dream and became a financial donor as well.

Our dream always lies outside our comfort zone. We will have to leave what's comfortable in order to achieve our dream. Every dreamer has a choice to either feel comfort but give up the dream or feel fear and pursue it.

Pursuing the dream is always scary. Courage is not being unafraid but moving forward in spite of your fears. We have to sacrifice and make big changes in order to pursue our dream.

CHAPTER 54

DREAM OPPOSITION

There are always people discouraging us from pursuing our dreams. Sometimes it shakes up their world and reminds them of their own failures to see us pursue our dream. It may even be people we love. It could even be people who have our best interest in mind.

Not everyone was as excited about me pursuing my dream. My mom, in particular, thought I had lost my mind. She said, "Please don't tell people God is leading you because God would not have you leave your 'good job' and be broke." She insisted that this was a bad idea. She would not share with our family and friends my plans because she held out hopes that I would come to my senses and change my mind. She said, "Why would you leave a great career when you can make good money and retire with a pension?" She was persistent in telling me how this was wrong. I thought she would get over it after a few months, but she didn't.

One day, Carol had finally had enough of her being negative toward me following my dream and yelled back at her, "Listen, you are going to have to stop being negative or you will break his spirit."

I was so glad I had Carol's support. I would not have had the strength to continue if she had not supported me. As I look back on it now, I know that she provided support not because she felt it was right but because she knew it was something that I had to do. She had her own doubts, but I was so glad she didn't share them with me. I was on thin ice as it was. Any added doubts would have cracked the ice right beneath me.

So we continued this path not knowing exactly where it would take us.

CHAPTER 55

WHY IS IT TAKING SO LONG TO ACCOMPLISH MY DREAM?

A couple years into pursuing my dream, it seemed we had hit a dry season. We were just getting by. Money was always tight. Very few people bought books or wanted our help in becoming financially free. I thought my dream was just around the corner. We had been tested before, and now we were ready to serve God by helping His people. With few people wanting our help and financial resources constantly on the edge of running out, I became discouraged and disappointed. Maybe my mom was right. Maybe it was time to abandon my dream.

When we follow our dreams, inevitably we go through a long dry season that Bruce Wilkerson calls "the wasteland." We thought surely our dream was right around the corner, but it wasn't. We go through a long dry season where it seems our dream has almost died. It's during this desert land season that God prepares us for our dream.

It's important to stay connected to God as we pursue our dream. We can't forget that He is more important than the dream.

Fulfilling the Dream

My dream morphed and changed a lot through the years, and I believe it will continue to change. But today I'm doing what I could only dream about. I love what I do. Every day, I get to do what God has called and gifted me to do. It doesn't feel like work. Yes, I get tired and worn out, but I'm truly fulfilled by what I do. I'm good at it and am able to help a lot of people. I wish everyone could feel the peace that comes along with pursuing your God-given big dream.

Tragically, a whole lifetime can pass without a person ever accomplishing the great thing he or she was born to do and wants to do.

There are five misconceptions that keep us from pursuing our God-given dreams (Wilkerson, *The Dream Giver*, 77):

- I don't have a dream.
- I have to invent my dream.
- I have a dream, but it's not important.
- I have a dream, but it's up to God to make it happen.
- I had a dream, but it's too late.

Which one of these beliefs is keeping you from pursuing your dream?

The Truth about Your Big Dream

The truth is before you were born, God put a purpose in your heart. A big dream always seems overwhelming at first. Ultimately a big dream is aimed at meeting a big need in the world. While you still have breath, it's never too late to act on your dream.

Your purpose or dream is never about you. It's about helping to meet the needs of those around you. There is peace in the pursuit of your God-given dream. It will aggravate you until you pursue it.

Some people suppress it enough with mundane activities so much that they can barely recognize their dream. But deep down, it's still there. Occasionally something reminds us of our dream and we become irritated.

You can suppress it or try to fill it with other things but nothing will bring the peace you want. That itch can only be scratched by the pursuit of a God-given dream that's much bigger than yourself.

It's like putting a square peg in a round hole. It's only when you are in God's will that you will have true peace.

To figure out your God-given dream, ask yourself these questions:

- What have I always been good at?
- What needs do I care about the most?
- Whom do I admire most?
- What makes me feel most fulfilled?
- What do I love to do most?
- What have I felt called to do?
- Whom do I feel called to help?

CHAPTER 56

IS IT NECESSARY THAT I LEAVE MY JOB TO FOLLOW MY BIG DREAM?

You don't always have to leave your job to follow your dream. I know plenty of people who are following their big dreams who did not leave their jobs. Businessman Alan Barnhart shares how he felt called to ministry early in his career as an engineer in his small family-owned business. He and his wife felt a desire to help spread the gospel throughout the ten-forty window of the world where most nonbelievers in the world lived. His parents convinced them that he was a talented businessman who could be more helpful using his talents in business and earning resources to fund his dream. Alan did just that. He turned his small family business into a large, successful business. Revenues of Barnhart Corporation have increased into the hundreds of millions of dollars annually. Alan continues to lead the business but decided to give the company to a nonprofit foundation so that profits could go toward furthering God's work. Whether you remain in your current vocation or not, you have to determine how God can best use you to accomplish your big dream.

What If I Am Not in the Right Vocation?

If you are not currently in the right career field, you should begin making plans to move into the career that best fits your abilities and desires. However, *do not quit your job today*. You can begin the process for discovery and transformation without destroying your monthly budget. Even though your current job may not be the best career fit for you, it provides financial means that can help you transition into a long-term career that best meets your abilities and passions. Many resources can help you identify that best career fit. I recommend you read Tim LaHaye's *Why You Act the Way You Do* and Larry Burkett and Lee Ellis's *Finding the Career That Fits You*.

It is worth the time and effort to invest in finding the best career fit. Even as you begin the discovery process, you should continue working hard at your current job and be careful not to waste or misuse your current employer's resources. Do not spend time on the job planning your transitions. Remember, God placed you there for a purpose. He is expecting you to be faithful to Him in your work while watching for open doors. We have to trust God to open the right career doors at the right time.

Revelation 3:7 says, "What he opens no one can shut, and what he shuts no one can open."

LaHaye explains in *Why You Act the Way You Do*:

> We just need to stay in close fellowship with the Master, who does have a plan for our lives. So we should busy ourselves cleaning up the room we are now in and God will, in his own time, open another door for us. Once inside, we will find it too needs a lot of hard work, so we should busy ourselves cleaning up the second room. About the time we get that room cleaned up, there will be a third door open to us, then a fourth and so on. Finally, we will look back and say, "Hasn't God been faithful to lead us into so many places of opportunity to serve him?" But in the meantime we need to be found faithful, cleaning in the room we are in.

Small Group Questions

1. Read Colossians 3:22–25. Do you typically see your work as your ministry? Explain.

2. What can you do to make your work more effective for God?

3. Are you currently working in a position you are skilled at doing, are passionate about, and can earn a living?

4. If not, what kind of work can you do to earn a living that may be more suitable for your skills and passion?

5. What have you always been good at?

6. What needs do you care about the most?

7. Whom do you admire most?

8. What makes you feel most fulfilled?

9. Whom do you feel called to help?

10. Do you have a God-given big dream? Describe it.

11. Have you decided to pursue your big dream? Why or why not?

CHAPTER 57

BUILD A GENEROUS SPIRIT

Generosity is an overwhelming characteristic of God. John 3:16 says, "God loved the world so He *gave* His only Son." He is a giver. In fact, God is the most generous being ever. If we are to reflect His character to the world, then we have to build a generous spirit. There is no such thing as a stingy Christian. That would be an oxymoron.

During His walk on earth, Jesus showed that He was an unselfish giver. Giving allows us to take on more of His character. By giving, we are able not only to meet the needs of others but also to position ourselves to receive more blessings from God. Jesus promises this very thing while teaching His disciples in Luke 18:18–30:

> A certain ruler asked him, "Good teacher, what must I do to inherit eternal life?"
>
> "Why do you call me good?" Jesus answered. "No one is good—except God alone. You know the commandments: 'Do not commit adultery, do not murder, do not steal, do not give false testimony, honor your father and mother.'"
>
> "All these I have kept since I was a boy," he said.
>
> When Jesus heard this, he said to him, "You still lack one thing. Sell everything you have and give to the poor, and you will have treasure in heaven. Then come, follow me."

When he heard this, he became very sad, because he was a man of great wealth. Jesus looked at him and said, "How hard it is for the rich to enter the kingdom of God! Indeed, it is easier for a camel to go through the eye of a needle than for a rich man to enter the kingdom of God."

Those who heard this asked, "Who then can be saved?"

Jesus replied, "What is impossible with men is possible with God."

Peter said to him, "We have left all we had to follow you!"

"I tell you the truth," Jesus said to them. "No one who has left home or wife or brothers or parents or children for the sake of the kingdom of God will fail to receive many times as much in this age and, in the age to come, eternal life."

Jesus's words confirm that by being a cheerful giver, we will be rewarded both in heaven and while on earth.

God expects His people to be generous. Generosity is not as much about how much money we have. It's about the attitude of our hearts toward money. Generosity is a mind-set, an attitude, and a lifestyle. It releases blessing in our life and allows us to partner with God to significantly impact the lives of others.

Four Reasons Why People Don't Give

1. Poor stewardship

Stewardship and generosity are two sides of the same coin. You can't be generous without good stewardship.

2. Greed

Luke 12:13–21 says,

Someone in the crowd said to him, "Teacher, tell my brother to divide the inheritance with me."

Jesus replied, "Man, who appointed me a judge or an arbiter between you?" Then he said to them, "Watch out! Be on your guard against all kinds of greed; life does not consist in an abundance of possessions."

And he told them this parable: "The ground of a certain rich man yielded an abundant harvest. He thought to himself, 'What shall I do? I have no place to store my crops.'

"Then he said, 'This is what I'll do. I will tear down my barns and build bigger ones, and there I will store my surplus grain. And I'll say to myself, "You have plenty of grain laid up for many years. Take life easy; eat, drink, and be merry."'

"But God said to him, 'You fool! This very night your life will be demanded from you. Then who will get what you have prepared for yourself?'

"This is how it will be with whoever stores up things for themselves but is not rich toward God."

Jesus told this story to warn us to guard our hearts against greed. This is not to say that every wealthy person automatically falls into the trap of greed. We can't look at a person's wealth or poverty to determine his or her heart toward God. A person who is a billionaire who commits to living on only 10 percent of his or her income will still live a much more lavish lifestyle than any of us can imagine. His or her idea of modesty is very different from most people's. The key to this scripture is "without being rich toward God." There is nothing wrong with being wealthy, but when we accumulate wealth in order to have an easy life without being generous toward God, we have fallen into this trap. Wealth without generosity equals greed.

3. Spiritual immaturity

Growing closer to God and turning our finances over to God go hand in hand. When Christians understand biblical truths about money, they are more likely to become cheerful givers. Our giving is a direct indication of our spiritual maturity. The Bible says God loves a cheerful giver, but I think it also could be said that a cheerful giver loves God.

4. No experiences with the freedom that comes with generosity

Most of us in America live in abundance and are in a position to give. In fact, most of you reading this book have enough food in your house or money in your pocket right now to feed someone else in need. So if we have so much abundance, why don't we give more? I believe if more people only knew the joy that comes with giving that they would give more. Scripture tells us that it is more of a blessing to give than to receive. That sounds backward to most of us. Would you rather be a person who doesn't have enough to maintain your life to the point that you need to receive from others, or would you rather be the person who has more than enough and is in position to help someone else? Giving to someone else is so much more enjoyable.

Recently, Carol and I were on a trip out of town and staying at a hotel. I heard a knock on the door from the maid, but Carol was inside sleep. I asked for a couple towels and told her we didn't need maid service today. A short moment after I closed the door, I had a thought that I should give her a tip even if she didn't clean the room. I went and found the young lady going to the next room. I hadn't noticed that the young lady was pregnant. I handed her forty dollars cash I had in my pocket and thanked her for the towels. I'm not sure whether the money meant a lot to her or not, but it meant a lot to me. It felt good to show generosity. When I give, I get excited. I left that young lady and floated back to my room. I'm sure my feet never touched the ground. It's true. It is more of a blessing to give than it is to receive.

Why don't you try it for yourself? Go get a cup of coffee at Waffle House, and leave a hundred-dollar tip. Don't leave a track or invitation to your church. Just give and see how that makes you feel. I promise you; it will do as much for you as it does for the person you gave it to.

CHAPTER 58

HONOR GOD WITH OFFERINGS

One of the most often quoted scriptures in the Bible that deals with the subject of giving is Malachi 3:8. In fact, most of us have heard this verse so often that we know it by heart.

"Will a man rob God? Yet you have robbed Me! But you say, 'In what way have we robbed You?' In tithes and offerings."

This is one of the few scriptures that make me cringe when I hear it in church. I know that can't be good for a stewardship pastor. It's not because it's not true or I didn't believe it but because it's so often abused or misunderstood.

Somehow when most of us read this scripture, we miss what I think is the key word in this scripture. This scripture says we "rob" God in "tithes *and* offerings" (emphasis added). That word *and* is a conjunction, meaning both of these are important. This scripture is addressing both tithes and offerings.

Both tithes and offerings bring honor to God because both represent what God did for us through Jesus Christ.

Christ was both a tithe and an offering. When God considered how He would restore His people, He chose to send His best. He never considered sending someone else. He didn't say, "Why don't I send an angel like Gabriel or Michael?" No. He didn't hesitate to send His best. He sent His son Jesus as a tithe. Jesus also served as God's offering as He willingly sacrificed His life for our sins on the cross.

Tithing is not generosity. It's only when we give offerings that we begin a lifestyle of generosity.

What Is an Offering?

So what's the difference between a tithe and an offering? Remember, a tithe is bringing the first tenth of my income to God through my local church.

The offering is symbolic of the sacrifice of Jesus Christ. The animals used in biblical offerings had to be "without defect" to be acceptable to God (Leviticus 1:3). In the same way, Jesus was "a lamb without blemish or defect" (1 Peter 1:19), an acceptable gift for our sins.

The Bible uses the words *offering* and *sacrifice* interchangeably. An offering is something that we give or sacrifice by choice. An offering is anything I give in addition to my tithe. Where a tithe amount was determined for us, the amount of an offering is determined by the giver.

So many Christians don't understand the word *offering*. It's not a word that we use often in everyday life. A member told me once, "Well, I can't tithe, but I can give an offering." Since an offering is anything I give in addition to my tithe, it's impossible to give an offering without also giving a tithe. Therefore, if we are not at least tithing, we are, by default, robbing God of offerings as well. For example, if you had $120 in your purse and a person stole $100 out of your purse but left a twenty, you would not say that person offered me $20. No that person robbed you of $100.

I think the most important word and most overlooked word of Malachi 3:8 is the word *offering*. The offering gets to the heart of building a generous spirit.

The term *offering* wasn't such a big deal to me either until one day I read a scripture that made me struggle with this thought. It may help you to struggle with it too.

"Just as there were many who were appalled at him—his appearance was so disfigured beyond that of any human being and his form marred beyond human likeness" (Isaiah 52:14).

Isaiah is prophesying about Jesus's crucifixion. Most of us have this image of Jesus quietly suffering on the cross, but this paints a different picture.

The truth is that Jesus was beaten so badly He did not look like a human being.

I couldn't believe what I was reading and asked myself, "How does this even happen?" As I continued to study, this is what I found out.

- He was beaten by the high priest (Matthew 26:68).
- Pilate's soldiers beat him with a staff on the head again and again (Matthew 27:30).
- Then Jesus was flogged (Mark 15:15).

In the Roman Empire, flogging was often used as a prelude to crucifixion. They used whips with small pieces of metal or bone at the tips to cause disfigurement and serious trauma. The skilled floggers would rip pieces of flesh from the body or cause the loss of an eye. These floggers were likely the best.

According to Jewish law, the punishment couldn't exceed thirty-nine lashes, but these were Roman soldiers who didn't abide by Jewish law. Jesus was beaten and disfigured to the point where they couldn't even tell if he was a human—eyes closed, flesh and hair ripped from his skin. Then, He was nailed to a cross that He couldn't even carry because of the heavy weight.

I was okay when I had this picture of Jesus quietly suffering on the cross, but this image messed me up. "Disfigured beyond human likeness." Yet the worst part was not the physical pain. The worst part was that for the first time, He felt separated from God.

When He took on my sin, for the first time in His existence, He felt what we feel when we sin. He felt separated from God. That's what sin does. He felt the isolation, loneliness, depression, guilt, shame, and everything else that comes along with feeling separated from God. He had never experienced this before. Jesus cried out, "My God, my God, why have you forsaken me?" (Matthew 27:46).

The only thing that kept Him on that cross is that He looked out in the future and saw my face. He loved me so much He couldn't stand to live without me.

See, the difference in the tithe and the offering is that the offering is a choice. We don't get to choose our tithe. It belongs to God. But the offering is ours to choose.

Jesus chose to give Himself as an offering. He chose to die for my sins, so I could live with Him forever in heaven.

He agonized over the decision the night before. He prayed to God, asking if there was some other way, but ultimately He said, "Not my will but Your will be done." Sacrifice is always a choice. I will never understand why He made that choice for me and why He loved me so much. But He did. He did this for me.

Scripture says we should give in proportion to the way God has blessed us (Deuteronomy 16:17). I don't know how to respond to that kind of love. I do know one thing: I can't read or hear this scripture ever again without seeing this image of Christ. It's the offering that stands out to me.

I'm not sharing this to condemn you. Condemnation doesn't come from God. That's the trick of the enemy. I'm sharing this with you to let you know how much Jesus loves you.

Isaiah foretold what Jesus would do for us that day on the cross in Isaiah 53:5:

But he was pierced for our transgressions,
he was crushed for our iniquities;
the punishment that brought us peace was on him,
and by his wounds we are healed.

How do I respond to what Jesus did for me? There is no way I can. But because of His love, I'm committed to honoring Him with a life of sacrifice. I'm committed to putting Him first in my finances, and I'm committed to honoring God with not only my tithes and offerings but my entire life. Generosity is a natural response to God's grace. What I give to God financially is just a down payment to let Him know that I am all in.

CHAPTER 59

HOW MUCH IS ENOUGH?

Recently, I attended the annual generosity celebration sponsored by the Hope Christian Community Foundation. During the celebration, David shared his testimony of how he and his wife decided that they would live on $5,000 a month and anything above that they would give it to God. David shared how the first month he received the largest commission check that he had ever received—in the amount of $75,000. Although it was a challenge, he and his wife kept their commitment and gave $70,000 as an offering to God.

I would have broken my neck backpedaling out of that commitment to God. "Did I say I would start this month? I really meant next month." I have heard his testimony before, but it never stops challenging me to want to give at a higher level of generosity. David's commitment does not make sense in man's economy. In man's economy, people are always struggling with "How much of my money should I give?" Carol and I spoke at a marriage retreat, and one of the husbands asked, "Do we *have* to tithe off the gross?" I could tell from his tone that the thought of giving all that money to God troubled him deeply. I have seen this look all too often. This is a constant battle because every dollar given away is a dollar not spent on what's really important ... me.

I love how David's testimony has nothing to do with tithing. That would have been the easy part. Cut God a check for $7,500, and I keep $67,500 for me. That's a sweet deal. Instead, David's commitment was to living a generous life.

Many of us believe that we do not have enough to even think of being generous, but 80 percent of the world is likely praying for what you have right now. When our focus is on this world, we will never have enough stuff or money. Remember when you were not working and your prayer was just to get a job. Then, you prayed for a $50,000 job, and when you got it, your spending went up to $50,000. Then you prayed for $100,000, and your spending went up to $100,000 or more (oh yeah, can't forget those credit cards). In man's economy, regardless of what we make, we just need a little more. Ecclesiastes 5:10 says, "He who loves money will not be satisfied with money, nor he who loves abundance with its income. This too is vanity."

For those who operate in God's economy, the question is very different. Instead of asking how much to give, the question is "How much of God's money is enough for me to live on?" Having this perspective keeps us from getting caught up in materialism. Our goal as Christians is to be known for our generosity. When we are generous, we honor God and reflect His character. God is the most generous giver ever. John 3:16 says, "For God so loved the world that he *gave* (emphasis added) his one and only Son." It is only because He was generous that we are able to give to others. Generosity is not just for those we consider to be wealthy but for all Christians. As we commit to God's economy, we stop comparing our standard of living to others and ask as David and his wife, "How much is enough?"

CHAPTER 60

THREE LEVELS OF GIVING

For Christians, there are three levels of giving to God. Let me give them to you, and then I will explain and give you a benefit for reaching each level.

1. What I should give
2. What I could give
3. What I would give

The first level is the *should* level — the tithe. As Christians, we are required to tithe. This is what we should do. It isn't an option for us. God commands it. Jesus spoke of it as an easy baby step for Christians. It's only 10 percent. Many people who intend to tithe and think they are actually aren't. I was counseling a couple recently who said they were committed to tithing, but when we looked at their finances, they had earned $130,000 but had given $8,000. Sadly, few people get to this first level and can never get a glimpse of the joy, fun, and blessings available at the higher levels. The benefit of getting to this first level is tithing removes the curse and opens the windows of heaven over your life.

The second level is the *could* level. At this level, we begin to give an offering to God. An offering is anything I give above my tithe. Most people who get to the first level usually move on to the second level if they are invited to give more and share a compelling vision.

At this level, we look at our budget with a different set of eyes and think, *If I change this area, I could give more.* I remember when I was first introduced to this level. One of our pastors asked me to become a vision partner at my church, which meant that I would give an additional $2,000 above my tithes toward the vision offering at my church. I thought to myself, *Two thousand dollars is a lot of money.* But I knew that if we tweaked this and that, we could do it. The benefit of giving at the *could* level is that the offering is where the blessing is. Tithing removes the curse, but giving an offering brings the blessings and moves us closer to God. Jesus said, "Where your treasure is your heart will be also."

If you are not currently giving above your tithe, I would encourage you to step into the could level by starting to give significantly above your tithes toward your church's vision this year. This will bring blessings to your life and allow you to partner with God to impact the lives of others through your church.

Giving at this level is a sacrifice, but it really still doesn't require faith. We are just moving things around or deciding not to do something in order to give more.

The third level is the *would* level. Few people actually reach the third level of giving. This is a level of extravagant giving. At this level, we ask ourselves, "What would I give as an extravagant gift to God?" Pastor David Griggs describes this as a gift that makes you sweat.

The key to giving extravagantly is that you have to make a decision before you get the money in your hands. Once you see the money, it's too late. There was a lady in the Bible who gave Jesus her last two pennies. I'm sure she made her mind up ahead of time. She probably thought, *If I ever see Jesus, I'm going to give Him all I have.* It doesn't matter how big or small the gift is.

The *would* level gift is symbolic of being all in with God. The benefit of giving at this level is that now we become men and women God can trust. Jesus said, in Luke 16:11, "If I can't trust you with money, how can I trust you with true riches?" When we give at the would level, then Jesus knows He can trust us with whatever. He says, "When you remain in me and my word remains in you, ask me anything and I will give it to you" (John 15:4–16).

Vision Partners

Every fall at our church, our lead pastors communicate our church's vision for the next twelve months and provide an opportunity for all members to make financial commitments over and above their normal tithes toward achieving the strategic areas of our church's vision.

Those who commit to give significantly toward the vision offering we call "vision partners." Vision partners are the people in our church who are engaged in our vision. Engaged people don't just show up. They sacrifice things that are important to them. When you are engaged, your lifestyle is impacted. As vision partners, we get to partner with God on the greatest cause ever. We sacrifice our talents, time, and money because we realize if we are going to impact our community for God, then it's up to us. It's an honor to partner together to see lives forever changed. Consistent, faithful giving always makes a significant difference.

Miraculously, every year our vison partners commit to a significant vision offering at our church. The miracle is not that God provides the money. The miracle is that God changes the hearts of His people so that they release the influence money has over their lives.

My goal is not to put pressure on you to give. But I have to be open and honest with you. My hope is that you will choose to become vision partners. It's not just for your church; it's for you. I'm praying that God will do a miracle in your heart and free you from the love of money and things. I want you to experience the peace and freedom that comes when you are giving your whole life as an offering and sacrifice to God.

CHAPTER 61

DOES THE AMOUNT MATTER?

A question I get often is, "Does the amount I give really matter?"

There is a story in the Bible that shines some light on this question. It is the story of two brothers, Cain and Abel. The brothers each brought a gift to God. But one gift was viewed as acceptable while the other gift was not. Why was one accepted by God and the other not?

Acceptable gifts are amounts that matter. When the gift matters to us, then it matters to God. If it doesn't matter to us, then it doesn't matter to God.

A friend shared this story of John. He was a twenty-six-year-old software engineer, making $85,000 a year. He made maximum contributions to his 401(k), enjoyed a $1,500-per-month apartment downtown, and drove a new SUV with the special edition sport package so he could haul his toys around. John was excited about beginning his new life with Amy, his soon-to-be bride. When she saw the black velvet-covered box, it took her breath away. But when she opened it, her reaction changed. She tried not to seem disappointed, but when she found out John had only spent $250 on the ring, she was devastated. It was not that she was materialistic, but she cried and asked if he really loved her. John responded, "The amount of the ring doesn't matter anyway. After all, it's the heart that counts" (Anderson, *Plastic Donuts*, 27–28).

A lot of Christians have this same opinion: "The amount doesn't matter … God knows my heart." While the heart is crucial, the amount does matter. In fact, it's the amount that engages the heart.

Jesus said, "Where your treasure is your heart will be also" (Matthew 6:21). Wherever we spend money, our hearts have to follow.

We all have amounts that matter to us, whether it's our home mortgage, car payments, and so on. Because these amounts matter to us, we are diligent to set aside the money for these items.

Our giving to God should be no different. We should give gifts to God that cost us something and that we value. This will require us to live counterculture and have a Christ-centered eternal perspective.

When a man wanted to give King David what he needed to give an offering to God, David replied, "No, I insist on paying you for it. I will not sacrifice to the LORD my God offerings that cost me nothing" (2 Samuel 24:24). An offering always causes us to sacrifice something we value. We sacrifice something we value for something we value more.

God accepts our gifts when we give gifts that matter to us. When we sacrifice things of this world to invest in things that matter to Him, scripture says, "It is like a pleasing aroma to God" (Exodus 29:18). If it matters to us, then it matters to God. If it doesn't matter to us, then it will not matter to God.

My challenge to you is to think about what amounts really matter to you. Make a list of the top three expenses you have that matter to you.

What do you spend money on?	Monthly $ Amount	Annual $ Amount
Example — Mortgage	$1,600	$19,200
1.		
2.		
3.		

Now make a list of your giving to funding kingdom building.

What do you give to?	Monthly $ Amount	Annual $ Amount
Example — My Church	$1,000	$12,000

How does this amount compare to the top three amounts that matter to you most?

Carol and I committed several years ago to giving 10 percent of our gross income to our local church as our standard of giving. As we grew in our understanding of generosity, we set a goal to increase our giving beyond just tithing by 1 percent a year. Today, we give about 15 percent of our gross income. It's still not where we would like to be. We battle the same things as everyone else. We try to balance our lifestyles while being good stewards and savers. We have our two older kids in college and the two younger ones not far behind them. Building a generous spirit requires us to resist the temptations of this world. It doesn't mean we avoid all pleasures in life, but we realize that it is hard to resemble everyone around us and be generous as well.

I believe you should prayerfully seek God's will about your level of giving. What would your giving to God look like if it mattered more than anything else you do or have? Take time to ask yourself, "What could I give financially to God that is a stretch of my faith?" Write the amount down, and commit to begin fulfilling that financial gift immediately. Whatever that amount is, ask God to help you be obedient to fulfill the level of giving you desire.

Small Group Questions

1. Read Proverbs 11:24–25, Matthew 20, Luke 12:34, and 1 Timothy 6:18–19. What are some benefits of generosity?

2. What truths have you learned about generosity that have impacted you most? In what way have they impacted you?

3. What do these scriptures communicate to you about lifestyle?
   a. Mark 8:36–37

   b. Acts 4:32–37

   c. I Thessalonians 4:11–12

4. Read Psalm 39:4–6 and Psalm 103:13–16.
   a. In your own words, contrast the brevity of life on earth with eternity.

   b. How does this impact the way you invest your time and money?

5. Read 2 Corinthians 5:6–10. How does knowing we will all go before God and account for what we have done make you feel?

6. How would you handle winning a $100-million lottery? How does that compare to how you handle money today?

7. If a stranger picked up your monthly bank statement, what would he or she say matters most to you?
   a. Explain.

   b. Does this reflect what you would like to have as your priorities?

8. As you reflect on eternity, answer these questions thoughtfully.
   a. What do I wish to be remembered for?

   b. What can I do during my lifetime that would contribute most significantly to the cause of Christ?

    c. In light of these answers, what actions or changes do I need to make now?

9. What adjustments in your life can you make to have your giving matter more to you and to God?

PART 6

AM I WINNING?

CHAPTER 62

TIME MANAGEMENT

Being a good time manager is vital to having a peaceful life. The one thing none of us can get more of is time. We can earn more money, but we all get only twenty-four hours each day or 168 each week. If we don't manage our time, then others will manage it for us. There will always be more requests or demands than we have time for. We have to be proactive about determining how we will best use our time.

Think back to the five-tier fountain and consider how your 168 weekly hours are currently spent in each tier. List this time in the first column. Then consider how your time would be spent if you were intentional about using your time in order to have a winning life. Write these target times in the second column. Finally, what changes have to take place in order to make the target times a reality in your life? For instance, you may have to delegate more at work in order to reduce the amount of time you spend at work or you may have to watch less TV in order to make time for exercise. List these changes in the third column in the following table.

Tier	Example	Current	Target	Changes
God/Church	10			
Relationships (family, household responsibilities, friends)	34			
Health				
Sleep	49			
Exercise	4			
Relaxation/ Personal time/ Sabbath	16			
Finances (earning and managing money)	50			
Purpose (preparing for and fulfilling a God-given purpose)	5			
Total Hours	168			

Have Margin in Your Time

Earlier in the book, I wrote on the importance of living with a margin when it comes to money. It's just as important to live with a margin when it comes to our time. I purposely don't schedule every minute of the day. I say no to most of the ways I can use my time in order to maintain a time margin in my life. I never know when God's going to bring a person into my life for me to help or to learn from. Having every minute allocated in my life could prevent me from doing something very significant. Saying no to something good could help me to say yes to something great.

Each week, I plan out my calendar by putting in the big items that are important to me, such as a date with my wife, Sabbath day with God, daily Bible time, time with the kids, and key work meetings or events. The majority of my time isn't booked. That positions me to meet my weekly goals while having the flexibility to adjust as needed. I aim to get as many of my goals done as early in the week as possible. The important thing to remember is that, just like money, you have to manage time in order not to waste it away.

CHAPTER 63

GOAL SETTING

Goal setting is another vital component to living the life God wants for you. When we set and commit to appropriate goals, we naturally stay focused on and energized about what's important.

In the five-tier water fountain example, each tier represents an area in which God wants to provide peace in your life. The flowing water represents the spirit of God.

"Now the Lord is the Spirit, and where the Spirit of the Lord is, there is freedom" (2 Corinthians 3:17).

So the question we must ask is, "How do I get more of God's Spirit in that area of my life?"

Below are four steps to setting and committing to goals that will lead you to the life of joy, peace, and freedom that God has for you.

Four Steps for Goal Setting

Step 1 — Self-Assessment

Go back to the peace self-assessment you completed in chapter 1. Make any necessary changes to your original assessment. Remember it's vital that you are totally honest. This assessment is only for you and those with whom you choose to share it.

Step 2 — Set SMART Goals

Now that you have completed your assessment, it's time to set some goals. Choose your goal topics from the "no" answers in the self-assessment. Set some SMART goals.

S = Specific

M = Measurable

A = Attainable/Achievable

R = Relevant

T = Time Bound

Specific

A specific goal has a much greater chance of being accomplished than a general goal. Provide enough detail so that there is no indecision as to what exactly you should be doing. An example of a general goal would be, "Eat more *fruits and vegetables*." But a specific goal would say, "Eat nine servings of *fruits and vegetables each day*."

Measurable

Choose a goal with measurable progress, so you can assess success or failure.

Attainable/Achievable

An attainable goal has an outcome that you can realistically achieve. All of us have goals that are God goals, which only He can do. But in your goal-setting process, set goals that you can do and you have control over. Ask, "Is this in my control to achieve?" Start small. Ask yourself, "Is this a realistic goal for me at this time?" You can always gradually increase the goal over time.

Relevant

You can't work on everything. Seven goals are enough. Make sure your goals cover each of the five key areas of your life. Start on the biggest issues first. It doesn't make sense to spend time thinking about your big dream if your marriage is falling apart or you don't have a relationship with God. Be sure that your goals address the most relevant issues in your life. By the way, I always have "Read the Bible daily" as a goal for every man I mentor. There is no substitution for spending time with God daily.

Time Bound

Set a time frame for the goal. Break your goal into weekly increments, for example, "Take my wife out on a date once a week."

Step 3 — Track Your Results Weekly

I know many people do not like to track results, but we have to have a plan to in order to meet our objectives. All of us will end up somewhere in life, but when we set goals and track our progress, we are more likely to end up somewhere close to our target. When we don't track our goals, we tend to end up somewhere far away from where we intended to go.

Every year, many of us start off with New Year's resolutions or goals only to find that we didn't stick with them more than a few months. One of the reasons why is that we didn't really have a good plan. A good plan includes having a way to track our progress.

One of my mentors helped me by suggesting I divide the year into four thirteen-week quarters and then track my results weekly. This helped me to just stay focused on having successful weeks.

Below is an example of my weekly goals. I know this level of detail may be overwhelming for most. Your goal-tracking tool does not have to be as detailed, but you have to track your goals weekly in order to stay focused on what's important.

Example

Travis Moody	pts	Goal	M	T	W	T	F	S	S	Actual		96%
Read Bible and pray for family daily	0.3	7	1	1	1	1	1	1	1	7	100%	0.30
Spend time weekly w/ Carol, Erica (via phone), TJ, Donovan, Gilana, Mom	0.25	6	1	1	3	1		1	1	6	100%	0.25
Spend at least 5 hrs. weekly working on new book	0.05	300	60	30	60		70	80		300	100%	0.05
Workout Aerobic/ weights at 124–144 heart rate for 150 min/week	0.1	150	45	30	30		30		30	150	100%	0.10
Eat less than 2600 calories daily	0.1	7	1		1	1	1			4	57%	0.06
Save $200/ week	0.15	200				200			200	100%	0.15
Meet with at least 2 members/ weekly outside of church	0.05	2			1		1			2	100%	0.05

I created this tool for me and my mentees in order to track our progress weekly. We are not expecting to be at 100 percent every week but at least maintain weekly results above 85 percent. That way, we at least maintain a B week if not an A week.

One of the benefits I enjoy from tracking my goals weekly is that when I have a bad week, it's not the end of the world. I can just start over the next week. I may not win every week, but if I can keep winning most of the weeks, I keep moving closer to my goals.

Just like in sports, stringing together winning weeks leads to winning quarters, which eventually lead to winning years. The goal is not perfection but progress. I know if I continue making progress each week, then I will win at living an overall healthy life.

Step 4: Ask for Accountability

Share your plan with a spiritually mature person you trust and ask him or her to hold you accountable.

"The way of fools seems right to them, but the wise listen to advice" (Proverbs 12:15).

If you would like our help with goal tracking and accountability, you can contact us for access to our online resources at thelomahgroup.com.

CHAPTER 64

GOD CARES ABOUT YOUR GOALS

In January 2013, I wrote my goals on an index card. On one side, I listed ten goals for 2013. I called these God's part. These were things I was hoping for but realized that God is in control of.

God's Part:

- $20,000 in emergency savings
- weight under 260 pounds
- family vacation
- new kitchen appliances
- Erica's restoration to God
- no student loans
- vision offering $5,000
- complete writing of new book
- read Old Testament
- four hundred vision partners

On the back of the index card, I wrote my weekly goals and called this "my part."

My Part:

- read Bible and pray daily
- fast and pray for Erica's restoration one day a week
- meet with at least two vision partners or potential vision partners weekly

- stick to my personal miscellaneous budget of $100 per week
- exercise at least 150 minutes per week
- eat a balanced diet of less than 2,600 calories daily and limit sweets to one day a week
- spend individual time with each family member weekly
- windfalls (plan for extra money)
  - 25 percent giving vision offering
  - 25 percent fun (vacations and home decor)
  - 25 percent emergency savings
  - 25 percent college funding

In April 2014, my friend William came over to install our new dishwasher. It was the last of the new kitchen appliances to be replaced in our home. We had slowly replaced appliances as they wore out. First went the microwave. It just stopped working. Then the washer and dryer went unexpectedly. A year later, my daughter and I were watching TV when we smelled smoke coming from the kitchen. We found the refrigerator having an electrical fire. I called Carol on the phone as she was leaving church and said, "Meet me at the appliance store. I will tell you more when we get there." We replaced the refrigerator. Later, we had enough money to replace the garbage disposal and oven, and the final piece on this day was the dishwasher.

William had been one of the men in my accountability group in 2013. When he finished the installation, I pulled out my index card and gave him the privilege of checking off the fourth item on my goal list. This felt like a big milestone for me. It felt good to meet one of my big goals. It also built my confidence that God cared about my goals and that He would grant the other big goals. I was excited about which goal would be achieved next. I specifically thought about my prayer for my oldest daughter, Erica, to have a relationship with God. I'm convinced more than ever that if I continue to do my part, God will do His part. If He cares enough to give us new appliances, then surely He cares enough to restore my baby girl.

CHAPTER 65

THE COUNTERFEIT PEACE

The enemy offers counterfeits for each of these five tiers of peace. He wants to distract you by having you chasing the outcome — chasing the perfect man or woman, the ideal weight, the dream house, the dream job, and so on. He knows that chasing these things keeps you away from the true purpose God has for you.

God wants us to succeed, but in order to succeed, we have to do our part. It's not changes in our situation that bring success but rather changes in our behaviors.

If we want success in our health, we have to eat better, exercise regularly, and get proper rest. We can't continue the same old behaviors and hope God will bless us. If we want success, we have to commit to behaviors that will bring it.

Carol and I received peace in our finances when we started following God's financial principles. We committed to tithing, committed no new debt, started saving, and followed a written budget. This is when we experienced the peace of God. We still were very much in debt for over $100,000, but our behaviors had changed. Since we had turned our financial behaviors over to God, we had financial peace.

Our behaviors led to our success. We have helped many people over the years overcome their financial debt challenges. But just as many start the process and never finish. We find that once some people get a little breathing room and their finances aren't that bad, they slack up and never finish the process. They started out hungry for financial freedom, but their appetite went away.

CHAPTER 66

YOU HAVE TO WANT SUCCESS

There is an old African proverb that goes like this. A man went to a wise old sage in his village and asked, "What is the key to success?" The wise sage took him by the hand and led him into the water. They went into the water, and the water was over his waist. They continued in the water until finally the water was over his head. The wise sage waited with the man in the water until finally the man couldn't breathe anymore. The man jumped out of the water and yelled at the sage, "You crazy old fool. I would have died if I had stayed any longer."

The sage responded, "When you want success as much as you wanted to breathe then you will have found the secret" (Kimbro, *Think and Grow Rich*, 74–75).

We have to stay hungry. The only people who ever get truly freed from their debts or whatever is holding them back are those who get mad at it. You can't be friends with debt, sickness, bad relationships, or whatever is holding you back. You have to get mad at it and kick it out of your life. You have to get hungry for change in your life. I find that the things I'm hungry for are the things I focus on. You have to get and stay hungry for the life God has for you. Be hungry for your ...

- understanding of God
- happy family
- good health

- financial freedom
- purpose
- church to accomplish its vision
- discipleship
- big dream
- success

CHAPTER 67

DAVE B. NATTO

But what if you never accomplish the success you are seeking? It's possible that we can follow all of God's financial principles and never become wealthy. We can exercise and eat right and never get to what we think is our ideal weight. What happens when you do everything right and you still don't achieve the success you were hoping for?

I heard a friend make the comment: "Not attached to the outcome." He used the acronym NATTO. He was saying we can't be attached to the results. We have to leave the outcome up to God. I agreed with his thoughts, but I felt something was missing. We have to let God do His part and trust Him to work things out. But as I thought more about it, I realized we have a part to play as well. Our part is exhibiting the right behaviors.

I gave this part an acronym as well, and now our success strategy has a name: DAVE B. NATTO—Diligent about Vision Execution but Not Attached to the Outcome.

Diligence is a commitment to work hard fueled by a drive to succeed. Diligence means putting our heart into it and working hard. It requires dedication of our time and resources to completing a task.

We have to do our part in order to expect God to do His part. We can't expect God to bless us when we haven't been diligent. God wants us to have some skin in the game. Oftentimes, He is waiting for us to do our part. He won't violate His principles.

"Do not be deceived: God cannot be mocked. A man reaps what he sows" (Galatians 6:7).

We have to really want success and be diligent about pursuing it while trusting God for the results. When we do both our part and trust God to do His part, then we have success.

There is a story in the Bible about when three Hebrew boys were told to bow down to the king's statute or else they would be thrown into a fiery furnace to die. The boys refused to bow down to anyone other than God and responded, "If we are thrown into the blazing furnace, the God we serve is able to deliver us from it, and he will deliver us from Your Majesty's hand. But even if he does not, we want you to know, Your Majesty, that we will not serve your gods or worship the image of gold you have set up" (Daniel 3:17–18).

These boys were diligent about executing the vision God had given them, and they were not attached to the outcome. Don't get me wrong; they didn't want to die, and they prayed for that earnestly. They believed that God would answer their prayer, but they didn't put their success in the outcome. Their success was in their behavior.

My wife and I have a single female friend whom we both love dearly. She wants to get married, but it hasn't happened for her. She has done everything right. She keeps herself looking good and her body in good physical shape. She maintains a great personality and attitude. She loves God and serves her church. She is a very loving and giving person. She has a great job and manages finances well. Yet she hasn't met the right man for marriage to this point. We pray along with her for God to bring her the right man in her life and believe it will happen.

We have to have that same kind of faith and trust in God. Even if I don't become rich, I will follow God. Even if I don't find the husband or wife I desire, I will trust God because I know He is able. God honors this type of faith.

We all know how the story turned out. The king threw the three boys into the fire, but they were not burned. In fact, they were untouched. The king noticed that there appeared to be a fourth person in the fire with them. When we do our part and trust God to do His part, He is sure to take care of us. God was right there with them in the fire. Their success was not in avoiding the fire; their success was in their God-honoring behaviors. Success is not an outcome. It's in the behavior. God wants to do the same thing for us. He wants to give us success, but we have to have the same attitude as these three boys. They exuded an attitude that said, "I know God can give me success, but even if God doesn't answer my prayer, I will trust Him anyway."

Diligence should be apparent in your life. Others should see it.

The following questions can help determine how diligent you are:

- What would others say are the defining characteristics of your life?
- What cause would others say you dedicate your time and resources to?
- My life makes a difference for the kingdom of God because of _____?

You may survive without diligence, but you will not live the life of significance that God has for you without diligence.

Be DAVE B. NATTO. Be diligent about vision execution but not attached to the outcome.

CHAPTER 68

LIFE AS A FOOTBALL GAME

First Quarter: Birth to Twenty-Two Years Old

It's important to get off to a good start. Do what you have to do so later you can do what you want to do. If you spend the first quarter doing whatever feels good, you will suffer in the second half. Good decisions in the first quarter give you a huge advantage in the second half. Commit to doing your best in school, stay away from the bad things, and choose the right relationships. You are making some of the most important decisions at a time when you have the least knowledge, preparation, and experience. It's important in the first half to have a good coach on the side line and to listen to what your coach is telling you. He or she has been there before and can help you by calling winning plays.

Second Quarter: Twenty-Three to Forty-Four Years Old

The second quarter continues to be important. If you made good decisions in the first quarter, the second quarter continues to be smooth. Your capacity expands in the second quarter, but your team expands. This is when you have a spouse and kids and your life becomes about building a successful team. You work harder in this quarter than at any other point in your life. It's important to make smart decisions during this time. You have more things, but you also have more responsibilities. These are your best years. Don't waste them by just trying to merely get through them. Enjoy the quarter. Enjoy the hard work and the struggles with your teammates. If not, you will look back at these times and think, *How did I not enjoy every minute of the second quarter?*

Half-Time

This is a time in your life when you look over the first half and contemplate what needs to happen so that you win the game of life. The first half is behind you. What adjustments do you need to make to win the game?

Third Quarter: Forty-Five to Sixty-Six Years Old

This quarter, you will enjoy the most, especially if you made good decisions in the first half. You finally start to see some of the benefits of the good decisions you made in the first quarter. You have more time, money, and wisdom. This is the quarter where you start to do the things you love and are actually good at doing. While before you relied on the coach for direction, now others are looking to you for direction. This will be your most productive quarter. Be aggressive. You begin to understand that you are more than your occupation. You start to see what winning in the game of life really means. Full steam ahead.

Fourth Quarter: Sixty-Seven to Eighty-Eight Years Old

You are in the final quarter of life. You continue to have life and purpose. There is no such thing as retirement in the Bible. Sure, your work changes, but you still have a lot of life and purpose. This is the quarter where you start to think about your legacy. Winning the game is not just about you; it's about helping others win as well. If you have made good decisions in previous quarters, then in this quarter, you are not concerned about your existence. Your focus is on how you can leave a legacy for others behind you. Enjoy your life, family, health, financial freedom, and purpose. You deserve it.

Overtime: Eighty-Nine Years Old and Beyond

Enjoy each day. Every day for you has purpose. Others need to know your life story—both your successes and failures. You continue to battle as the Bible says Caleb did in his old age (Joshua 14:10–12). You will leave an inheritance for your children's children.

CHAPTER 69

DID I WIN THIS WEEK?

Regardless of where you are currently in life, it's never too late to make adjustments in order to win in life. It's too big a task to try to have a good life or a good ten years. You have to just focus on having a good week and let the months and years take care of themselves. At the end of each week, I ask myself these five questions to determine whether I had a winning week.

1. Did I spend time with God?
2. Did I spend time with my loved ones?
3. Did I invest in my physical, mental, and emotional health?
4. Did I spend less than I earned and wisely invest the difference?
5. Did I do something meaningful to benefit someone other than myself and my family?

You may not get everything done that you had hoped you would, but if at the end of the week, you can answer yes to these five questions, then you had a winning week. Consistently having winning weeks turns into having winning months and years, and before you know it, you will have a great life of significance. Along the way, you will find the peace your heart has been seeking. More importantly, you will receive the ultimate peace when you stand before your Father and He says to you, "Well done, My good and faithful servant! [You Won]. You have been faithful with a few things; I will put you in charge of many things. Come and share your master's happiness!"

My prayer for you is that you will be encouraged to put into practice what you have learned in this book and that it will richly bless your life. I also hope that you will share a copy of this book with others and help them to win each week and live a life full of God's peace as well. Thank you for supporting my big dream!

Small Group Questions

1. What outcomes are you hoping God will produce in your life?

2. What do feel is your part in making those outcomes a reality in your life?

3. After taking the peace assessment, on which tier do you feel you are lacking God's power the most? How do you get more of God's influence in that area of your life?

4. What are your seven SMART goals?

5. Are you good at managing time? If not, what is your largest time management issue?

6. What cause would others say you dedicate your time and resources to?

7. At the end of your life, what will determine whether you had a great life?

8. Did you win this week?

    a. Did you spend time with God?

    b. Did you spend time with your loved ones?

    c. Did you invest in your physical, mental, and emotional health?

    d. Did you spend less than you earned and wisely invest the difference?

    e. Did you do something meaningful to benefit someone other than yourself and your family?

9. What can you do to have a better week next week?

BIBLIOGRAPHY

American Heart Association. "American Heart Association Recommendations for Physical Activity in Adults." Accessed May 2014. www.heart.org.

Anderson, Jeff. *Plastic Donuts*. Acceptable Gift Inc., 2012.

Bach, David. *The Automatic Millionaire*. New York: Broadway Books, 2004.

Centers for Disease Control and Prevention. "How Much Sleep Do I Need?" CDC.gov. Accessed August 29, 2014. http://www.cdc.gov/sleep/about_sleep/how_much_sleep.htm.

Chen, Tim. "American Household Credit Card Debt Statistics: 2015." Nerdwallet.com. Accessed October 23, 2015. Coleman, Robert. *The Master Plan of Evangelism*. Grand Rapids, MI: Revell, 1993.

Collins, Jim. *Good to Great*. New York: HarperCollins, 2001.

Dayton, Howard. *Your Money Counts*. Wheaton, IL: Tyndale House, 1997.

Dupree, Janet Rae. "Can You Become a Creature of Habit?" *New York Times*, May 4, 2008.

Eggerichs, Dr. Emerson. *Love & Respect*. Nashville, TN: Thomas Nelson, 2004.

Exley, Richard. *The Making of a Man*. Tulsa, OK: Honor Books, 1993.

Forbes. "What Not to Wear to Work." Accessed July 2009. http://www.forbes.com/2009/07/22/office-fashion-sexy-forbes-woman-style-clothes.html.

Henley, Daniel. *Every Woman, Every Man*. Cordova, TN: Double-Edged Publishing, 2010.

Hogan, Eve. *Affirmations: Why They Work & How to Use Them.* Accessed December 2011. https://spiritualityhealth.com/blog/eve-hogan/affirmations-why-they-work-how-use-them. https://www.nerdwallet.com/blog/credit-card-data/average-credit-card-debt-household/.

Huffington Post. "Phil Jackson on Michael Jordan: I Didn't Want Him to Be the Scoring Leader." Huffingtonpost.com. Accessed September 23, 2015. http://www.huffingtonpost.com/2013/06/17/phil-jackson-michael-jordan_n_3451199.html.

Jacques, Renee. "9 Reasons to Take a Vacation ASAP, According to Science." Huffingtonpost.com. Accessed August 8, 2014. http://www.huffingtonpost.com/2015/09/05/take-a-vacation_n_5701215.html.

Jet. "Why Money Is the Leading Cause of Divorce." November 18, 1996.

Kimbro, Dennis, and Napoleon Hill. *Think and Grow Rich.* New York: Fawcett Columbine, 1991.

LaHaye, Tim. *Why You Act the Way You Do.* Tyndale House, 1988.

Mental Health Foundation. "10 Ways to Look after Your Mental Health." www.mentalhealth.org. Accessed August 28, 2014. http://www.mentalhealth.org.uk/help-information/10-ways-to-look-after-your-mental-health/drink-sensibly/.

Miks, Jason. *Why Sugar Is Worse than Fat.* CNN.com. Accessed September 11, 2014. http://globalpublicsquare.blogs.cnn.com/2014/09/10/why-sugar-is-worse-than-fat/?hpt=hp_t3.

National Poverty Center. *Extreme Poverty in the United States, 1996 to 2011.* Npc.org. Accessed February 2012. http://www.npc.umich.edu/publications/policy_briefs/brief28/policybrief28.pdf.

Parrot, Drs. Les and Leslie. *Saving Your Marriage before It Starts.* Grand Rapids, MI: Zondervan, 2006.

Perlow, Leslie and Jessica Porter. "Making Time Off Predictable—and Required." *Harvard Business Review.* Accessed August 2014. http://hbr.org/2009/10/making-time-off-predictable-and-required/ar/pr.

Ramsey, Dave. *Financial Peace: Revisited.* New York: Viking Books, 2002.

Shelton, Danny, and Shelley Quinn. *Ten Commandments Twice Removed.* Remnant Publications, 2007.

Siebeling, John. *Fresh Start with God*. Memphis, TN: The Life Church, 2010.

Smolinski, Julieanne. "Women, How Often Do You Look in the Mirror? Study Says 8 Times a Day." Today.com. Accessed May 15, 2012. http://klgh.today.com/_news/2012/05/15/11716823-women-how-often-do-you-look-in-the-mirror-study-says-8-times-a-day?d=1.

Sports Illustrated. "How (and Why) Athletes Go Broke." Si.com. Accessed March 2009. http://www.si.com/vault/2009/03/23/105789480/how-and-why-athletes-go-broke.

Stanley, Thomas J., and William D. Danko. *The Millionaire Next Door*. New York: Longstreet Press, 1996.

Talbott, Shawn M., PhD. *Exercise Vs. Diet: The Truth about Weight Loss*. HuffingtonPost.com. Accessed August 2014. http://www.huffingtonpost.com/2014/04/30/exercise-vs-diet-for-weight-loss_n_5207271.html.

The Fatherless Generation. Accessed May 2014. https://thefatherlessgeneration.wordpress.com/statistics/.

Tracy, Brian. *Maximum Achievement: Strategies and Skills That Will Unlock Your Hidden Power to Succeed*. New York: Fireside, 1995.

Warren, Rick, and Mark Hyman. "Amen, Daniel." *The Daniel Plan*. Grand Rapids, MI: Zondervan, 2013.

Warren, Rick. *The Purpose-Driven Life*. Grand Rapids, MI: Zondervan, 2002.

Wilkinson, Bruce. *The Dream Giver*. Sisters, OR: Multnomah, 2003.

Williams, Ray. "Good Looks Can Get You that Job, Promotion, and Raise." Duke University. Accessed September 2011. https://faculty.fuqua.duke.edu/~charvey/Media/2011/FP_September_8_2011.pdf.

World Bank. "World Bank Sees Progress against Extreme Poverty, but Flags Vulnerabilities." Web.worldbank.org. Accessed October 23, 2015. http://web.worldbank.org/WBSITE/EXTERNAL/NEWS/0,,contentMDK:23130032~pagePK:64257043~piPK:437376~theSitePK:4607,00.html.